This book was written to address a growing need. It is for single parents who want to do a better job of parenting and live happier, more successful lives; for their families and friends who need to understand them better; and for those who would minister to their needs more effectively.

Single parents can be healthy and happy people who raise healthy and happy children.

BEING A SINGLE PARENT

André Bustanoby

BALLANTINE BOOKS • NEW YORK

Contents

Preface

Not too many years ago, American parents had a broad base of support in their task of child rearing. The extended family of grandparents, aunts, uncles, cousins, nieces, and nephews all had a part in rearing children and providing them with good role models. But with the growing mobility of the American population, the extended family began to shrink, and the task of child rearing became the exclusive task of the nuclear family—husband, wife, and siblings.

Over the past forty-five years, however, the nuclear family has taken a battering. Today there is one divorce for every two marriages. The high incidence of divorce has left the task of child rearing on the shoulders of the single parent, though joint custody is an attempt to rectify this. When we realize how far we have come from the care of the extended family to the care of the nuclear family, and now to the care of the single parent, it becomes clear what a staggering responsibility the single parent has. Child rearing—which was once the task of *many*—is now the task of *one*.

Single parenting is a task that is falling on the shoulders of more and more people. Demographers expect that by 1990, almost half of all children under eighteen will be living with a single parent. The prospects for black children are dimmer still; it is estimated that two-thirds of all black children will be living with one parent.

This book was written to address a growing need. It is for single parents who want to do a better job of parenting and live happier and more successful lives, for their families and friends who need to understand them better, and for those who would minister to their needs more effectively. Single parents can be healthy and happy people and raise healthy and happy children. We who are not single parents can make their job easier by letting them know that we understand and care.

André Bustanoby
Bowie, Maryland

The Single-Parent Explosion

Ogden Nash once said, "A family is a unit composed not only of children, but of men, women, an occasional animal and the common cold."[1] Today's families still are composed of children, an occasional animal, and the common cold. But a mother or father is missing in almost seven million households with children under eighteen.[2]

American has experienced a single-parent explosion:

- Between 1950 and 1982 the single population increased by 385 percent—from 4 million to 19.4 million.[3]

- Since 1970 the number of two-parent households with children under 18 declined by 4 percent while the number of one-parent households maintained by a father alone increased 99 percent and those maintained by a mother increased 105 percent.[4]

The impact on children has been great:

- 13.4 million children under 18 live with one parent—an increase of 66 percent in ten years. This is all the more striking in view of the 10-percent decline in the total number of children. The impact on the black population

is greater: 58 percent of black children live without one
or both parents.[5]

- In 9 out of 10 cases the mother, usually divorced, is the
custodial parent.[6]

- Demographers expect that by 1990 almost half (44 percent) of all children under 18 will be living with one
parent. The prospects for black children are dimmer still.
It is estimated that two-thirds will be living with one
parent.[7]

What these statistics reveal is interesting; what they fail to
reveal is vital. They fail to reveal the fact that many more families must function with one parent for other reasons than divorce.
No one knows, for example, how many families are deserted by
one of the parents. One estimate places it at one million a year.[8]
Other families are missing a parent because of separation, hos-
pitalization, military duties, out-of-state employment, and incar-
ceration. The prison population of single parents may be as high
as 282,000.[9]

Because of the diversity of the single-parent population it is
incorrect to refer to the single parent. One expert redefines this
population segment in terms of lifestyle.[10] Another, lamenting the
stigma attached to the divorced family, says that we must not
describe it as "a broken home," "disorganized," "fractured,"
"incomplete," or "single-parent family"—as though divorce is
"an index of social disorder."[11] This expert says that divorce
frequently results in the establishment of two new households—
therefore the proper terminology would be a "binuclear family."[12]

All this may be clinically sound, but it fails to use terminology
that the public is familiar with and fails to allay the suspicion
that we cannot raise well-adjusted children without two parents.

This book attempts to use familiar terminology and at the same
time eliminate stereotyping. It is impossible to deal with every
single-parent situation, but the book attempts to deal with the
more common ones:

- Divorced mothers with custody
- Divorced fathers with custody

- Divorced parents without custody
- The single, never-married parent
- The single widowed parent

Experts Ask the Single Parents

One group of researchers, wanting to find out more about single parents, asked three thousand single men and women across the country about their singleness. The singles were never-married, divorced, or widowed. They were asked the following questions: *What aspects of the single household are the most difficult for you or your child/children? How do you feel about remaining a single parent? As a single parent, what have you done to ensure the psychological and emotional health of your child? How has she or he reacted to the one-parent household situation? What have been the major pleasures and problems of being a single parent?*[13] The answers were enlightening.

What Problems Do Single Parents Face?

Mothers and fathers answered the first question differently. The biggest problem for the mother was depression, worry, and self-concern. The second greatest concern was a lowered standard of living.[14] The concerns of these mothers directly affected the children. They were unable to provide child care and other necessities for their children as they felt they should. The study found that

with women, earning capacity proves to be a direct determinant of happiness and well-being. Women who did not attend college and who are in the lowest income group are approximately twice as likely to cite depression as the problem of child-raising as those who are educated and hold high-paying, professional jobs. Blue-collar women earning low incomes are three times more apt to complain of lowered standards of living than those in the higher bracket. High wage-earners, on the other hand, have a different problem. Almost a third of them claim that their involvements with members of the opposite sex are the most trying part of single parenting.[15]

The single father's concerns were different. New to the task of being the primary caregiver, he is not completely aware of the magnitude of the task. He is concerned, however, that the child gets good care while he's at work.[16]

Will You Remain Unmarried?

When asked how they felt about remaining a single parent, approximately one-third of the respondents said they preferred to remain unmarried. Older single mothers felt this way especially. Mothers with older children tend to be influenced by their relationships with their children. The opposite is true of men. Almost half of those over forty-five would like to marry again.

What About Your Child's Psychological Well Being?

When asked what they were doing to ensure their child's psychological and emotional health, parents gave a variety of responses. They made wise use of resources—day-care centers, family, baby sitters, counseling services, and friends. The child's grandparents were the resource mentioned most often. Sometimes the ex-spouse was mentioned as a source of genuine support.[17]

Single parents repeatedly emphasized the importance of their own attitudes. One single father said, "Single parenting is a difficult road, though at the end you're glad you saw it through because the real rewards are having a happy, healthy kid and being a better person for it."[18]

Single Parents Ask The Experts

Single-parenting is a rough road. Single parents are concerned about good child care, the safety of the latchkey child, and how to raise a healthy child without the benefit of two custodial parents. What do the experts say about these concerns? Should single parents be optimistic about success? The experts do not agree.

For several years magazines and child-rearing books have been sending soothing messages to single parents: children are very resilient, and whatever harm they experience is the result of prejudice and the stigma of being "the product of a broken home."[19]

Can You Reassure Us?

Single parents want to be reassured that they are not damaging their children. Some experts are reassuring, as in an article that appeared in a professional journal. This review of social psychological research into female-headed families conducted between 1970 and 1980 concludes that

> theoretically, children do not need the presence of the same-sex/opposite-sex parents in the family in order to develop sex-role behavior. Children in female-headed families are likely to have good emotional adjustment, good self-esteem except when they are stigmatized, intellectual development comparable to others in the same socioeconomic status.[20]

The author of the review attempts to give single parents reassurance in several areas.

1. *The effect of the missing parent.* The review maintains that boys and girls don't learn sex-role behavior from the same-sex parent. They are influenced by the most powerful and competent parent. The sex-type-behavior that the parent considers appropriate is what they will adopt.[21]

2. *Emotional adjustment and self-esteem.* The review says that after the initial trauma of divorce, children in single-parent families become as well-adjusted as children from two-parent families. They were even better adjusted than children from two-parent families in conflict. The report does concede that there is some evidence that single mothers treat their sons differently than mothers in two-parent homes. The review contends that self-esteem suffers when the family is stigmatized. The social environment, not the family, causes a child to suffer—when he or she is labeled "the product of a broken home."[22]

Authoritative parenting is said to produce competency and good behavior in children. Single parents report that lack of conflict with the absent parent enables them to lay down rules and be more authoritative and consistent.[23]

The review maintains that poor school performance is not to be blamed on the fact that a parent is missing. The reason for poor performance is that most single-parent households are headed by mothers who are forced to live at a poverty level. It is poverty, not the absence of a parent, that explains poor performance. The attitude of the mother toward her economic situation, her children, and the absent father is all-important.

3. *Juvenile delinquency.* The review reports, "The highest level of violence among male juvenile delinquents is found among males from large two-parent families and not from female-headed families."[24]

Why Can't You Reassure Us?"

Some experts take issue with these findings and are not so reassuring. An ongoing study of eighteen thousand children in elementary and secondary schools in fourteen states arrived at a different conclusion. The study, undertaken by the National Association of Elementary School Principals and the Kettering Foundation, reports that children from single-parent homes have much more trouble than children from two-parent homes. This report drew much criticism and angered single parents when it reported that their children achieve less, are absent more, have more disciplinary problems, and at the secondary school level have more health problems.[25] More is said about this report in chapter 10.

James Herzog, a psychiatrist at Children's Hospital Medical Center in Boston, studied seventy-two young children, the majority from single-parent homes in Brookline, Massachusetts. He concludes that the absence of an active father figure was harmful, and most harmful to male toddlers eighteen to twenty-four months old. Boys between two-and-a-half and four-and-a-half years old were highly macho—hyperactive, aggressive, and fond of stories about stern male disciplinarians. The age group five and older showed marked depression in both girls and boys. Herzog attributes their sadness, withdrawal, and aggression toward self to their belief that they were responsible for the breakup of the home.[26]

A Chicago children's psychiatrist echoes the same theme: "I see an awful lot of kids suffering from depressive symptoms of loss. They often appeared very bored, with no motivation, but actually they're depressed."[27]

Some children swing between timidity and aggression. An Illinois school principal says that a child will act up at school to express frustration or hurt, but quiet down at home for fear of abandonment by the remaining parent.[28]

Even if fear of abandonment can be isolated, some researchers say that the single-parent family is likely to have more problems because of the overload on the single parent—working and raising a family with no help from the other spouse.[29] The load is particularly crushing for a single-custodial mother who earns approximately half of what a man earns at a comparable job. Even if she is awarded child support in the divorce settlement, the chances of her receiving any of it are less than 50 percent. New and better-enforced laws on child-support payment will probably change this figure.

Single-custodial fathers also have problems. They have many of the same problems custodial mothers have, but in addition are often less prepared for nurturing. New York psychoanalyst Wolfgang Pappenheim says, "They often have an appalling ignorance about the emotional needs of children."[30]

Single parents crushed by feelings of sole responsibility often force their children into the role of pseudo-adult and confidant. Child psychologist David Elkind, author of *The Hurried Child,* says that this may serve the parent's needs, but it is not clear that this is what the child needs. Erica Abeel, author of *I'll Call You Tomorrow,* who is herself divorced and a joint-custody parent, says, "The greatest problem with single parents is that the children are forced to grow up too fast, to behave as adults. My son said he was nostalgic for his childhood. He said that when he was eight years old."[31]

Another single mother said that her three-year-old son talks about picking up the check at restaurants and sometimes tells her in comforting tones, "I'll be in the other room. Call me if you need me." Child psychologist Judith Wallerstein says that many children are overburdened. At age nine or ten they simply can't be asked to give advice about the stock market, marriage, or divorce. Elkind sees this problem as that of an overloaded parent trying to relieve some of the burden by dumping it on the children. Psychiatrist Alfred Messer says that the young child pushed into such a role "always suffers later in life from lack of self-esteem, because so much was expected by the parent, consciously or subconsciously."[32] Small children can't live up to such expectations, whether imagined or real.

The target of particularly harsh criticism is the unmarried, middle-class woman who, in her thirties, decides to have a child and raise it alone. Single parents and their children can be taught to cope. But professionals feel that there is a big difference between coping with unfortunate circumstances and deliberately making them happen.[33]

Why The Confusion?

Why is there so much confusion among the experts, particularly when it comes to the effects of divorce on a child? A major reason is the difficulty researchers have in isolating divorce from the stresses that go along with it: financial burdens, the child's belief that he was responsible for the breakup, the child's fear of abandonment, and the emotional (and sometimes physical) debilitation of the custodial parent.[34]

There is one place where research does agree. The stronger and more positive the custodial parent, the less likely it is that the child will have problems adjusting to the single-parent household. Interviews with adult children of divorce seem to confirm this. After talking to a number of adults whose parents divorced, one interviewer concluded,

> The success children have in resolving that early conflict has many causes, but some help seems to come from having had at least one honest, loving and reasonably guilt-free parent willing to take responsibility for a new way of life. Continued evidence that the damage is not permanent, that divorce does not ruin children's lives, should make it easier for us to find ways to help them through the experience—which, though it will almost certainly hurt, will not cripple.[35]

The fact of the matter is that *all* single-parent homes need this type of parent, not just the divorced. In this book we will see again and again that a positive attitude in the parent is all-important.

🚶 2

Divorced Mothers With Custody

"Being single isn't sad anymore," gushed the magazine. "It's positively sensational. On these 16 pages, beginning with Farrah Fawcett—and what a beginning!—you'll find out the whys and hows of successful single life."[1]

On the pages that followed, Farrah appeared in her Calvin Klein blouse ($310) and pants ($180). The article cooed, "Always provocative: black lace and ruffles at night."[2]

This article, which appeared in a slick women's magazine, was titled "Single and Loving It." It drew a smile from me and probably a big laugh from most of the 6.5 million single mothers who saw it—women whose median income seldom permits clothes purchases, let alone Calvin Klein.

Singleness in America today is *not* "positively sensational" for most single mothers, nine out of ten times divorced with the custody of their children. Many of these women are living close to the poverty threshold, which, as of February 1984, was $9,900 for a family of four.[3]

Even median income figures are dismal. White women, listed by the 1980 census as "female householder, husband absent," have a median yearly income of $13,076. For black women the figures is $7,921 and for those of "Spanish origin," $8,129.[4]

Not only do the black and Hispanic women have lower median incomes than whites, they bear a greater burden of child rearing.

In 1982, 47 percent of all black children lived with a separated or divorced mother. Only 15 percent of white children lived with a single mother. Though black children make up only 15 percent of the child population, they accounted for one-third of all children living with one parent. For Hispanic children, 27 percent lived with one parent, typically a separated or divorced mother.[5]

The concerns of the single-divorced mother are many: adequate day care for her child, dangers to the latchkey child, the effects of divorce on the child, the effects of single-parent rearing, the effect of the missing father, school performance, custody and visitation problems, coping with her own feelings, and dating again. These are concerns of most single parents and will be discussed in the following chapters. This chapter deals with a foundational problem: the tyranny of economics. How single-divorced mothers—and for that matter, all single mothers—deal with financial matters will determine the outcome of many other problems. The usually neutral Bureau of Census puts it well when it says:

> The increasing prevalence of one-parent families must certainly carry with it some potentially harmful effects for both the adults and the children. The socialization of children is a tremendous responsibility for a parent, usually the mother, who under these conditions must bear the greatest burdens without the aid and support of a steady adult partner. In many such single-parent families, the mother is forced to seek employment for financial reasons, thus further complicating the problem. Pressures undoubtedly build on both parents and children, producing significant strains on all persons involved.[6]

You've Come A Long Way

Virginia Slims cigarette ads assure the modern woman that she has come a long way since the repressions of the Victorian Era. The ads contrast modern women with the repressed, "weaker sex" of the bygone era. Today's women are bouncy, energetic and many-talented—women who juggle a prestigious job, children, household, and husband or lover. But this is not reality.

Women today are concerned about their physical and emotional health, more so than men,[7] Sixty-six percent more women than men suffer depressions.[8]

The Tyranny of Poverty

A study made by nine women for the National Institute of Mental Health (NIMH) bears out this finding—and much more:

- The highest rates of depressions are in the 25-to-44-year-old age group. .

- Suicide attempters (usually depressed) overwhelmingly are females between 20 and 30 years old and increasingly are coming from the ranks of separated and divorced women and women whose marriages are in trouble.

- The typical suicide-attempter tends to be a young woman from a lower middle-class background with recent marital problems or separation or divorce.[9]

In this study, single parenthood itself emerged as a major stress factor. One mother, feeling the stigma of single parenthood, said,

I found that as a single so-called "separated parent," going to school to attend to my children's affairs had put me in jeopardy—many a day, because there was no man with me. I don't feel that quite as deeply anymore. I feel that if I would go up by myself, if the children's father wasn't there, around to go with me, then I'd get someone, a man to go. I would not go there myself anymore. . . .[10]

Another single mother, who had begun to cope, looked back on her desperate circumstances and said,

I had no appetite and as I said, lost weight. I slept a lot but had a lot of nightmares. Patience? Ah, I had plenty of that. You might say I was in a total coma. I got to the point where I couldn't feel anything. Tears, hate, anything. I couldn't feel sad. I forgot what "happy" meant, just fear,

that's all I could feel. There was terrible tension in the air
all the time and nothing was spontaneous. Everything was
mechanical. The children were in the same shape I was in:
tense.[11]

According to the study, "High rates of depression seem to be
associated with stress that derives from life conditions such as
single-parenthood, low income, poor education, and responsibility for young children."[12] This has a tremendously negative impact on the children. These mothers spent more time prohibiting
or proscribing behavior and less time nurturing and giving emotional support. The mothers had no emotional reserves for themselves, let alone for their children. They tended to be more
dominating and hostile-aggressive in their child-rearing styles and
more likely to say no to their children's requests.[13]

The findings of the study adversely reflected on single mothers.
But I am not suggesting that all single mothers are beaten down
and depressed. Some of them have a great deal of stamina and
are able to live courageously under incredibly difficult circumstances. Their children are most fortunate.

"Those Lazy Welfare Leeches"

Single-divorced mothers on welfare can expect little sympathy
from the public. They are often viewed as lazy and quite capable
of lifting themselves up by their bootstraps if they would only do
it. They are frequently dismissed out of hand as sexually promiscuous.

One welfare recipient who had a child out of wedlock re-
counted her experience of going to an agency looking for a job.
She said, "People look at you, write down how many children
you have, and [when] you say you're not married [you get] the
expression . . . , you know, the expression, like it shows in their
faces . . . , like you catch them whispering and mumbling."[14]

But it's not just the agencies. These women feel it from people
in general. One woman said, "Like people on the street. Maybe
they'll say, oh, you know, 'Wow! So many kids and not married!' "[15]

This is not mentioned to condone illegitimacy but to point out
that the public often carries a cruel stereotype of the poor welfare

recipient. The response these women get does not reflect the compassion Jesus showed the woman at the well. She told Him that He didn't want a Samaritan woman drawing water for Him; after all, He might catch a social disease if He touched her water jug. He replied that He knew all about her, but He still wanted a drink (John 4:6—26). Jesus also showed compassion to the woman caught in adultery (John 8:1—1). *Christian morality does no preclude Christian compassion.*

In the NIMH study, many women reported that they were either the victims of sexual assaults or were unwilling participants in sexual acts.[16] Doubtless, much of this sexual activity results in unwanted pregnancy.

The public is also misinformed about child support. Divorced mothers are sometimes portrayed unfairly as typically sprawled on a couch and eating bonbons as they watch "All My Children" on TV. Meanwhile their poor ex-husbands are slaving away to make child-support payments.

There is no child-support "gravy train." As we have seen, only half of court-mandated child support is ever paid. When it is, it amounts to only $1,800 a year on the average. Moreover, alimony is a thing of the past. Only 14 percent of women are ever awarded it, and fewer still collect it.[17]

Let's suppose that these women *do* apply themselves, get an education, and hold a full-time job. Even then they cannot expect their earning power to equal a man's. In 1981 the median income for male year-round, full-time workers, age fifteen and older, was $20,690; the woman's was $12,460.[18] And the situation is getting worse, not better. In 1950 a woman earned 64 cents for every dollar a man made; in 1980 it was 62 cents, and in 1983, 59 cents.[19] (See appendix A for more information.)

Why is this? There are several reasons. Most job-training programs train women for predominantly female occupations where pay is low and chances for advancement are slim. Since more women than men have the custodial care of their children, they are less able to work overtime; lack of adequate day care often keeps them from taking advantage of job opportunities.[20] Some employers believe that the female-custodial parent will miss work when her child is ill and will quit her job for the first man who comes along and promises to support her. The latter belief has

ne justification, as we will see shortly in the discussion of "the
nderella Complex."

x and the Prestigious Job

But poor motivation and lack of education are not the only
sons why women often end up in low-paying "women's jobs."
r some reason men with impressive family backgrounds and
od academic records are more likely to obtain high-status jobs.
men who do well in college are just as likely to pursue "fe-
le" occupations such as public school teaching or nursing as
y are to pursue the more socially prestigious professions of
ctors and lawyers.[21]

Lawmakers are attempting to help those who are economically
advantaged and face barriers to employment. The Job Training
rtnership Act of 1982, actively lobbied by the Displaced
memakers Network, specifically provides for homemakers un-
r Title II: Training Services for the Disadvantaged. It provides
on-the-job and classroom training, work experience, remedial
ucation, counseling, job development, and supportive services.
ditional information is available from Displaced Homemakers
twork, Inc., 1531 Pennsylvania Ave. S.E., Washington, D.C.
003.

But lawmakers can do nothing about the key issue of attitude.
particular, self-confidence is believed to be the single most
portant personality trait a woman must have to be a successful
der in a profession.[22] And one major reason for the lack of
f-confidence is that many women are troubled by "the Cinder-
a Complex."

he Cinderella Complex

e Victorian woman was plagued with a disorder known as
onversion hysteria." Its symptoms were weakness and faint-
. It as called *conversion* hysteria because the patient, quite
inst her knowledge or will, converted her mental distress into
ysical symptoms, which offered a certain benefit—escape from
severe emotional conflict of doing her duty as a woman in a
n's world and keeping her mouth shut. The conflict was con-

verted to *bodily* distress, and the symptoms sent an importa
message to others that the lips dared not speak: "You're expec
ing too much of me!"

Modern women, as we have seen, suffer from depression. B
they are also plagued with an equally debilitating, more subt
disorder, popularly called "the Cinderella Complex"—a fear
independence that prompts them to look for a man to take ca
of them.

Colette's Story

Colette Dowling, author of the best-selling book *The Cinder*
la Complex, tells how she discovered her affliction.[23] In 1975 s
left New York and a solitary four-year struggle to make en
meet as a single parent. She moved to a large house in a sm
rural village ninety miles north of Manhattan where she set abc
to support herself as a writer. There she settled down with h
children—and a man who seemed to be a perfect companion. B
she said, "What I hadn't anticipated—what I'd had no way
foreseeing—was the startling collapse of ambition that would c
cur as soon as I began sharing my home with a man again."

This "collapse of ambition" came on slowly, almost impe
ceptibly. Rather than writing, she found herself making a ne
insulating it with the soft bits of fluff of bedspreads and curtain
and stocking it with homemade treats from the kitchen. She w
quite content to leave the paying of the bills to Lowell, her col
panion, until he confronted her. He told her that she was r
living up to her part of the bargain—both had agreed that th
would be self-supporting.

Colette realized how easy it was to let her writing slide. S
didn't feel the *need* to be working. She enjoyed the luxury
being a "wife." What did Lowell mean, "It isn't fair"? Wh
isn't fair? Isn't this the way it's supposed to be?

Colette tried to bring in money, but her writing just did
click. Lowell grew impatient. He wanted to know how long s
was going to go on like this. Suppose it goes on a year? Wh
then?

"The 'What then?' was chilling," Colette recalled. "To me
seemed proof that his care was not very deep, or else why wou

he be pushing me like that? Why would he be saying, in effect, 'I don't *want* to take care of you'?"

Colette began to feel intimidated and powerless. She had lost respect for herself and felt that the only way she could stand up was if someone *lifted* her up.

She eventually saw that her distorted view of her weakness and Lowell's power was really a neurotic dependence on her part, designed to get what psychologists call a "secondary gain"—someone who would relieve her of her fear of independence and take care of her.

The tremendous burden of being a single-divorced-custodial mother is in itself enough to drag any woman down and alarm her children. But when a lack of self-confidence and the secret desire to be taken care of is added to this burden, the combination is lethal.

This is not to minimize discriminatory economics or the failure of the ex-husband to pay child support. Many women, particularly those living at the poverty level, are so depressed by their circumstances that they give up. Their children, cast adrift on the sea of uncertainty, await their fate—some stoically and some angrily.

But discriminatory economics does not explain the behavior of single mothers who are bright and talented and have good jobs. They feel the terrible pressure and demands of single parenting but are determined to take care of *themselves*. They do not suffer from the Cinderella Complex, which generates lack of self-confidence, fear of independence, and a wish to be taken care of.

Lucy's Story

Lucy is a good example of a woman who beat the Cinderella Complex. Like a growing number of women I am seeing in my practice, she was suffering from agoraphobia. This phobia's essential feature is a terror of being alone, or being in public places from which escape might be difficult, or where help is not available in case of sudden incapacitation.

Lucy couldn't come for her appointment by herself. Her sister had to bring her. In addition to her fear of being alone and fear of driving, she had many physical symptoms that the doctors could only attribute to anxiety.

In discussing her past I discovered that she never felt loved by a man—neither by her father nor her husband. And she always felt dependent. Her husband encouraged her dependency by reinforcing her helplessness. He did it by being particularly attentive to her when she was phobic. But in her rare moments of good health he wanted nothing to do with her. In terms of psychological dynamics Lucy *needed* to be phobic. It was her way of saying to her husband, "I need you. Can't you see I'm a weak, helpless person!" When she was weak and helpless, he responded.

I explained to Lucy what my suspicions were and that I believed she could overcome her phobia if she stood on her own two feet and was willing to risk her husband's rejection. She followed my advice to perfection. She stopped her sick, helpless dependence on her husband and began to take care of her children, herself, and her home. She joined a women's crisis recovery group, and in a matter of weeks her phobia and physical symptoms were gone. She was driving everywhere by herself.

Lucy's husband was irate. He told me that he didn't know what I was doing to his wife, but he didn't like it. She wasn't "the loving person she used to be." What he really meant was that she had broken her neurotic dependency on him, and she was angry with him for his part in the conspiracy. He ultimately divorced her, accusing me of ruining his marriage. But Lucy did marvelously—until she met Scott.

With the nastiness of the divorce out of the way, Lucy decided she would like some male companionship. She met Scott at a singles' retreat, and he seemed like a decent guy. By now I was seeing Lucy only periodically to monitor her progress. One day she called to say she had to see me. She had another phobic episode and was devastated. "I thought I was through with this," she sobbed.

What happened? Her relationship with Scott was beginning to get cozy. Lucy began to feel that old dependency coming back. She fantasized that Scott was the man who would take care of her and her children.

I explained to Lucy that she was falling back into the same pattern she had with her husband. The male was to fill the role of the strong, caring partner, and she was to fill the role of the weak, dependent one. Her body was simply accommodating to the old role and was helping her get across the message, "See how weak and helpless I am and how much I need you!"

Lucy confessed that this was true. The more we talked, the angrier she became for permitting such a lapse. But rather than turn the anger inward and become depressed, she let it out and used it to survive—*by herself.*

She survived Scott and one other relationship before she learned that *both* men and women can be strong and healthy and yet have rewarding relationships.

A Hopeless Situation?

The Cinderella Complex goes deeper than many psychologists are aware of. The problem touches on theology and the Bible.

The health and wholeness of human beings must take into account God's creative intent and the impact of the fall of man, particularly the curse that followed (Gen. 3:16–19). In the Fall, woman was cursed with a sense of dependence on man. The tragic irony is that she who contributed to the fall of man is made dependent on this fallen, fallible creature.

Is her situation hopeless, then? Not if she acknowledges the God of *grace,* who desires not only to save us from the penalty of the Fall and its sin through Jesus Christ, but who also wants to help us live successfully by His grace. The apostle Paul put it well when he said that if God was willing to give us the greatest gift of grace, His Son, is He not willing to give us every lesser gift necessary to live successfully (Rom.8:31–32)?

Attitude Is The Key

If dependency, lack of confidence, and poor self-image all hurt the single mother, what can she do to change? Attitude is the key. It is the difference in attitude among divorced mothers with custody that makes it difficult for experts to agree on whether divorce hurts the children, and if so, how much. .

The Importance of Positive Attitude

Some women, because of their physical and emotional makeup, are able to perform heroically under conditions that debilitate and

embitter other women. Since the custodial parent is the primary
means by which the child assesses his well-being and the meaning of what's going on around him, *the attitude of that parent is
all-important.* If the custodial parent is so battered by circumstances that she alarms the child's sense of well-being and distorts
realities, he will be an anxious child with a skewed view of life.
If she is able to make the child feel loved and secure in spite of
adversity, the child will thrive.

The evidence regarding depressed mothers in the NIMH study
cited earlier confirms this contention.

> Children of depressed mothers were more likely to report
> themselves unhappy with their mothers and turned to their
> mothers for emotional support less frequently than children
> of less depressed mothers. Children of depressed mothers
> also more frequently reported that they were punished or
> rejected at home. The interviews showed that children tend
> to be sensitive and understanding of the stresses in their
> parents' lives, as long as they feel loved by them. Depres-
> sion appears to seriously impair a mother's ability to con-
> vey the sense of being loved, and hence the relationship of
> the mother and child.[24]

It should be remembered that even though the mother is the custodial parent, she may be an ''assenter'' rather than a ''seeker.''
An ''assenter'' is a parent who accepts custody not because she
wants it, but because no other choice is feasible. The ''seeker''
is the custodial parent who wants custody and aggressively seeks
it. This parent is much more likely to accept the burdens of single
parenting and constructively look for ways to cope.

Resentment over having to care for a child can poison the parent-child relationship and increase the likelihood of having to deal
with a problem child. The child is far better off in a home where
there is peace and where he's wanted than in a home where he
feels that he's a burden. The single mother who resents the burden of child care *must* get help in resolving the problem before
she creates problems for her child. More will be said about
''seekers'' and ''assenters'' in chapter 3, where the issue of divorced fathers with custody is discussed. With fathers the problem is more pronounced.

Single mothers with custody who do not have a positive attitude about single parenting may be caught between what society expects them to do and what they really feel they are capable of doing. When marriages break up, even though more and more fathers are asking for and getting custody, the majority of the time the mother is expected to be the primary caregiver and custodial parent. If she doesn't want the job, she is regarded as a bad mother. The father doesn't receive this criticism because he isn't expected to be the primary caregiver. So, to avoid looking bad, a mother may assent to custody of her child but have serious reservations about it—reservations that she can't hide from a child, who in turn feels insecure.

The Problem of Guilt

One of the major enemies of a positive attitude is guilt. Many single mothers can't be positive about single parenting because they feel that they have done wrong to their children, their ex-spouses, their extended families, and even themselves. Some single mothers feel guilty justifiably. Psychological damage has been done. Sin has been committed. But the single mother should remember two things:

First, it's important to distinguish between theological and psychological guilt. All guilt feelings are not the result of God's convicting us of our wrong (theological guilt). A lot of guilt comes as a result of how our circumstances play on our minds. Perhaps we have been raised with an overdeveloped and, hence, neurotic sense of guilt. Our children, ex-spouses, or parents can control us by taking advantage of that neurotic flaw (psychological guilt).

Second, it's important to know that the opposites of sin and guilt are grace and forgiveness. Sin and guilt actually provide God with opportunities to show how gracious and loving He is. The apostle Paul expresses it, "Where sin increased, grace increased all the more" (Rom. 5:20). If guilt is the result of actual sin, the answer is not to deny it but to accept the remedy—forgiveness by God's grace.

If You're Not A Guilty Mother . . .

Sometimes a good laugh helps our attitude. A recent book suggests new ways to revel in guilt. First, there's "the Working Mother's Guilt." The scenario goes this way:

Hello, Mom? Is that you? I know you don't like me to phone you at work and all, but where's the Sweet 'n Low? Huh? Oh, it's for the firemen. No, everything's real okay now, Mom. Nothing to worry about. The firemen put out the fire right away. The fire? Oh, that was when I tried to make grilled cheese sandwiches and forgot to take the plastic off the cheese so it caught fire. I *know* that I was supposed to make peanut butter and jelly sandwiches. But I couldn't, Mom. Huh? No peanut butter, that's why.

Well, Mom, I have to give the firemen their Sweet 'n Low now, and then I'm going next door to Mrs. Jones's house. Well, when she saw the firemen come she invited me over for soda. She said she didn't believe that mothers should be working all the time to pay the mortgage and that they should stay home until their kids went away to college, just like she did. Well, bye.[25]

Then there's "the Single-Parent Guilt." This hits when your third-grader's teacher tries to be helpful and says, "Annie, you don't have to make Father's Day presents with the class because you come from a broken home." No wonder the poor child feels that her home needs fixing.

Finally there's "the Latchkey Guilt.":

Well, Bobby, I had the hardware store put a little plastic ring with a different color on each key, see? So you can tell them apart. Now *this* key is for the lobby door, only don't ever let anyone in you don't know. Wait outside until one of our neighbors comes.

Now *this* key is for the top door lock—the orange key. And *this* one is for the bottom door lock. You know that's the one that sticks and sometimes you have to push the door in and kick it and then turn the key really hard to the left while kicking the door again. But that's easy to remember! I'm sure you'll have no trouble with it.

And then if you'll just remember to keep the keys on the string around your neck, and when you're home never open the door for anyone and never answer the telephone unless it's me, but *I* always ring three times first, so you'll know. Why, it'll go just *fine*, right?[26]

t's one thing to recognize these as the sober realities single par-nts must live with. But it's quite another to use them to whip urselves with guilt. When single parents can begin to see the umor of the guilt games they play with themselves and others, hey can be sure they're beginning to rid themselves of guilt games.

🏃 3

Divorced Fathers
With Custody

Though more and more fathers are gaining custody of their children, single fathering is still looked upon as an unusual phenomenon. The successful single father is capable of inspiring awe. Unlike single mothers, single fathers are often viewed as extraordinary parents who do little wrong and receive support of both friends and relatives. They are also sought after by women looking for someone to be a father to children they may be raising on their own.[1]

One researcher suggests that the single father may feel odd at times and unsuited to be the primary-care parent. The single-parent family is often regarded as a "pathological model." When the father receives custody of the children, people tend to feel "something has gone terribly wrong." The single father is challenged to explain why he has the children, particularly when traditionally it's "in the best interest" of the children to be with their mother.[2]

Generally males are not socialized to be the nurturing, primary-care parent. So what is this ill-equipped man doing with a tearful preschool boy or a teenage girl with premenstrual cramps—children who obviously need a mother's care? Or, what's this *man* doing at the parent-teacher conference. Where's the child's mother?

Though some people question the ability of a man to be the

nurturing, primary-care parent, a typical response is the woman's magazine that emphasizes the success of the single father:

> At 5:45 every morning Craig Knutson wakes up his children, Jennifer and Chad, and supervises their dressing, washing, and shoe-tying while he gets himself ready for the business day. Then the whole family sits down for breakfast. After washing up and doing a few other household chores, Craig feeds Princess, the family Collie, bundles up the children, drives them to their nearby school, and kisses them good-bye. "Have a nice day," he calls to them. "I'll see you this evening."[3]

The story goes on to tell about Craig's eight-hour day in a busy office and his return to full-time parenting duties in the evening. As I read, I began to feel that the story was a bit idyllic. I know of few two-parent homes, with both parents working outside the home, where the day begins on such an organized, cheery note. My eye then caught a picture of little Chad and Dad at the bathroom sink over the caption, "Dad is always available if a little fellow needs some help with brushing."

That was more than I could stomach. For the peace of mind of both single mothers and single fathers, we must not promote the idea of the Super Single Parent. Teeth will not always be brushed well and may, in fact, miss some brushings. The single parent must be able to let some details slip through the cracks without feeling he's a failure.

How Many Single Fathers?

Though single fathers are still an uncommon phenomenon compared with single mothers, the figures may go as high as 1.5 million fathers raising 3.5 million children.[4] Single fathers are surprising themselves and the female population with their ability to nurture. The response of a female therapist counseling a steelworker, Roger, and his teenage daughter, Danielle, is typical:

> Roger just blew me over because of my stereotype of a steelworker. He knew what it meant to be a good parent—

to feel his children's pain as well as his own. He could be sensitive and warm and vulnerable.[5]

It may help our perspective to remember that American society historically has not expected the father to be the primary-care parent—the one who is responsible for the day-to-day physical and emotional care of the children. So when he does it well, Americans are surprised. When he does it well and also holds down a full-time job, he is ready for canonization.

Mothers have been achieving success at this for years, married or single. Because society *expects* the mother to be the primary caregiver, she doesn't receive praise for doing it well. She's just doing what she *ought* to do and, as indicated earlier, often with fewer financial resources.

This is one criticism I have regarding the study done in 1982 by the Parents Without Partners magazine *Single Parent*. This study of eleven hundred fathers reported that they were doing very well as single parents. But the figures in the report reveal that the *average* yearly income of these fathers was $30,000. This is not to denigrate the good job these fathers are doing. But in fairness to single mothers, who often labor with an economic handicap, it is very difficult to draw any comparisons between the performance of single-custodial mothers and fathers. The white male single parent who earns $30,000 a year is light-years away from the black female single parent who earns $7,500.

Remember, we really can't talk about *the* single parent. We may establish certain principles of successful parenting mandatory for all parents. But we must be thoughtful in our application of those principles and appreciate the difference between the black single mother making $7,500 and the white single father making four times that amount.

Why Do Men Become Custodial Fathers?

How do we explain the social phenomenon of the single-custodial father? Why do men become custodial fathers? The answers vary, and their success largely depends on the circumstances under which they become single fathers.

Seekers

Some fathers become the custodial parent because that's what they want. The fathers who *seek* custody have a better chance at success than those who merely assent to it. This doesn't mean that support from family, friends, and church is unnecessary. It just means that generally his chances are better than the nonseeker's.

One caution should be mentioned. If the *reason* for seeking custody is not positive, the single father may *appear* to be a good father but may damage his child in subtle ways. For example, the father, angered over his wife's leaving him, may use custody as a means to get even. He may not admit that this is why he wants custody. He may even establish an elaborate rationale for seeking custody. But if his motive is to get even, he will do two things wrong: (1) he will weaken the bond between the child and his mother and may go as far as to encourage negative thinking about her. He will do this by obstructing contact with the mother—her letters, phone calls, visits—and negatively interpreting to the child all she says or does; (2) he will be an indulgent parent. To maintain the "good-guy" image, he will tend to indulge the child's whims and overlook bad behavior that requires a firm hand.

Custody by the father is most successful when both he and the mother agree that it would be best for the children and the father welcomes the opportunity to be the primary caregiver. He must be aware of the difficulties of single fatherhood and receive support from family, friends, and the church. Just as the attitude of the single mother must be positive, so must the attitude and motive for gaining custody on the part of the father.

A studied, dispassionate approach to custody is possible. I remember one father who initiated counseling. This in itself was a clue to the direction of the case: usually the mother, not the father, is the one to initiate family counseling.

The man came alone for the first visit and gave me the family background. He was twenty-one and his wife eighteen when they married. They had a child right away, and the wife seemed to resent being tied down. Now, five years later, she wanted to get out of the marriage. "I want custody," he said. "And I think she'll agree to it. I've always been closer to our son, except when he was a baby. For the first month or two she treated him as a plaything. But when he grew older, she lost interest. He's been pretty much 'my' son for five years."

When I talked to his wife I found that she was willing to let her husband have custody. "He's a good father," she said. "He's ready for parenthood, but I'm still a kid and not ready."

The father sought and received custody, and his we're-going-to-do-just-fine attitude created just the stable climate his son needed for continued development.

Assenters

The assenter is the parent who does not seek custody of the child but either has it thrust upon him or, when presented with the opportunity, gladly accepts it.

The first type of assenter is usually angry and resentful. He often has custody forced on him when his wife deserts. One angry assenter said, "She got tired of us and split." Another said, "She saw herself as needing personal growth that was inhibited by the children. She felt hemmed in by the marriage. She said that she just couldn't meet my needs or the children's needs."[6]

These men felt they had little choice in the matter of custody. Their sense of duty toward their children and guilt over their previous neglect prompted them to assent to custody. But they tended to interact with their children less than custodial fathers who seek custody, and they tended to feel greater anxiety about their success as single parents.

Both the seeker and the assenter with wrong motives tend to be poor parents, but for different reasons. A child knows whether or not he's wanted. The assenter, in the way he handles and talks to his children, easily conveys the message, "You're a bother; you're in the way."

It is not divorce and single-parenting per se that produce problem children. It is the attitude of the parents. Do the children feel unwanted or in the way? Do they feel that they are a burden to a parent already struggling for survival? It is far better for the child to be with *neither* parent if they are both crippled emotionally.

The type of assenter most likely to succeed as the single father is the one who had good relations with his children prior to divorce and still values harmonious relations with his wife. Not all marriages break up in explosive acrimony. Some marriages die in their sleep. The funeral is quite civilized, and the survivors do quite well as individuals.

One exception is the father who is not close to his children, has neither positive nor negative feelings about them, but discovers the joys of parenting when the opportunity is thrust on him. One assenter was separated for two years, during which time his wife had custody of their three children. When she had a nervous breakdown, her doctor told him that he had to help relieve the pressure she felt. She was not hospitalized, and the doctor prescribed bedrest and medication. The father agreed to take the children for six months or until she recuperated.

To his surprise he discovered that single parenthood did not drastically change his lifestyle and that family, friends, and neighbors were a great help. What is more, the interaction with children and community made his life more interesting.

After his wife's health improved, she wanted the daughter to come live with her. Her husband refused and said the children were a package deal: if she took one, she took all. She declined the offer, and he assumed permanent custody. A year later they were divorced and he was granted legal custody of all three children.[7]

Seekers tend to be more successful as single parents than assenters simply because parenthood is what they want, not something that is forced on them. The exception is the seeker who wants custody to punish his wife or for reasons other than wanting to be a good parent. But this Super Single Parent (like his female counterpart) does not make a good parent because he tries too hard. He does not accept his failures well, and they will come. Nor does he accept the unresponsiveness of his children. He will tend to be an angry or petulant parent, feeling that the little ingrates don't appreciate his heroic efforts.

Seekers tend to avail themselves of social services and the support of family, friends, and church. Assenters tend to isolate themselves and their children and become demoralized. Those who care should take the initiative to offer aid and comfort. The church can do a great deal for the assenter, particularly the older women skilled in child rearing who are willing to teach the men how to do it.

When Dad Becomes "Mr. Mom"

One of the surprise movie hits of 1983 was *Mr. Mom*, a story about a man named Jack Butler who is laid off from his job while his wife goes to work. One reason for the success of this movie is that many single fathers identified with the way Jack developed new feelings for his children when he became the primary caregiver.

Single Fathers Speak Out

Many single fathers say that the word *father* doesn't adequately describe them. They refer to themselves as the "primary-care parent" or the "primary caregiver." This role carries a greater responsibility and burden than the word *father* conveys.[8]

One father identified with Jack Butler's boredom. He said, "There are days when I get very lonely and bored. After seven years at home, it's starting to be a drag. Eventually you start to get lobotomized."[9] This man realized that he could not make the home his sole interest and needed something outside the home just for him. How many times have mothers said the same thing! Perhaps one good thing that will come out of the disruption of the traditional two-parent home is a greater appreciation by both mothers and fathers for what the other must contend with.

Another single father said,

> To have a career, to have a home that's well-kept and to raise children the way you want to raise them cannot be done in twenty-four-hour days. You either have to devote yourself to one or the other, or do them all less well than you could if you devoted yourself to one. . . .[10]

If single fathers are to maintain their sanity and not become angry and frustrated parents, they *must* realize their limitations. Moreover, if a man becomes a single-custodial father grudgingly, if he's a halfhearted assenter, he will have big problems with his role as a single father. Or, if he is a seeker with the wrong attitude, he will also have problems. This would be the single father who thinks he is going to punish his wife by suing for custody or by showing her, "Anything you can do I can do better."

If adults are truly concerned about how divorce and single parenting affect their children, they must take a hard look at their attitudes toward single parenting and toward the absent spouse. Anger or resentment in either case will hamper the wholesome development of the children who, in the normal course of growing up, have enough adversity to contend with. Single parents who can't give up anger and resentment ought to seek therapy. It may be that the disruption in the home is caused not by a problem child, but by a problem parent.

Special Concerns

Some of the concerns of single fathers are the same as those of single mothers. They want to know what constitutes normal childhood and adolescent behavior. Chapters 12 and 13 give specific help in answering the more common questions about child rearing, along with warnings about special pitfalls to avoid. Suggestions for further reading are also given.

It must be remembered that no one is born a good father. It is a matter of patience, study, and love. But more than that, it is a matter of *information*. Fathers must learn everything they can about child psychology and teaching methods. If they don't know the great psychological difference between a three-year-old and a four-year-old, how can they possibly guide and discipline intelligently?[11]

Above all, watch out for parental guilt. No father (or mother) will do everything right. To whip ourselves with guilt will rob us of the alertness and stamina we need to do a good job. And worse, we leave ourselves vulnerable to manipulation by our children. The child who grows up angry and feeling that he's gotten a rotten deal in life is often the child of a guilty parent who, by his words and behavior, says, "You poor kid; you've gotten a rotten deal."

An excellent resource for single fathers is Fitzhugh Dodson's book, *How to Father*. Dodson devotes almost three hundred pages to child development from infancy to late adolescence. He adds an extensive index and several helpful appendixes to guide fathers in choosing books, toys, and play equipment.[12]

Another resource that Christian dads will appreciate is the monthly magazine *Dads Only*. It is published and edited by Paul

Lewis, P.O. Box 340, Julian, CA 92036. The magazine is advertised as "a news and creative ideas resource for Christian dads and husbands." It is intended for both married and single dads, and the latter will find it helpful in relating creatively to their children as Christian parents.

Another special concern of a father is his daughter's sexual development. He must be *informed*, first of all, so he can answer questions as they arise. Sex education is a gradual process whereby the parent informs the child as she becomes aware of her sexuality. He provides a growing body of knowledge for the child over the years as books, television, and friends bring up the subject and make her curious. Before she experiences her first period, if he feels awkward about preparing her with information and sanitary aids, he could have a female friend prepare her.

Sometimes fathers feel ashamed of their own sexual feelings toward their daughters who are blossoming into womanhood, and they don't always handle their feelings constructively. A father is responsible both to reinforce the incest taboo and to affirm his daughter's sexuality. Sometimes a girl will test her sexual prowess on her father by getting too familiar or exposing too much flesh. The father can affirm her and yet reinforce the incest taboo by letting her know that she's no longer a little girl but is becoming a very attractive woman. And because of this she will have to put on more clothes and be a little more reserved in kissing and body contact. The fact that a girl has the ability to seduce her father is a compliment to her feminine prowess. When this matter is handled in a forthright way that reinforces the incest taboo, the girl will grow up to be a confident, morally prudent woman.

Household management and child care constitute an area of special concern. Cooking, cleaning, budgeting, shopping, and even hair styling are skills that men need to master. Churches can help by offering courses on parent effectiveness. A course for single fathers ought to have a specific masculine orientation, perhaps led by a man who is a successful single parent. Women could be invited to teach specific skills such as styling a little girl's hair.

The indispensable quality the single father must develop is a sensitivity to his children's emotional needs. Men by nature and socialization tend to view emotions as irrational and quite incidental in formulating a solution and doing something about it. Many men need to know that recognizing children's feelings and talking about them is often *the* solution. When a parent *understands* the child's feelings and *cares* that he feels as he does, the child is relieved of the fears and low self-worth that lie at the core of most problems. The parent conveys most effectively that he loves the child and will provide for the child's security when he understands how and why the child feels unloved or insecure. The child will wonder how his father can possibly meet these needs when he doesn't understand.

Fathers who view feelings as "irrational" will either avoid emotionally charged issues or become angry because the child "shouldn't feel that way." Whether or not the child *should* feel as he does, that's where he is, and the father must understand why. I repeat: *Sometimes understanding and caring are themselves the solution.* [13]

The chart of emotions in appendix B is designed to help fathers identify in themselves and their children the nuances of positive and negative emotions. Remember, when a parent is perceptive enough to understand what a child is feeling and why he feels that way, he communicates love and caring, which in turn produce self-worth and security in the child. The parent cares enough to pay attention to the child's feelings and is wise enough to provide a secure environment for her.

Tempting Solutions

When the burden of being "Mr. Mom" overwhelms the single father, he may be tempted to grasp an attractive but unwise solution. If he lives near his parents, he may be tempted to move in with them and let his parents become surrogate parents to his children. He could then easily slip back into the routine of going to work, knowing that his children are well-cared for, and coming home at night to a clean house and hot meal. Sometimes sympathetic in-laws who are concerned about their grandchildren's welfare are open to a living-together arrangement.

This is unwise and not recommended unless financial necessity leaves no other choice. Grandparents have raised their families and don't have the stamina to keep up with young children. Furthermore, they are at a time in their lives when they ought to be winding down activity and enjoying the fruit of their labor.

A father is in danger of taking advantage of this situation and treating the children's grandparents as built-in baby sitters while he gets on with his career and social life. This can only lead to resentment by his parents, who feel used, and ultimately end that living situation—an unfortunate experience for the children who have already gone through the breakup of one household.

Another tempting solution is marriage. I deal with this subject extensively in *But I Didn't Want a Divorce* and *The Readymade Family*.[14]

The divorced person who marries to establish a two-parent home is heading for trouble. He should be marrying to have a companion for himself, not a parent for his children. Making a marriage work is a mammoth task itself and is even more difficult when there's a readymade family. The person who marries to have someone share the parenting job will likely become an absent parent and dump the responsibility on the new spouse. Marriage for the purpose of getting help in raising the children ignores the reality that one day the children will grow up and leave home. Will the marriage look good then?

Being a single father and being an unmarried person are two distinct dimensions of life. One has to do with being a parent. The other has to do with being a spouse. The single parent must be careful to look at the two dimensions separately and ask himself the question, "Quite aside from the issue of being a single parent, why do I want to marry?" The answer should be revealing and helpful.

4

Parents Without Custody

Custody battles, with the children caught in the power struggle, are what we usually think of when a marriage breaks up. This may be true initially. But once sole custody has been granted, the noncustodial or separated parents become missing parents. As a rule this does not disturb the custodial parent. In fact, the feeling is often relief.[1]

A recent study of noncustodial parents revealed that most of them saw their children rarely or not at all during the previous year. Only 16 percent of the children in the study saw their noncustodial fathers as often as once a week, and 40 percent had no contact with their fathers for the previous five years. They didn't even know if their fathers were alive. Noncustodial mothers fared better: 25 percent of the children saw their mothers at least once a week. Another 25 percent had not seen their mothers during the previous five years.[2]

Father-child contact was linked primarily to three factors: level of support, race (white children saw their noncustodial parents more often than black children), and education of the mother. Remarriage had a major impact. If both parents remarried, only 13 percent of the children had weekly contact with their fathers. The figure was 50 percent when neither parent remarried.

Mothers Without Custody

Why is it that noncustodial mothers tended to see their children more often than noncustodial fathers? I believe that the answer lies in *guilt*. Traditional motherhood is still highly valued in America, and many mothers without custody feel guilty and condemned.

Guilt-Ridden Mothers

One mother expressed her feelings this way:

> My husband and I have decided to divorce after 12 years. Our marriage died of boredom, so there was little emotion felt for fighting, only sadness. The decision took a long time, as we had developed a security in being a couple that was scary to end. Now I face an even bigger decision. I want to let my husband have custody of the children. He is a wonderful father and is emotionally more involved with them. (He is more willing to raise them, but he insists on sole custody, although I'll be able to see them.) My fear of the stigma attached to a woman who gives up her children is keeping me from making this final decision, and holding up our divorce. I'm not a bad person or unfit, and I don't want to be labeled as such. Since I know my reasons are right, why do I feel uncomfortable, even ashamed about telling our friends?[3]

This woman's fears are justified. Ellen Kimball knows this is true. When chronic illness incapacitated her, she relinquished permanent custody of her two children, aged eleven and twelve, to their father. She had spent years being a Super Mom in a household that included the three children of her second husband, a widower, but now she could no longer keep up. Her world caved in, and she felt terribly alone—as if she were the only person in the world who had done such a thing. She lost a couple of good friends. Her mother was aghast and her father upset.[4]

As a result of her experience, Ellen decided that noncustodial mothers need help. She became the national director of an organization called Mothers Without Custody. Their newsletter, the

MW/OC Associate (P.O. Box 602, Greenbelt, MD 20770), offers valuable information: regional board members with their phone numbers, books and articles relating to mothers' needs, advice on particular problems mothers face, and legislation affecting mothers without custody. The organization is designed to help four categories of women: those who have voluntarily given up custody, those who have lost custody to their ex-husbands in court, women whose children have been stolen by their ex-husbands, and those whose children have been taken by the state and put in foster or alternative care.

Why Give Up Custody?

A mother may choose to give up custody for a variety of reasons:

1. She often feels almost totally responsible for the breakdown of the marriage and therefore has no right to ask for child custody.

2 She wants to avoid a custody battle.

3. She feels a lack of emotional support in her role as mother. She feels she can't do it alone.

4. She has extreme feelings of non-worth as wife, mother, and person.

5. She is afraid that her low self-worth may rub off on her children or hurt them in some way.

6. She feels economic pressure.

7. Anger at the husband for not assuming his responsibility as a parent over the years. Now he can do it all!

8. She would rather build her own career and find self-worth in that than in being a single-custodial parent.[5]

It is remarkable that so many mothers without custody feel alone and isolated when approximately three-quarters of a million mothers live apart from their minor children.[6] Because of their guilt, mothers without custody tend to keep their "sin" a secret. They cut themselves off from others in similar circumstances, or from those who are sympathetic and may help them—a remarkable contrast to noncustodial fathers who have organized self-help groups all over the country. One psychologist interviewing noncustodial mothers discovered that out of the twenty interviewed, not one knew another noncustodial mother. They simply didn't seek out women in similar situations.[7]

A self-help group is one of the most pressing needs a noncustodial mother has. Local churches can do a great deal to help make noncustodial mothers feel at ease by having a compassionate spirit and expressing understanding. This attitude will free these mothers to talk about their situations without fear of being stigmatized. By making these mothers more visible, the church will increase the chances of these women finding each other and helping each other through an informal network of friendship or a more formal self-help group.

A noncustodial mother must make a great emotional adjustment. Not only does she mourn the loss of the marriage and loss of the children, she must also face the children's confusion and hurt over her leaving them and the "bad mother" label her former husband may hang on her.[8]

The most unforgiving, guilt-provoking person is often the noncustodial mother's own mother. One mother told her daughter, "I hope your ex-husband remarries, because your kids need a mother." The daughter protested that the children already *had* a mother, but her plea fell on deaf ears.[9]

Another mother said, "I never thought my daughter would abandon her children." In time she realized that the grandchildren were better off with their father, but she had already won the "foot in the mouth" award.

It is difficult for a grandmother to understand why her daughter chooses not to ask for custody. Sometimes her anger or criticism is the result of displaced fear—fear that she might not see her grandchildren anymore. She must believe that in time she will understand her daughter's decision and visitation arrangements will be made.

Caution on Coping With Guilt

Noncustodial parents must be cautious in dealing with their guilt so they don't go to one of two extremes.

1. *The chronically guilty mother.* This is the mother who accepts all the bad things that people say about her and what she has done to her children. She lives a joyless life. She seeks no improvement of her living conditions and may even neglect her appearance. The unconscious strategy of this method of coping is to show others that she is doing penance for "abandoning" her children. Even though she may have opportunity to improve her lot, she chooses not to because she feels she doesn't *deserve* any better out of life. The secondary gain of this strategy is to lessen the guilt she feels. People will see that she's already suffering enough and that her sackcloth and ashes are ample evidence of penance.

   This behavior may not be deliberate or conscious, but it is neurotic nevertheless. It does her children no good, to say nothing of what it does to her. It robs her children of the assurance that even though she's not living with them she still loves them. It robs her of the energy and inclination to be a loving long-distance parent.

   This is not said to condemn the mother without custody. She feels enough guilt. But she as well as those around her need to be aware of the neurotic quality of her "adjustment." The church can help counsel such mothers on the difference between theological and psychological guilt.

   The neurotically guilty mother must not be confused with the beleaguered mother who has done everything in her power to hold herself and children together but has exhausted all her physical and emotional resources. She sincerely wants to cope, but she is at her wit's end.

2. *The "I will not feel guilty" mother.* Some mothers cope with guilt by going to the other extreme. They may appear to be utterly indifferent to their children and excessively narcissistic in their declaration, "I've got to be me!" This type of mother runs the risk of being criticized by her family and the general public. Most people do not see extreme narcissistic behavior as neurotic adjustment. In fact, many see it as selfish sinfulness. But rare is

the woman who is truly heartless toward her children and so totally self-absorbed that she thinks only of herself.

There is great danger, in pastoral counseling or church ministry, of alienating this woman and hardening her in her narcissism. The wise counselor knows that the narcissist is not without feelings for others. She is covering her feelings with steel and concrete so they won't get through to her. Unfortunately, the extreme narcissist is so complex and unlovable that it takes a great deal of wisdom to understand her and a Christlike compassion to love her. The public opposes many of the legitimate goals of women's movements for this very reason—its narcissism.

The balanced woman is to be found somewhere between these two extremes. She understands her children's need to know she still loves them, but she also knows that to be a fully functional mother without custody she must get on with her life. There is a mutual respect of both her needs and her children's needs. It is the kind of attitude reflected in the following letter of a mother without custody to her children. She acknowledges that the separation was painful and then says:

This is difficult for all of us. . . . You are part of my life and will be always. . . . In future years, when you are grown, there would have come a time when you would have to leave me and go on to live a life on your own, but our separation was so premature. I let go of you before either of us was ready. . . . I care about you every day. I care that your body is well. I care that your emotions and mind are well, just like when I lived with you. I love you as much as always. I am here whenever you need me. I am either one ring away on the phone or one hour away in my car, but I am as close to you as your skin. In my heart, I love you . . . MOM.[10]

Fathers Without Custody

"Where is justice for the man who is divorced? He is going to lose if he is a working man [and] if he has a good-paying job he might as well forget it."[11] So editorializes Darlene Newberry, second wife of the founder of a local fathers' rights organization. She assures her readers that the intent of the fathers' rights organization is not to get out of child support but rather to obtain "justice in the court for divorced fathers."

It is remarkable that neither mothers with custody nor fathers without custody feel they are treated justly by child-support laws and enforcement. In chapter 2 we looked at the mothers' complaints. But what injustice is felt by fathers?

The Child-Support Issue

Fathers who have been ordered by the court to pay child support feel that they in turn ought to have their visitation rights honored. But when the relationship between the divorced parents is antagonistic, the custodial parent, who is usually the mother, will often deny visitation. She may feel that this is justified on the ground that the father is a negative influence on the child. The father's response to denial of visitation is nonpayment of support. One father said, "If she's not going to let me see my kids, why should I pay any support? All I'm good for in her eyes is a paycheck. She needs to know that there's more to being a father than that!"

Under the law, however, the courts view support and visitation as separate issues. Divorce settlements specify the amount of child support, but visitation rights are not spelled out. "Reasonable visitation rights" are what usually appears on paper. What is reasonable for one parent often is not reasonable for the other. But no law is broken if visitation is curtailed. The noncustodial parent must get a lawyer and have the court decide if the custodial parent is being unreasonable.

Child support is another matter. Failure to pay child support is a violation of specific terms of the settlement. The nonpaying parent stands in contempt and is either subjected to being hailed into court or having a federal tax refund diverted by the Internal Revenue Service for child support.[12] Mothers whose spouses fail to comply with court-mandated child support can get the money from diverted tax refunds and can depend on the IRS to seize the husbands' assets to pay for back support.

Regulations require that there be a minimum back payment of $750 owed before the IRS arrests the offender. Regulations also require that the state child-support enforcement agency must have made reasonable efforts to collect before the IRS will consider the matter. All requests must include the debtor's social security number and verification of his last known address.

In 1982, $166 million in back support was collected by the IRS. Congress seems interested in tightening up the system even more. One bill would require states to set up mandatory collection systems from wages. Another would require states to notify credit bureaus when debtors fail to pay support.[13]

Sometimes an irate father without custody will threaten to quit work to avoid paying child support. This is inadvisable. The Supreme Court of New Mexico in 1982 ruled on the case of a father who did this. The court said:

> The respondent claims that he used all of his funds for business and personal living expenses. If he did so, it was bad judgment on his part and clearly a willful violation of his obligations. It is unfortunate that he ignored his most important single obligation, namely, the support of his minor child (Niemyjski v. Niemyjski).[14]

Texas has pioneered legislation attempting to redress what is felt to be the inequity of support without visitation. The bill provides that visitation in divorce decrees be made specific and enforceable and be defended by the child enforcement network. This means that the state enforces the collection of support and the visitation rights of the parent without custody according to the terms stated in the divorce decree. Children are protected, however, by provisions that can deny visitation to an abusive parent. One attorney believes that the new law will eliminate 30 percent of noncompliance child-support cases.[15]

Fathers Dispute Support Statistics

According to the American Child Custody Alliance, a fathers' rights group, nonsupport statistics are being manipulated to make fathers look bad. The Alliance lambasted a Texas politician who said that only 9 percent of children deserving support receive it. They maintain that more than one-quarter of Aid to Families with Dependent Children (AFDC) cases involved a parent who *could* not contribute because he was incapacitated. Of the remaining number 80 percent were paternity cases, uncollectable because the mother could not identify the father.[16]

Even though the figure of nonsupport is still high (about 25 percent, according to the Alliance), the statistics are still not accurate. AFDC rules encourage divorced parents to slip money under the table but continue to claim nonsupport so they will get aid.[17] What is happening in Texas is probably happening nationwide and is probably skewing national nonsupport figures.

Angry and Depressed Fathers

We have seen that mothers without custody tend to be guilt-ridden. Fathers without custody tend to be angry and depressed. They are angry over the support/visitation inequity, and depression is one of the major reasons why fathers without custody fail to continue relationships with their children. They deal with depression by avoiding what makes them depressed.

Fathers who feel rejected by their wives often expect the same from their children. Shame, grief, lowered self-esteem, and a feeling of expendability gather in a cloud of depression that appears every time they visit. Depression saps the energy needed for the demands of a visit. The father will often begin to drink heavily, particularly after visiting with his child.[18]

Some men who felt consciously or unconsciously guilty for the breakup of the marriage found it difficult to initiate and maintain visits with their children. For many, their relationships with their children prior to divorce had been very important. But after divorce their guilt made it difficult for them to face their children.[19]

One father without custody wept after a visit with his ten-year-old son. "I love him so much—and he loves me," the father sobbed. "But my boy loves his mother too, and I wouldn't put him through the pain of asking him to choose between us in a custody fight. And it would be a fight because his mother would never give him up.

"Do you understand what I mean when I say that I love him so much I can't see him any more?" He paused, stopped his tears, sighed, and said, "I'm not going to see him any more." This father turned to stone before my eyes. He had regained control of himself and would no longer permit himself to have feelings.

I understand this man's agony, but I knew his son would not understand that his father didn't come around anymore because he cared *too much*.

The experience of this father is common. One researcher writes:

> Divorced men in one study felt shut out, rootless and at
> loose ends two years after their divorces were final. The
> biggest problem these men faced was the pain of mourning
> the loss of constant contact with their kids. All too often,
> they dealt with this hurt by cutting themselves off from
> their youngsters in order to avoid the regular torment of
> saying hello only to say goodbye again.[20]

Easing the pain by avoiding the children is good neither for the children nor for the father. A study of 128 fathers without custody found that the ones who recovered from divorce the fastest were those who were busy making a home for the children to visit and making arrangements for visits. Contact with the children resulted in the fathers' feeling less inadequate and depressed and feeling they had a part in the children's lives again. The pain of repeated separations was offset by a growing sense of involvement in the children's lives.[21]

The children also benefited. They seemed to have a lower incidence of school problems, antisocial behavior, and low self-esteem. The National Institute on Drug Abuse goes so far as to say that children who have contact with a warm and caring father as a role model are less likely to turn to drugs than those with an absent or uncaring dad.[22] An interesting side effect is that a good relationship with the biological father correlates with a good relationship with a stepfather when the mother remarries.

Parents don't intend to hurt their children. But the harsh realities of life often prevent parents from doing what they know they should be doing. Such parents need our compassion, not our condemnation.

The need for compassion is highlighted by the report of a Vancouver psychiatrist who calls these men "abandoned husbands." He says that they are poorly understood and underserved by sychotherapists. He sees them as socially isolated, ill-prepared or separation, and incapable of dealing with injury to their egos.

All too often, as clinicians, our unconscious sex-role stereotypes and bias toward these men have aggravated this process. We have underestimated the magnitude of their confusion, fear, isolation and anguish in our inability to look behind their rage and its behavioral manifestations. Many of these husbands can be assisted in treatment with the correct approach: warm, non-threatening invitations with clear guidelines and responses to queries. A coercive and/or patronizing approach will fail.[23]

nvolved Noncustodial Parents

tatistics tend to encourage the stereotype of noncustodial parents s missing or uninvolved parents, but many noncustodial parents re very involved with their children—and would be more involved if they were not obstructed by custodial parents. Such bstruction is particularly tragic when the noncustodial parent is ctually the more interested and more "fit" parent. But the courts, nable to assess who the more fit parent is, will often award ustody for reasons other than fitness:

- to the mother because the "tender years presumption" still exists (a child of "tender years" should be with his mother);

- to the father because a male judge or master (though he wouldn't admit it) is not impartial and is upset by women getting the man's money and children;

- or to the parent the child chooses to live with—a questionable basis of awarding custody, as we will see in the next chapter.

Three such cases come to mind.

When the Courts Let You Down

The first case involved a prejudiced (in my view) master who awarded the father custody because the teenage daughter requested it. That may have been enough justification for his decisions, in his own mind. But when he forgave five thousand dollars that the father owed in back child support because the mother now "was earning enough money" to care for the second child still in her custody, he raised serious questions about his impartiality. The husband's attorney was astonished at the decision—and, of course, delighted. The case is now under appeal.

I counseled this couple before they divorced, and there is no question in my mind that this angry and violent man is an unfit husband and father. He was verbally and physically abusive to his wife and is verbally abusive to both his children. His self image is severely crippled, and rather than own it as his problem he lashes out at others whom he thinks thwart and obstruct him— even his children.

The two other cases involve noncustodial fathers who both are doing their very best to have active roles in the development of their children. But in both cases the custodial mothers are uncooperative and obstructive.

One of the mothers seems indifferent to reports from school about the rebellion of the youngest child and the poor work of both the children. The father has spent a great deal of time on the phone, long distance, with the children and with the school teachers trying to solve the problems. He has even been going over every school assignment with his children—his phone bill must be horrendous! When the children come to visit him, the mother shows her lack of cooperation by refusing to pack adequate and appropriate clothes. The father has had to buy completely new wardrobes for the children so they will have something to wear when they visit.

Both this man and his wife, the noncustodial stepmother, ache for the children and feel that there has been a miscarriage of justice. But what can be done?

They have already taken two constructive steps. One is to insist on the noncustodial parent's right of access to all records—school and any others that affect the child's health and well-being. Second

e noncustodial father, with his wife's support, continues to remain
tive with the children. This leads me to make a third suggestion.
A noncustodial parent who feels that he or she is the more fit
rent should keep a daily log in ink in a bound record book.
e entries should include the day and time of contacts with the
ildren, the purpose of the contact, and any obstruction or lack
cooperation on the part of the custodial parent. The purpose
the log is to amass evidence to support the parent's contention
at he is the more fit parent, that he is more involved in the
tterment of the children than the custodial parent, and that the
stodial parent is obstructing the noncustodial parent. The names
d comments of all other interested parties should be included,
ch as school officials, doctors, and family therapists who may
subpoenaed to testify in court when a "petition to modify"
custody arrangement is issued. This is very time consuming
d expensive. Yet there are noncustodial parents whose com-
tment to their children is so strong that time and money are
cidental.

The noncustodial parent should be sure that his motives are
re. He should be certain that the interest of the children is his
me concern and that they are not being used as pawns in a
ntinuing power struggle.

e Noncustodial Stepmother

Since writing *The Readymade Family*, I have been hearing from
ore and more noncustodial stepmothers about the burdens they
rry. They are trying to make their marriages to noncustodial
rents work. They stand by with heavy hearts watching their
sbands try to be effective, involved noncustodial parents but
structed and thwarted in their efforts by "the other woman"—
custodial mother.

Celia, a noncustodial stepmother, who wrote to express her
stration, said, "My letter to you was going to be a 'help me'
ter, but things worked out—almost too late." She is childless
d would dearly love to be an active role model for her hus-
nd's children. But the ex-wife, the custodial mother, does not
nt Celia involved in any way with her children and even ob-
ucts her husband's involvement. Celia was frustrated not only
being cut out of the children's lives, but also in feeling that

the ex-wife was running her life. She said, "I don't like the wa
she thinks she can run our lives. She demands that my husban
Frank, call every other weekend and come up on a weeke
every six weeks. We will do what is convenient for us and n
her."

Celia continued, "It's hard to be a part-time stepmother.
realize that [stepson's name] needs to adjust to me and know m
I have to earn his trust and love. I also have adjustments to mak
and it isn't easy. Now, I feel that Frank wants what I want. I
told his son that we would not visit at his mother's house an
more because 'Daddy and Celia have their own place.' I fe
better about things now."

Helpful Hints for Parents
Without Custody

In chapters 5 and 6 the issues of custody and visitation will
treated in detail. But let me make some suggestions here to pa
ents without custody.

One single father who had difficulty keeping up with his tee
age son, who moved from Miami after the divorce, develop
ideas of ways to keep in touch. He collected them into a bo
called *1001 Ways to Be a Long-Distance Super Dad*.[24] Mothe
without custody can use these ideas too:

- Arrange beforehand what time you'll telephone your
  child. If it's inconvenient, phone back later.

- Keep a running list of topics to talk about over the phone;
  your conversations will be more meaningful.

- Choose a distinctive stationery so your child will immediately pick out your letters.

- Clip and send newspaper or magazine articles or pictures
  that would interest your child. Mention them in your
  next conversation.

- Find out your child's favorite TV programs and watch
  them. Watch the first 10 minutes of special shows or
  sporting events "together" via telephone.

- If your child's community has a science museum, planetarium society or film club, s/he might enjoy a year's membership in the junior division.

- Send your former spouse pre-addressed manila envelopes and several dollars' worth of postage so you can help with homework. Once you've received the schoolwork, offer your youngster feedback. On your next trip to visit your child's teachers, ask how you can help your child.[25]

In chapter 3 I mentioned a helpful publication for Christian fathers called *Dads Only*. The publisher also publishes *Dads and Moms*.[26] the latter is for all parents, but the single parent can glean a lot of ideas from it. It is chock-full of ideas to involve parents with their children. We can't always keep our marriages together. But we don't have to divorce our children.

⚶ 5
Custody: The Struggle Goes On and On

The official-looking document arrives in the mail, and printed on the cover is the Latin phrase *A Vinculo Matrimonii*. It means literally, "from the bonds of matrimony." It is a full-fledged, legal divorce, sometimes called, "the final decree."

But those who have children, are divorced, and have ex-spouses who have decided not to become "missing spouses," know that divorce is anything but final. Laws governing custody, child support, and visitation often leave the door open to a struggle that goes on and on. No matter who is initially awarded custody by the court, that award may be challenged by the noncustodial parent by filing a "petition for modification." It may be filed when the circumstances of either parent or of the children have materially and substantially changed since the entry of the order of the decree, or if it would be in the children's interest to make some change in the original custody arrangement.[1] Also, the court may challenge the custody and visitation arrangements. Indeed, the court, not the parent, acts as the custodian of the children and has the right to take them away, assign them to a foster home, or even declare them adoptable if neither parent is considered fit.[2]

Given this state of affairs, it is important that the single parent understand how custody can affect him and his child's relationship with both parents and how he might approach ongoing custody challenges constructively.

How It All Began—A Short History

To understand how the court decides an equitable custody arrangement, it may be helpful to review the history of custody.

The Absolute Power of the Father

Our modern notion of parent-child relations evolved from Roman law (about 500 B.C.). At that time a child was viewed as the property of the father, who in turn assumed the physical care of his property. The idea of a child as property and later the provider of services and income to his father didn't begin to change until the sixteenth century. The law was slow to adapt to this changing philosophy. Even then, when a marriage was dissolved, the custody of the child went to the father, who retained his property rights. If, however, the father was deprived of the child for any reason, he was absolved of financial support. The state respected the father's common-law right to custody and did not intervene except in the case of the father's default.[3]

This tradition of noninterference was broken in England in 1839 with the Talfourds Act. For the first time in history, the idea of the father's absolute authority was challenged and the court claimed the right to determine the custody of children under seven. This move set the stage for one of the main governing principles of custody that carried over into the twentieth century—the "Tender Years Presumption."[4]

Mother Knows Best

In 1880 a judge presiding over the *Hart v. Hart* custody dispute ruled in favor of the mother with the argument, "The claim of a mother during the years of the infant's life to care for her child is to be preferred to that of the father." This decision revealed that judges were beginning to distinguish between the physical support and the psychological well-being of the child. Though this set a precedent, maternal custody was still considered the exception, and when a child turned four, the court usually returned the child to the father.[5]

The mother's importance in the child's life had now been established. This was gradually expanded upon until the early twentieth century, when the mother's right to custody and the father's duty to support a child not in his custody became law. Now the accepted belief, supported by the moral and cultural climate, was that the mother was better able to meet the physical and psychological needs of the child with the father's financial support.[6]

But What About the Children?

For almost two thousand years no one seemed to speak for the children and their rights except in the case of an abusive parent. The battle in the courts focused on fathers' rights versus mothers' rights. In 1925 Judge Benjamin Cardozo, in *Finlay v. Finlay*, did something about this oversight when he introduced the concept of "the best interest of the child." The judge ruled that neither a father nor a mother has cause for action against the other or against anyone else. It is their responsibility to act in the best interest of the child. The guidelines were:

1. The young child should be placed with the mother.

2. A girl should be in the mother's custody; the boy in the father's custody, providing he no longer requires the mother's constant care.

3. If the child is old enough he can voice his preference.

4. The noncustodial parent has visitation rights.[7]

This ruling seemed to break new ground. Yet the application of the new doctrine was criticized because it favored the mother. Historically she was the primary caregiver and in fact knew far more about the child's physical and emotional needs than the father, and the ruling recognized that. But now, with modern role changes, fathers are claiming that they can be just as nurturing as mothers. Just as mothers are breaking into the man's world of business, fathers are breaking into the woman's world of nurturing parent, the primary caregiver. Fathers maintain that thinking must shift from a "mothering" role to a "primary caregiver role," be it mother's or father's.

Thirty-one states eventually developed statutes that establish the best-interest-of-the-child standard. The others let the courts decide if the standard is met. The basic considerations are the kind of relationship the child has with the parent; the desire of the child; the health, welfare, and social behavior of the child; and that no presumption shall exist that one parent is more fit than the other. In spite of these guidelines, what is in the best interest of the child requires more information and understanding of the family than the court can possibly acquire.

The Child's Preference

In trying to arrive at a decision of what is in the child's best interest, lawmakers and the courts felt that the child's preference was to be taken into account. Which parent did he want to live with? In 1974 the American Bar Association attempted to establish guidelines to facilitate this. One of the guidelines provides a court-appointed attorney for the child. All fifty states now inquire into the child's preference.[8]

The idea of the child's preference sounds good when we consider that the parents are battling over what *they* believe to be *in their best interest*. Most parents believe they are also arguing for what is in the child's interest. But the court wants to know the *child's* preference. Is this a good thing? Consider the following:

1. *What child, even a teenager, can anticipate the future implications of a decision as important as this?* Can he, at his maturity level, really determine what is best for him?

2. *Is the child's decision truly his own?* Or is the preference coached, directly or indirectly, by his parents or extended family? Does the child know that one parent would show more hurt than the other parent if he made the "wrong" choice and is thus manipulated?

3. *The idea of having to make a choice runs contrary to God's pattern for the family.* It's like being asked, "Which do you want, your left leg or right leg?" It divides a child's loyalty and places on him the responsibility to reject one of the parents. This is why a strong depressive reaction is seen in children who express a preference, no matter which parent is granted custody. One researcher put it well when he said, "Out of concern for insuring the child's right to choose be-

tween his parents, it seems that the legal and cultural system often parentifies the child it seeks to protect."[9]

The Best Interest Of The Child

The "best interest of the child" has spawned a number of custody arrangements, all of which lay claim to the best interest of the child. There is, however, one custody arrangement that isn't bogged down by "the best interest" argument. It is promoted in the book *Beyond the Best Interest of the Child*. It proposes that if continuity between the custodial parent and child is to be uninterrupted, "the noncustodial parent should have no legally enforceable right to visit the child, and the custodial parent should have the right to decide whether it is desirable for the child to have such visits."[10]

A major criticism of this position is that it ignores the child's right to maintain a relationship with both parents and ignores his deep-seated need to be loyal to both parents—a loyalty that idealizes even the most unloving and brutal parent. Such a position also assumes that those who decide which parent should have sole custody are choosing the most fit parent. It further assumes that they know this parent is capable of determining objectively whether or not the child should be exposed to the noncustodial parent. Even the courts are reluctant to lay claim to such cosmic wisdom.

Custody Arrangements

There are two basic types of custody arrangements: sole custody and joint custody. But actually there are various kinds of arrangements, and five are usually mentioned.[11]

1. *Sole custody.* This is custody granted by the court to one parent (the custodial parent) with the other parent (noncustodial) maintaining rights to see the child periodically. The custodial parent is legally and physically responsible for the child's activities, conduct, and well-being. He or she is the administrator of the child's custody and therefore, in effect, controls the child's access to the parent without custody.

2. *Joint custody.* There are three kinds of joint custody: *legal* custody, joint *physical* custody, and joint *legal* and *physical* custody.

   Joint legal custody means that both parents share the legal responsibility for the control of their child. If little Johnny has a run-in with the law, both parents answer in court. Theoretically both parents have a say in all decisions. However, if both parents have legal custody but only one has *physical* custody, the absent parent can't be much of an influence. In fact, the absent parent may find himself seriously compromised. He may have legal responsibility for the child with no practical way to have an influence on the child and guide his life. Joint legal custody is more realistic if it includes joint physical custody. Joint legal and physical custody is also called *shared custody, co-custody,* or *co-parenting after divorce.*

3. *Divided or alternative custody.* This may sound like joint custody, but it is actually sole custody for each parent in part of a year or in alternating years. Unless the parents agree to make all decisions about the child together, no matter who the child may be living with, the arrangement is not joint custody. As with sole custody, the impact of the absent parent is minimal. Children need frequent and meaningful interaction with both parents.

4. *Split custody.* In this arrangement one child lives permanently with one parent and another child lives with the other parent. Each child visits the other parent. Split custody is not joint custody unless both parents agree to assume responsibility for the actions of all the children and they jointly make all decisions regarding the children. Split-custody arrangements are workable when the children are of different sexes and ages—three or four years or more different.

5. *Genuine shared custody.* This is achieved when there is a time-sharing formula that involves two parents committed to being involved in all the important decisions regarding the children and maintaining as much physical contact as circumstances and geography allow.

The Disadvantages of Sole Custody

Sole custody has two serious defects:

1. *The first defect is that it may cut off the noncustodial parent from contact with the child.* If the custodial mother remarries and moves out of state with her new husband, the noncustodial father will be deprived of regular visiting rights.

   Not all noncustodial parents caught in that situation are as fortunate as Michael Konczewski of Queens, New York, whose ex-wife, Gail, moved to Florida with their six-year-old daughter and her new husband. Gail happened to be wealthy enough ($80,000 a year) to absorb the court-ordered ruling that she pay $4,000 a year to her husband so he can make monthly visits to his daughter.[12]

   The custodial parent as the administrator of the child's custody can decide whether or not it is in the child's best interest to see the noncustodial parent. Unless the custody decree spells out the terms of visitation, the noncustodial parent faces a long and expensive court fight to correct the problem.

   In Texas the crowded court dockets require the noncustodial parent to wait six months. Moreover, the custodial parent is unlikely to be punished for obstructing visits. Every time visits are obstructed, the noncustodial parent must hire an attorney and wait another six months. This invites the "no visit no support" response of the noncustodial parent.

2. *Another defect in the sole-custody arrangement is that it requires the court to decide which parent is "most fit" to be the primary caregiver.* One women's-rights attorney argues that the court should give much weight to "the experience of the primary caretaker in feeding, clothing, sickness care, educational and social development, discipline, companionship and to the need for continuity in these and many other areas of child care."[13]

   Because most women are socialized to be caregivers, this argument favors them. In a custody battle a father can be made to look unfit. Visualize, for example, a father on the witness stand responding to his wife's attorney:

Attorney: Do you love your children?

Father: Yes, of course.

A: Who is their pediatrician?

F: I'm not sure.

A: Who has been called when there was an emergency in the past?

F: I'm not sure.

A: Do you have a phone number for such a person?

F: No.

A: Your wife has taken care of these details in the past, hasn't she?

F: I guess so.

A: Then she really can take care of the medical needs of the children, can't she?[14]

To counter this problem in representing their male clients, attorneys are preparing fathers for custody with the help of family therapists.[15] The father learns how to be a primary caregiver and how to answer questions on the witness stand:

Attorney: Do you love your children?

Father: Yes, of course.

A: Who is their pediatrician?

F: Dr. Moore is now, but I'm going to relocate, and Dr. Smith has been recommended. I have conferred with him and he will accept the children as patients and Dr. Moore has said he will transfer their records.

A: Who has been called in an emergency in the past?

F: Dr. Moore, Dr. Smith now can be called, and there is a medical facility with an emergency room three blocks from my apartment.

A: What's the phone number?

F: Seven-four-eight-four-five-oh-five.

A: Your wife has taken care of these details in the past, hasn't she?

F: Yes. I worked and she stayed at home. Now we both will be working, and I am prepared to assume the care of the children.

A: Then she really can take care of the medical needs of the children, can't she?

F: We both can.

The scenario is sad but necessary, because a battle for sole custody requires the court to find out which parent is most fit. Even though a child's ongoing and frequent contact with both parents is important and even though either parent may be equally fit as primary caregiver, the court must decide which parent will have sole custody. This conjures up the scene in Solomon's court where the two women laid claim to the same child (1 Kings 3:16–28). The wisdom of Solomon is still needed today; the baby can't be cut in two. Yet, children are torn. One five-year-old boy actually told his mother that he wanted to cut himself in half so he could be with both parents at the same time.[16]

Some states are tipping the scales against mothers by giving a great deal of weight to economic circumstances. Some judges believe that economic conditions are important to providing a "stable" home environment and good child care. One women's rights advocate says, "Since most women have less earning capacity and poorer employment prospects than their husbands, this places women at an immediate disadvantage in winning child custody."[17] She maintains that these considerations are severely hurting mothers, who are losing two-thirds of all litigated custody disputes.[18]

The "fitness" of the custodial parent should not be based on either caregiving expertise or income. Both have a bearing. But the child needs both parents—except, of course, an abusive parent. The most fit custodial parent is the one who is able to provide an ongoing relationship with both biological parents and as many members of the child's family of origin as possible. The most fit parent is the one who is able to tolerate and collaborate in such an ongoing relationship.

This type of fitness doctrine would help stop the horrible civil war that is common in sole-custody cases. Thirteen-year-old John was the victim of such a war.

John grew up in a home with a very dominant mother, Betty, and a passive father, Jack. As the marriage began to deteriorate, Betty decided she had had enough and told Jack to get out. Jack consulted an attorney, who advised him to stay put and not forfeit his property and parental rights.

That did it. Fort Sumter exploded, and Betty launched an offensive to strengthen John's loyalties to her and undercut his loyalties to his father. She pulled incredible stunts. She told her son that his father was playing around with other women and had turned their summer cottage into "a whore house." When Jack attempted to have time alone with John, Betty deliberately obstructed it. For example, Jack arranged for John to go out to supper with him, with Betty's full knowledge. About the time they were to go out, Betty cooked supper and acted angry and hurt because John was not going to eat at home. To pacify his mother, John stayed home.

At his attorney's suggestion, Jack brought John to see me. I was to find out what the boy wanted. I was not surprised to learn that the boy wanted his parents to stop putting him in the middle of their fights and to stop fighting.

About fifteen minutes into the session I heard a knock on my door. When I opened it, I was confronted by an angry woman with blazing eyes who demanded, "Is John _____ here?" I told her he was. She then pushed her way into the room and said, "He was brought here against his will. John, get your coat! We're going home!"

I said, "Just a minute! You're on my turf right now. Perhaps you'd like to call the police and register your complaint. And if you don't, I will."

She stormed out in a huff. The boy just sat there with a blank expression on his face as if to say, "So what else is new?"

Making toleration and collaboration a primary test of fitness would help prevent scenes like this.

Sole custody does offer an advantage in that some people are unable to function as parents and need the other parent to take over. Sometimes a parent's physical or emotional liabilities are so great, their children are better off with the other parent. As they return to health they are able to have more meaningful contacts with the children.

There also are people who have no business being parents. They have no tolerance for the demands that parenting places on them. Children in the custody of such parents run the risk of physical and emotional harm. Sole custody with a parent who encourages contact with the absent parent is far better than custody by a parent who can be damaging to the child.

The Disadvantages of Joint Legal and Physical Custody. It should be remembered that joint *legal* custody without joint *physical* custody makes a parent legally responsible for the child with limited opportunities to guide the child. The two should go together for greatest effectiveness. But joint physical custody can entail problems. Some legitimate arguments are mustered against joint physical custody:

1. *It is disruptive for a child to have two homes rather than one.* But one researcher replies on the basis of her findings that children adjusted readily to a two-home routine and there was less pain in separation than in families with sole-custody arrangements. Parents and children knew they would be together again soon.[19]

2. *The "yo-yo" problem.* The child's loyalties may continue to be tested by the parents' continuing dislike of each other. This is a distinct possibility, and children may even look for it.

   One joint-custody mother reported that her thirteen-year-old daughter told her that her father had bought a new car and had paid cash for it. The mother innocently—and, I believe, sincerely—remarked, "It must be nice to be able to do that." The daughter demanded, "What do you mean by that?" When the mother tried to explain that no offense was intended, the daughter didn't believe her. They just dropped the matter.

   The mother said, "Jackie is always doing this. It's as though she expects her father and me to be at odds with each other and continually tests to see if it's so." The mother is probably right. Jackie is engaging in some "security testing" to make sure her parents are still in a cooperative mood.

   In defense of joint physical custody, it should be noted that though loyalty battles may occur, they are more likely to occur in sole-custody arrangements where there is more need to vie for power and position.[20]

3. *Divorced parents will not cooperate.* If the parents can get along so well with a joint physical custody arrangement, why did they divorce? The answer usually given is that former spouses who are successful at joint custody are able to separate their problems with each other from their parenting responsibilities.[21] One researcher goes so far as to claim that 85 percent of divorced couples are able to do this.[22] That figure sounds a bit high, however.

One thing is certain. Given the choice between sole custody and joint custody, children prefer joint custody.[23] Here are some typical comments:

- I wouldn't like a visiting [noncustodial] relationship with my dad. That would be like having only one parent.

- The good thing about joint custody is that I get a chance to be close to both my parents.

- I get to know both of them and to see each parent more as a person.[24]

One man tells of lessons he has learned from the joint-custody arrangement involving his thirteen-year-old son. The father said that at first he was overprotective of his son, which played into the boy's fears. He also admitted doing things to show his former wife as an unfit mother. For example, his son called to ask him to come and get him because his mother went to a party and "dumped" him at his grandfather's. At one time the father would have done just that rather than talking about it over the phone and encouraging the boy to talk out the problem with his mother. The father said:

Organizing joint custody so that the child spends blocks of time with each parent is very important. We alternated too often in the beginning, with the result that my son felt fragmented or split all the time, rather than still having a connection with both parents. This has also given me more time to have with my own life, in that I can go out when he is not with me. My son wavers. At times he wants more space and freedom, but at other times he accuses me of trying to get rid of him.

One of his major fears was that because he didn't have a mother his friends would make fun of him. This was *in spite* of the fact that many of his friends' parents were divorced. He still was living with the TV family myth. At times he was feeling so rejected that he alienated his friends, his teachers *and* me.

A year later, he still expresses reconciliation fantasies telling me, "If you get divorced, I'm leaving." When I introduced him to a female friend, I got a lot of resistance and hostility.

One good thing is that my son has begun to express more positive emotions toward me: touching, showing affection.[25]

Louisiana's Joint Custody Bill

The State of Louisiana adopted a joint physical and legal custody statute effective January 1, 1983, that is being watched carefully by attorneys and marriage and family therapists. Under the statute, joint custody is presumed, unless the parents agree to award custody to one parent. Other provisions include:

- Order of preference: custody shall be awarded in the following order of preference, according to the best interest of the child: (1) to both parents jointly; (2) to either parent, without preference to sex, considering which parent is more likely to allow contact with the other.

- Plans prior to decree: the court shall require the parents to submit a plan for implementation. The plan may include housing arrangements for the child(ren), right of access and communications between the parents and the child(ren), and child support and any other matter deemed in the child(ren)'s interest.

- Burden of proof: the burden to prove that joint custody

is not in the child's interest rests upon the parent re-
questing sole custody.

- Information exchange: the award of joint custody obli-
gates the parties to exchange information.

- Option in determining rights: unless rights are already
allocated, apportioned, or decreed, parents should confer
in the exercise of decision-making rights and responsibilities.

- Terminating joint custody: an order for joint custody or
any plan may be modified or terminated if best interest
requires modification.

- Not modify existing orders: the act does not modify existing custody orders.[26]

At least one feminist group opposes joint custody as "harmful
to women and children."[27] They present a number of arguments:

1. *Men use joint custody as a bargaining tool to intimidate and
threaten their wives in order to extract more favorable property and support agreements*. They believe the ploy is particularly successful where women feel joint custody is not in the
child's best interest and the statute favors the parent seeking
joint custody.

   The argument does not appear valid in view of the provisions of the Louisiana model statute. A woman may block
joint custody by proving it is not in the child's best interest,
but the burden of proof rests on her. The problem with joint
custody may arise in part from the mother's inability to distinguish *her* best interest from the *child's* best interest.

2. *Men use joint custody to avoid paying outstanding support
orders*. This argument ignores the provision that the act does
not modify existing orders.

3. *Joint custody does not force fathers to become responsible
parents; it only gives them the right to interfere*. This argument ignores the burden-of-proof provision of the law. If she
can prove her allegations, she should.

4. *Joint custody is not in the child's best interest because it doesn't provide any more of a continuing relationship with both parents than sole custody, yet it allows the nonresponsible parent to make things difficult.* This argument ignores provisions of the Louisiana model: (a) the law provides for both *legal and physical* custody, allowing for a continuing relationship with both parents, and (b) it ignores again the burden-of-proof provision. If a woman's husband is not responsible, she should tell it to the judge. But she should remember that the burden of proof is on her.

5. *Joint custody forces a remarriage of hostile parties, which brings more disruption into the child's life.* This is a valid point, and the situation may require some monitoring by the court. The court could impose penalties such as fines or community service if it finds that the parents are not acting in the child's best interest. An uncooperative parent stands in contempt of court.

6. *Joint custody is being ordered in cases involving battered women.* When the woman opposes joint custody out of fear for her own safety, she is viewed as uncooperative and custody may be awarded to the batterer. The failure here is not in the statute itself, particularly the Louisiana model, but in its application. Once again, burden of proof is the issue.[28]

The Benefits of Mediation

No discussion of custody is complete without mentioning mediation. People who are about to become divorced single parents or who are considering a modification of the present custody plan may want to give serious consideration to mediation.

1. *What mediation can do.* Mediation is a nonadversarial alternative to the lawyer-adversary process of the courtroom. A mediator is neither an attorney nor a psychotherapist. He is a counselor skilled in helping a couple come to a mutually agreed decision regarding child and spouse support, child custody, and the division of property.

   Some mediators prefer "structured mediation," which involves an orientation session followed by the signing of a contract formally agreeing to mediation and to abide by certain rules. These include preparing financial statements and meeting with the mediator according to a fixed schedule. Appendix C shows a sample contract.[29]

Most couples require from four to six sessions of two hours each. The husband, wife, and mediator meet together. At least one session is held in the presence of an attorney, who draws up the agreement.

The couple usually meets with the attorney outside the mediation sessions to discuss the legal ramifications of their agreement. They may also meet with a financial consultant. Additional legal consultation may take two to six hours, and financial advice one to five hours.

The mediator, attorney, and accountant receive separate fees. The contract may state that if the couple reaches an impasse at certain points they will be subject to arbitration by an impartial third party, possibly someone from the American Arbitration Association.[30]

Mediation is cost effective. One study found it one-third less expensive than the lawyer-adversary process (an average of $764 compared with $2,359).[31]

2. *What mediation cannot do.* Mediation is not a substitute for therapy, though it may have therapeutic value. For mediation to be effective there must be a certain level of trust between the couple that they will work together in good faith.

Not all mediators like the structured contractual method. They feel that not everyone is ready to enter binding arbitration. Some people are not ready to deal with their spouses face to face. In such cases meetings are arranged separately until the people are ready to meet face to face.

Disagreement among mediators over the best approach is understandable when we realize the practice is only about ten years old. But it offers a viable alternative to the adversarial system. More information on mediation and mediators may be obtained from Family Mediation Association, 5018 Allen Road, Washington, DC 20016.

Marriage Therapist As Divorce Counselor

Every marriage therapist finds himself in the position of being unable to save a marriage. To release the couple from care to go their separate ways and find divorce lawyers at that point only encourages escalating the adversarial behavior. The therapist is in a position to guide the couple in nonadversarial dissolution of their marriage.

Usually a marriage on the brink of dissolution has a faulty communication pattern. The therapist can help the couple work through their communication difficulties to achieve a divorce settlement with fewer emotional wounds than they might sustain without his help. Going through the steps of planning the dissolution of the marriage sometimes presents a therapeutic paradox: the marriage may not look so bad after all. Such a move emotionally releases the couple from a communication deadlock and frees them to reconsider relating to each other in a different way. Moreover, the emotional and financial penalties of divorce sometimes make the marriage look positively attractive.

A more common situation is when only one spouse remains in counseling after the decision to divorce. The therapist is able to guide her (which is usually the case) as to where to go next. Though legal advice is not given, the therapist is able to explain the divorce process and give the client direction and support and then coordinate her needs with other professionals such as attorneys, mediators, and financial advisers.

One woman who was married to an angry, possessive, suffocating, and intimidating husband wrote to me of her experience after her husband dropped out of counseling:

> This may sound odd, because I know you are in the business of saving marriages and ours failed, but I really want to thank you for what you did. You managed to make me see that I should not feel guilty about making room for my own needs. I only wish that I had realized that sooner.

As a Christian therapist I consider it important to collaborate with my Christian clients' attorneys, particularly if the attorney is not a Christian. Some attorneys regard a Christian's attempt to be loving, even in the face of a lawsuit, as neurotic. Through collaboration I am able to help the client and the attorney prepare a defense that is consistent with Christian behavior.

Single parents sometimes use family therapists when they are facing a petition to modify a custody suit. The therapist's expertise in family systems and communication is essential. A divorced family with children *is still a family*, even though the husband and wife would like to be done with each other. A therapist who understands the new family structure created by divorce may be in a position to make suggestions that will ensure the healthy development of the child caught in the middle. His understanding of communication and interpersonal dynamics will enable him to cut through what *appears* to be the truth to what really is happening.

A case in point is the "deaf and dumb" marriage in which the wife exercised control through weakness and continued to do so after divorce. I was consulted by this woman's ex-husband, who was alarmed over the "feminizing" of his eight-year-old son in the custody of his mother. This was a "deaf and dumb" marriage because the husband didn't listen and the wife didn't speak up. This pattern continued after the divorce. The husband was more interested in contending for the logic of his position on everything rather than understanding what his wife was trying to tell him. His interpersonal posture was verbal and aggressive. But her style was to say as little as possible and leave others in doubt as to what she really wanted. Her interpersonal posture was soft spoken, almost nonverbal, and extremely passive. But she always managed to win through weakness. She was able to thwart her husband's efforts at developing a relationship with their son by helping him to make a fool of himself. Whenever she failed to communicate adequately, he became frustrated and tried to facilitate communication by becoming more verbal and aggressive. As he stepped up these behaviors, she withdrew, and then he responded by becoming even more aggressive and verbal. She was able to encourage this process until he looked absolutely unreasonable.

Her son began to adopt her style of communication and began to control his father exactly as she did. I had to help the father see that both his wife and his son were helping him to make himself look bad. Consequently the wife was able to use his "bad behavior" to justify keeping their son away from him. The son was able to control his father and get his way whenever he wanted by using the same tactics.

The father is not bad. He is a devout Christian. And he wanted to be a good husband and father. But he had to see that his assertiveness and verbalness taken to an extreme made his Christian zeal look like fanaticism—that he had a cult mentality. His wife and son managed to help him make a fool of himself in their ongoing custody disputes.

Mediation is good, and it is particularly useful with couples whose interpersonal dynamics are not extremely neurotic. But divorced couples who relate destructively are unable to deal constructively with custody issues. They need to learn how to break the relational pattern. This can be accomplished when either one recognizes what the game is and chooses not to play. For example, the aggressive, verbal father had to see that he was being baited. He needed to learn how to keep the lines of communication open without stepping up his aggressiveness.

For information on family therapists in your area, consult your pastor and consult the person whom he recommends. Or contact the American Association for Marriage and Family Therapy, 1717 K Street N.W. / Suite 407, Washington, DC 20006.

ŤŤŤ 6
Visitation: You Can't Divorce Your Children

Custody statutes keep a divorced couple from ever being entirely free of each other. But more than that, visitation arrangements make the former spouse an everpresent reality—unless, of course, the ex-spouse chooses to drop out of the picture entirely.

Children Need Two Parents

Some divorcés would like nothing better than to see the former spouse "get lost." This is particularly true if the marriage and divorce were stormy.

Good Riddance?

One woman who remarried shares her experience. She had asked her nine-year-old daughter how she felt about her absent father. Would she write down her feelings? The girl wrote:

> Sometimes I feel confused. I have two fathers. One of them lives with me. But the other one lives in Texes [*sic*]. I don't get to see the one who lives in Texes at all. I feel hate and love for him but I don't know how to show it. I don't hear from him at all seen [*sic*] I was 3 years old.

69

And I feel like he doesn't care. But just for once I would like to reach out and love him, but how can I do it, if I do not feel he wants me. I feel sad and sometimes I feel like cring [*sic*]. I have one stepbrother and sister. I get to see them once in a while. But it is better than never.[1]

Most of those who work with families agree that children need two parents or parent figures. Even unmarried single or widowed parents attempt to bring a surrogate, opposite-sex parent figure into the lives of the children.

The child who has no parent because of death may not wonder where his parent is. But he still needs the model of two parent figures.

The child who has a living parent who is absent often seems to have a great curiosity about that person. Even adopted children, when they grow older, seem to have a need to find out something about their biological parents. Adolescents especially need two adults for positive behavior development. One sociologist writes that even if the other parent is not available, the presence of *any* other adult "brings adolescent control levels closer to those found in two-parent households. . . . The raising of an adolescent is not a task that can easily be borne by a lone parent. It may take two to raise an adolescent."[2] The sociologist contends that two adults are able to teach societal norms to adolescents and to exercise surveillance over behavior that is potentially deviant. The additional adult provides social support for the single parent who must deal directly with the adolescent.

Family therapists helping single parents often find rapid improvement in child and teen behavior, particularly when the therapist and parent are of the opposite sex and work in close harmony with each other. This often has the psychological impact of a two-parent home.

How Children Perceive Missing Fathers

Since 90 percent of the time the mother has sole custody and the father is missing from the home, how children perceive these missing fathers is important to the question of visitation.

A study of ninety-six black, white, and Hispanic mothers and children using the projective technique of doll play was revealing.

The children, five and six years old, had lived in the sole custody of the mother since age three. More than eighteen thousand play fantasies with the dolls were tabulated by observers. Forty-six percent involved the father and 43 percent involved the mother. Carol S. Michaels, the therapist heading the study, said, "Even if father is physically absent, the symbolic image occupies much psychological space and time. These findings dispel notions that once father is out of sight, he is out of mind."[3]

Michaels believes that the child uses fantasy to help him or her understand the father's departure, separation, and nonresidency and to reclaim him, at least in fantasy, as a good figure who will always be there. She says, "In this way the child can at least use the fantasy father in the continued movement away from mother toward greater ego autonomy."[4]

The father's impact on a daughter's life is especially important. Roberta Chaplin teaches a course at Hunter College in New York City to help fathers see that they are important as nurturers and not just as providers. The father's failure to nurture has been "devastating for women," according to Dr. Chaplin. To a young girl entering puberty, and even beyond puberty, her father is the most influential man in her life. Because he is a male, he can validate his daughter's femininity as the mother cannot. Verbal and nonverbal messages that his daughter is turning out to be a fantastic woman are vitally important to the girl's self-image. Dr. Chaplin also says:

> Too often this role has been overlooked, especially in divorce cases. For example, psychoanalyst Anna Freud preaches a doctrine whereby the child of divorce should remain with the mother, having no contact at all with the father. Therapists need to be able to show that fathers are therapeutically important to their children, especially their daughters, so that the legal community will also recognize the fact.[5]

But it is not possible for a caring father to have a positive impact on the child if the custodial mother is determined to destroy the father-child relationship. Joan M. Lewis, a family court investigator, goes so far as to say that the overwhelming majority of custodial mothers refuse to recognize that the child's relationship with the father is imperative to the child's development. Acting out of their own pain and anger, they wind up negating the father. They feel a need to punish him, but they wind up punishing the children too. Lewis says that mothers often go to incredible lengths to isolate the child from the father—create distance by moving, change the child's name, or tell the child terrible stories about the father to elicit loyalty.

Lewis also questions statements by the mothers that the fathers are unavailable or uninterested. The courts, she feels, need to investigate to determine whether the fathers really are indifferent and not take the mother's word for it.[6]

Ten Divorce Myths

No therapist is so naïve to suggest that all absent parents, mothers or fathers, ought to be actively involved with the children. One divorcée says, and rightly so, that it takes two people to make a divorce work and that single parents need to be aware of some myths that can make them feel guilty and drive them crazy.[7]

Myth 1.

"Since I've gone past the bad feelings that came with divorce, my ex-spouse should be over them too." Sometimes this happens and makes constructive visitation possible. But when it doesn't, it keeps the naïve parent locked into the destructive games played during the marriage. The single parent can choose not to play any longer. A single custodial parent must not be naïve about "civilized" divorce, but he or she must also be careful not to look for excuses to keep the noncustodial parent away from the children. Likewise, the noncustodial parent must not use the children as pawns in a continuing power struggle.

Myth 2.

"My ex-spouse will change for the better after the divorce." The former spouse's involvement with the children prior to divorce is not *necessarily* an indicator to postdivorce involvement with them. Studies have found that some fathers, close to their children prior to divorce, are unable to cope with a fractured

family and disappear entirely. Other fathers, realizing their loss, make new attempts at relating to their children. Families restructure in different and unpredictable ways after a divorce.

Myth 3.

"My ex-spouse will want joint custody or coparenting." Some divorcés may desire this kind of arrangement. But though it is preferred by most children, if they have to choose between two parents at war and an absent parent with peace, the children will opt for peace.

Myth 4.

"Nice people always have civilized divorces." This is a myth commonly held by Christians, ignoring the fact that even the most godly people part ways in a huff. Consider the experience of Paul and Barnabas (Acts 15:36–41).

Most Christians are unaware of a phenomenon that I call "sanctifying a neurosis." The neurotically aggressive Christian, for example, gains much comfort and support from the conduct of Bible characters such as Joshua (see Josh. 8:1–28) and the words of the psalmist who declared such warriors blessed—warriors who in the spirit of total annihilation bashed the heads of Babylonian babies against the rocks (Ps. 137:8–9). Conversely, the neurotically self-effacing Christian finds a great deal of support in all the Bible verses that speak of meekness and humility. Needless to say, these are sick people who twist the Bible to support their neuroses. For more on the "sanctified neurosis," see my book, *Being a Success at Who You Are* (Zondervan, 1985).

Myth 5.

"In a short while the ex-spouse will settle gracefully into the role of noncustodial parent." Try to encourage this. If it doesn't happen, try to be objective and discern how much of the problem is truly your ex's and how much offensive behavior you are encouraging. You may need the objective opinion of a therapist. Don't rely on the opinion of family and friends. They already

want to side with you and are not trained in spotting game playing.

Myth 6.

"You will always agree on how the kids should be raised." You won't. Even married couples don't. The objective is to talk about the difference, out of earshot of the children. If you can't resolve the issues with your ex-spouse, you may need the opinion of a family therapist.

Myth 7.

"You should do everything in your power to foster a relationship with your ex-spouse." A balance is needed. Do not cut down your ex-spouse in front of your children; allow them to develop a realistic view of the other parent. It will help them deal with their idealistic fantasies. Parents who try to protect their children from ugly truths about the other parent often hinder the process of reality testing, which is part of a child's maturing process.

Myth 8.

"You should always praise your ex-spouse in front of your children." Wrong. This can be as defeating as cutting him down. A child may ask, "If he's so great, why did you divorce him?" or you may even encourage reconciliation fantasies. Try to represent reality as accurately as you can without attack or praise.

Myth 9.

"Since you're both adults, you and your ex-spouse ought to be able to sit down together and rationally work out the differences between the two of you when it comes to the children." Though a person may be an adult chronologically, it does not mean he's mature. An immature ex-spouse can be impossible to deal with.

Myth 10.

"What the ex-spouse does or doesn't do with the children will ruin their lives (and yours too!)." You can minimize the damaging effects of an ex-spouse's influence by choosing not to play

manipulative games. Even though the involvement of two loving parents is an ideal that children desire, a surrogate parent may make up for the lack.

Making Visits Work

Parents who are able to cooperate and continue contact between the child and noncustodial parent should be aware of some principles and guidelines for making visits work.

How Much Time For Your Children?

Deciding how much time the noncustodial parent will spend with the child depends on a number of factors. It depends on the demands of the noncustodial parent's life and the custodial parent's wishes.

It is probably unrealistic for the noncustodial parent to think of seeing his child every day. But frequent visits are preferable to long infrequent ones. Frequent contact provides continuity and enables the parent to keep up with the rapidly changing child. But "frequent" does not mean visits ought to be short or brief. The visit must be long enough to go comfortably through the three stages of the visit, called by one father, the "Hello, How Are You, Good-by."[8] There is the renewal stage, followed by the living-together-again stage, followed by the good-by stage.

The longer the gaps between visits, the greater the need for time to get reacquainted and to prepare for a painful good-by. If the visits aren't long enough, there is little time in the middle for enjoying each other. Visits should be spaced so that a lot of time need not be spent getting reacquainted or dreading the good-by. This is especially important for the long-distance parent who may see the children only two or three times a year.[9]

Suggestions for the Long-Distance Parent

The long-distance parent is at a particular disadvantage. It is difficult to maintain continuity when parent and child may be together only two or three times a year. Here are some suggestions:

- Maintain regular contact. Send cards and notes and call the children. It's often convenient for all concerned to call the same time each week.

- Don't expect too much. Children who are out playing or engrossed in a TV program aren't going to make good conversationalists if called to the phone. Even if the call is planned, don't be hurt if they don't sound enthusiastic about talking to you. Remember, the important thing is that you made contact; you cared enough to call. They will remember that. Even parents who are not divorced sometimes feel unloved and taken for granted by their children.

- Get used to having children around. When your children visit, the noise and clutter can be a shock if you're not used to it. Keep involved with children in church or clubs so you don't lose perspective.

- When your children visit, give them time to adjust. When we travel we need a little time to adjust to our new surroundings. So do our children. Don't push for affection too fast. It may alienate the children and make you feel unloved.

- Make it the children's home too. Keep some of their toys, clothes, and other personal belongings there so they will have the feeling it is their home too. Let them personalize their space with their own artwork and posters.

- Don't pry. Many single parents want to know what the former spouse is doing and are tempted to ask the children. Resist the temptation.

- Don't try to do too much at once. You can't cram a year into one visit. Make your time together as normal and relaxing as possible. Don't feel you need to entertain constantly—you wouldn't if you were the custodial parent. Nor should you be alarmed if your children are bored. They get bored at your ex-spouse's home too.

- Learn to set limits. Out of fear of alienating the children, parents sometimes become permissive. If we fail to set limits we damage the relationship and may encourage our children to manipulate us. They quickly recognize the "I-need-to-please-you-and-make-you-happy" syndrome that afflicts many noncustodial parents.

- Learn to be a *single* parent. Some joint activities with other people are fine. But remember that your child is there to see *you.*

- Be a *parent* to your child. You are not a friend, buddy, or playmate. Though you may be friendly and playful, you are and always will be a parent. Give direction and support to your child, and don't look to him for direction or to dry *your* tears.[10]

The "Reentry" Problem

Custodial parents frequently complain that when their children return from visiting the noncustodial parent, they are difficult to handle. One mother writes:

It's gotten to the point that I just hate sending the kids to visit their father because they are so difficult to handle when they get back. I don't know if it is something he is doing to them, something they are doing to themselves, or something I do when they return. But it is really causing me problems. What can I do?[11]

The problem may have its roots in a marriage that broke up because of "irreconcilable differences." When a couple finally live apart they are able to live as they wish, often in a manner that underscores how different they are.[12]

For the child, time spent with each parent is an experience characterized by different freedoms, rules, responsibilities, parental temperament, likes, and dislikes. One fourteen-year-old girl said:

It's hard now for me to believe my parents were even married. They have so little in common anymore. In a way, it's fun having two homes to live in; but it's also hard. I

have a lot to get used to when I come back from visiting
my dad. My mom just expects me to pick up where we
were when I left. But it's not that easy.[13]

She's right. It's *not* easy, and the single parent must understand
what's going on in the child's thoughts in order to manage the
situation well. Any of three motivations might be at work as
child returns to a custodial parent:

1. *Keeping the feelings alive.* If the visit was particularly good
   the child may be unresponsive or withdrawn because she's not
   ready to give up the good feelings of being close to the other
   parent she loves. It's her way of hanging on. The custodial
   parent should permit the child time to relegate the good feelings to pleasant memory. Getting angry or hurt or pressing
   for conversation will only make matters worse.[14]

2. *An invitation to testing.* Because visits are usually short, noncustodial parents sometimes unwisely suspend responsibilities
   and restrictions that are a normal part of a well-ordered home
   and make the visit a gala event. Chores and discipline are
   forgotten.[15]

   When the child returns home he can't help but notice the
   difference and wonder why he has to carry out normal responsibilities. He may begin to test by covert or even overt behavior. He may "forget" to do things, or he may become
   belligerent with comments such as "I don't get hassled like
   this at Dad's house!"

   The custodial parent will accomplish nothing with anger and
   impatience. In a determined, no-nonsense voice the custodial
   parent must say, "You may do things differently at your dad's
   house, but this is the way we do things here." If the child
   threatens to leave and go live with dad, the custodial parent
   should calmly say, "If that's what you want, call your father."
   Chances are that if the father were custodial parent, the child
   would have similar responsibilities there. Even in those cases
   where a child might choose to live with Dad in order to get
   more freedom, he would eventually translate the freedom to
   mean "Dad doesn't care enough to be concerned about what
   I do."

A conflict of loyalties. The most difficult reentry comes after a visit in which a bitter noncustodial parent has enumerated the many injustices the custodial parent has been guilty of. This produces a terrible conflict of loyalties. The child wants to love both parents but finds it difficult when he hears one cut down the other. It does no good for the custodial parent to rage at the ex-spouse for doing something so contrary to good parenting, even though the ex-spouse's behavior raises serious questions about fitness even to be a noncustodial parent.

What should the custodial parent do? If pressed for a response, answer the child as rationally and calmly as possible.[16] The custodial parent can take refuge in the fact that even though the child doesn't understand the truth of the matter, he will as he grows older. This is why it's important for a child to see his parents realistically and have them neither cut down nor built up. Part of the maturing process for a child is developing the ability to compare his *impressions* of reality with *reality itself.*

pecial Concerns of Christian Parents

hen a Christian gains sole custody of children, he sometimes ars that their spiritual life will suffer at the hands of the noncus-ial parent. This is particularly true when he feels that the life-le of the noncustodial parent is worldly.

Joan, who attends church faithfully and neither smokes nor nks, was concerned about the example her ex-spouse set for ir fourteen-year-old daughter Karen. After the divorce Joan's -spouse took up drinking and began to date women who smoked d drank. Often his girl friends would go to his place to smoke, nk, and dance—behavior that was scandalous to the conserv-ve church Joan and Karen attended.

On one occasion Joan's former husband wanted Karen to come er to his place and celebrate his birthday with him and his girl end. Joan didn't want Karen to go because of her ex-husband's estyle. But Karen put up a fuss: "What's wrong with smoking, inking, and dancing? You're always down on Dad. He can't anything right!"

Finally Joan relented. She said that her instincts told her s had more to lose by keeping Karen home than by letting her g She set a time for her ex-husband to bring Karen home, and th all agreed.

When Karen returned from the party she was thoroughly d gusted. She wasn't prepared for the culture shock. "That wom blew smoke in my face all night," she complained. "Then th sent me down to the basement to watch TV while they danc and smooched. I don't know why Dad wanted me to come ov there anyway!"

Joan's instincts had served her well. She was able to set asi her own prejudices and deal wisely with a daughter who need a jolt of reality.

This does not mean that Christian children are to be turn loose whenever they raise a fuss. It means that the task of bei a Christian single parent is complex. Worldliness is not the on issue involved in raising a child by yourself. The child's loya to the other parent and an idealization of the other parent powerful forces to contend with. Worldliness is not a great co cern to a child who is afraid of appearing disloyal or fearful losing the absent parent's love.

Parents should be aware, however, that serious violation of child's religious upbringing can jeopardize their legal rights custody or visitation. A court of appeals in New York withdr a mother's custody rights because she had "violated" orthod Jewish teachings by "permitting a male friend to stay in apartment and share her bed."[17]

A California judge removed an eleven-year-old girl from mother's custody because of her political activities. The moth Tina Fishman, a Communist and supporter of the Commun Party, U.S.A., faced felony charges. She had been charged i rock-throwing melee between protesters and police in Washir ton, D.C. The court said that it "cannot disregard the impact such charges upon Riva [the daughter]." The judge felt that Ri would be considered an oddball by her peer group because of mother's behavior.[18]

The Christian parent who is not sure what to do about worldly influence of the noncustodial parent might consult a p tor or Christian therapist. It is difficult to be objective about " best interest of the child'' when we have been wounded by a divorce and are still close to the situation.

A Check List of Visitation Dos and Don'ts

A number of principles dealing with visitation have been covered in this chapter. Here is a check list of dos and don'ts that summarize what has been said:

✔ *DON'T argue with what the other parent may have told your child.* Your child won't hear the different points of view presented by you and the other parent. What he will hear is an angry difference of opinion between two people he loves and feels equally loyal to. This doesn't mean that you can't tell your child that his parents see things differently.

✔ *DON'T try to cut down the child's positive image of the other parent.* Remember, your child needs both his parents, and you will invite a heated defense of the other parent if you belittle him. Children tend to idealize their parents and choose not to see anything bad about them. This is how they build their world of security.

✔ *DON'T try to persuade the child that you are always right and the other parent is wrong.* Remember the need for two parents and loyalty to both. This doesn't mean that you have no right to guide the child as you see fit when the child visits you. You can say, "I know you do this differently at Dad's (or Mom's) house. But when you're here, we'll do it this way."

✔ *DON'T react defensively when the child reports that the other parent is telling unkind stories about you.* You may say to the child, "I'm sorry to hear that. I hope you don't feel that's true. But let's talk about us!"

✔ *DON'T attempt to get the child to offend the religious, moral, or social values of your ex-spouse.* It's one thing to maintain the right to do things your way in your own home. But a little sensitivity at this point will keep your child from being a pawn in a power struggle. You need to respect the *child's* need to please both parents.

✔ *DON'T turn times of picking up and dropping off into opportunities to argue or attack.* If you must have words with your ex-spouse, do it when the child is not present.

✔ *DON'T change plans capriciously.* If you must change plans, give as much notice as possible.

✔ *DON'T expect or allow your child to "spy" on the other parent for you.*

✔ *DO listen to what your child is saying and take a friendly interest in him.* One of the criticisms directed toward fathers is that they don't know how to "tune in" to the feeling world of the child. It's immaterial whether or not your child *should* feel as he does. You don't help by telling him he *shouldn't* feel as he does. That only alienates you further. How can he expect you to help if he feels you don't understand? Making a child feel understood is the first step toward helping him.

✔ *DO answer questions in a way that minimizes conflict.* You can explain your way of doing things and set rules without being testy.

✔ *DO be aware of any problems your child may have and what you can do about them.* This will come as you spend time with your child and observe him in various situations. Should you need to talk with the custodial parent about these problems, do so in a way that does not suggest she (or he) is at fault. Custodial parents are very sensitive to what noncustodial parents feel about their performance.

✔ *DO be available on a reliable basis.* Your child needs the confidence that you are there and that he hasn't lost you. Your dependability and reliability can do a great deal to set his fears to rest. Remember the importance of continuity in your relationship with him.

✔ *DO show that you have consistent standards of behavior, even though they may be different from those of the other parent.* Standards of behavior and consistency are evidence of maturity. You can have a positive influence on your child's growth by modeling this maturity.

✔ *DO make a visit enjoyable rather than looking at it as an opportunity to impress your child.* The noncustodial parent is tempted to impress his child to make up for limited contact. Since the child is not on his own turf and near his friends, he is often at a loss for things to do. It is easy to fall into the habit of entertaining the child. Try to make your home a second home. If it's a small apartment, provide a bed or even a sleeping bag that he can call his own. Keep certain extras there for him such as toothbrush, clothes, and toys. Encourage him to get acquainted with the neighborhood and the children in it so his time with you has more of a normal family routine where he comes and goes. But remember that he's there to see *you*, so don't spend your time with others at his expense.

✔ *DO have your child ready on time for the visit if you are the custodial parent.* You expect the child to be returned on time, so render the courtesy of promptness to your ex-spouse. Likewise, if you are the noncustodial parent, be on time for picking up and dropping off.

✔ *DO understand that emergency situations arise that require a change in plans.*

✔ *DO be as friendly and courteous to your ex-spouse as you are with other adults.* Remember that you are modeling the behavior that you want your child to show.

✔ *DO remember that your ex-spouse loves the children too.* Share with your ex-spouse important things such as school pictures, report cards, and photos of special events.

7

The Never-married Parent

The number of children under eighteen living with never-married parents has increased dramatically in the past decade—2.8 million, which is a fourfold increase.[1] These children are being raised by almost 1.1 million never-married mothers and, surprisingly, 64,000 never-married fathers.[2]

The never-married parent often evokes the stereotype of a careless teenage girl who has had a child out of wedlock or perhaps a welfare mother who has had several children by different fathers, none of whom she ever married. It is an unfair stereotype, however. Some never-married parents are adoptive parents who, at the sacrifice of their own personal comfort, give a home to an unwanted child. Labeling never-married mothers as careless or promiscuous reveals a superficial understanding.

This chapter will attempt to shed light on the never-married parent with a view to problem solving rather than condemnation. Even if a never-married parent were a wayward sinner, the compassion of Jesus Christ is called for—a compassion that says, "Woman, where are they [your accusers]? . . . Go now and leave your life of sin" (John 8:10–11).

Illegitimate Parents

There is one type of parent that is of special concern to religious leaders, social scientists, and family therapists. He or she is most often described as an "illegitimate parent."[3] This is the person who, not feeling legitimate, conceives and raises a child in order to gain a sense of legitimacy he or she otherwise does not feel.

Deliberate Pregnancy

"Having children no matter under what circumstances is something that makes single people feel a little more legitimate," says Melvin Silberman, family therapist and professor at Temple University in Philadelphia. He says:

> There is still something shaky about the status of being single, you see. It is still not quite okay. This is why, especially in the lower-class cultures, there are so many pregnancies among teenagers, because having a child for them is a measure of their self-worth. It just may be that same process is at work for [other] single people too.[4]

Dr. Silberman is probably right. This is why sex education for teenagers is not doing anything to bring down the rate of illegitimate births. For many unwed parents the problem lies in their view of themselves, not in a lack of contraceptive information or availability.

A Growing Problem

The trend toward "illegitimate parenthood" (deliberate pregnancy out of wedlock) is rapidly moving out of the ghetto into middle-class communities. The national survey mentioned in chapter 1, which queried three thousand single men and women, asked whether they would consider having children even if they were not married. Almost 25 percent of the men and 20 percent of the women said they would. Here are some other findings:

- 3 percent of both sexes said they tried it and it turned

out well, but another 3 percent tried it and said they wouldn't advise others to try it.

- About 13 percent of both sexes believed it would be too hard on the child.

- 59 percent said they would never do it.[5]

The profile of the man most willing to have and raise a child out of wedlock reveals that he is usually in his early twenties, never married, has some college education, and has a low income. The older a single man gets, the less inclined he is to have a child out of wedlock. Single men in their forties and fifties are only half as willing as single men in their twenties to father a child out of wedlock.[6]

The profile of the woman who is willing to have a child out of wedlock is very much like the male. She is in her early twenties, a student or white-collar worker of low income, and never married. The study reported:

> In both cases, male and female, the idea of having a child out-of-wedlock is the notion of the young, liberal, inexperienced and experimental single. As single people grow older, as they learn the realities of child-rearing and perhaps raise a child themselves, enthusiasm becomes far less evident.[7]

Researchers look dimly at a trend among older unmarried women who decide to have an out-of-wedlock child and raise it alone. Alfred Messer, psychiatrist and family research specialist in Atlanta, says that these women "are the most narcissistic group of people you'll ever see."[8] He does not believe this kind of woman makes a good parent.

Messer has also had homosexual males confide that they want to "hire a woman" to have a baby so they can "reproduce themselves." The doctor looks dimly at this as well.

The Church and the Moral Issue

Churches, particularly those that are conservative and biblical in orientation, often have difficulty helping the never married, particularly those who fit our definition as "illegitimate parents." They tend to stereotype these parents, which is most unfortunate. Many of these parents are not consciously bent on disobeying God.

But it is difficult to ignore the moral issue when a person deliberately sets out to conceive a child without the benefit of marriage and the commitments that go with it.

Christians attempting to deal with the critical social issues discussed in this chapter must apply the doctrine of grace to their methodology. Three concepts are important in a "grace methodology": (1) God reveals Himself and His plan for our successful living through His creation in addition to His revelation in Scripture; (2) God reveals Himself as a gracious God through His creation in addition to His revelation in Scripture; (3) the gracious offer of salvation from sin naturally grows out of the above. Let me explain this.

God's Revelation of Himself in Creation

The Bible clearly states that God reveals Himself and His plan for our successful living in creation (Ps. 19:1-4). The psalmist says that creation tells us God is glorious, that He created the heavens and earth, and that through creation He tells us how we may live happily and successfully on His earth. The apostle Paul picks up this theme and points out that our problem is not that we are ignorant of God and His works. Our problem is that we *suppress* the truth we see (Rom. 1:18-20). We want to do things our own way, so God lets us have our way, and as a result we become spiritual and social misfits (Rom. 1:21-31).

The sexual promiscuity we have seen for the past thirty years is mankind's answer to God: we're going to do things *our* way. God says: Okay, do them your way. But you're going against the pattern I have laid down in creation for a happy life, and you're going to get hurt. God wants us to know that we cannot violate the social laws He has woven into the fabric of His creation

without paying the consequences any more than we can violate
the laws of gravity and inertia without a great deal of pain.

God Reveals Himself as a Gracious God

In spite of man's willfulness, God reveals Himself in His creation as a *gracious* God. Theologians call it "common grace." This is the work of God toward all men in which He holds down the evil of the race and promotes that which is good. It is this that Paul has in mind when he calls God "the savior of all men" (1 Tim. 4:10). This is not universalism. It is common grace. The word *save* is used in the sense of preserving. God is saying to the rebellious sinner, "See how I love you! I hold down the evil and promote the good. I am a gracious God."

He makes this message clear in Acts 14, where Paul says that God left Himself a testimony in His creation—a testimony that He is a gracious God. "He has shown kindness by giving you rain from heaven and crops in their seasons; He provides you with plenty of food and fills your hearts with joy" (Acts 14:17).

The Gracious Offer of Salvation

Out of this bounty comes God's gracious offer of salvation from sin. Through common grace God offers sinners an opportunity to live happily and healthily in His creation. He *is* the savior of all men. But He wants to be Savior in a special way. He wants to be the Savior of those who believe (1 Tim. 4:10). God wants to give us more than happiness and health through common grace. He also wants a personal relationship with us and offers it in special grace—the gift of His Son. He wants us to recognize that sin stands between Himself and us, but the sin can be removed; we can be reconciled to Him if we believe that Jesus Christ died on the cross and rose again from the dead to make atonement for our sin. When we believe that, God is not merely the savior (preserver) of all men, but He becomes the Savior—the reconciler—of those who believe.

The "grace methodology" involves gently showing people that as long as we live on God's earth, there are serious consequences to ignoring His creative design. But there is great reward, both here and hereafter, for accepting His gifts of grace—both common grace and special grace. The illegitimate parent may not be concerned about the moral issue. But he has to face the fact that he is living on God's earth. There are consequences, for both parent and child, for ignoring God's laws of creation and willfully choosing to become an illegitimate parent. Dr. Messer put it well when he said, "There's a difference between coping with an accident and setting out to have one."[10] Once people are willing to admit that there is a God who has put the world together according to His pattern and graciously offers us happiness and health when we follow that pattern, it is only a short step to seeing the greatest gift of grace, Jesus Christ. "God did this so that men would seek him and perhaps reach out for him and find him" (Acts 17:27).

In writing about the "illegitimate parent," I do not intend to condemn those who may fit that description. Furthermore, these remarks are in no way designed to encourage the never-married parents of an out-of-wedlock child to marry just because they have conceived a child. They may have exercised poor judgment in conceiving the child, but they should not further complicate their lives and the life of their child and marry simply because they are biological parents. That is not a sound basis for marriage.

A single parent is better than no parent at all and better than two parents who destroy the child's sense of security by constant welfare. I take issue, however, with the parent who *deliberately* sets out to conceive a child with no intention of giving the child the benefit of the loving care of *both* biological parents.

The Never-Married Mother

Quite apart from those women who *seek* to have a child out of wedlock are those who do not plan on it. These include the middle-class teenage mother and the lower-class welfare mother who may be either an unwilling or a willing sexual partner, becoming pregnant for psychosocial reasons they don't understand.

The Teenage Mother

Twenty years ago family researchers warned of the effect motherhood had on the life of the adolescent:

The girl who has an illegitimate child at the age of 16 suddenly has 90 percent of her life's script written for her. She will probably drop out of school; even if someone else in her family helps to take care of the baby, she will probably not be able to find a steady job that pays enough to provide for herself and her child; she may feel impelled to marry someone she might not otherwise have chosen. Her life choices are few, and most of them are bad. Had she been able to delay the first child, her prospects might have been quite different, assuming that she would have had opportunities to continue her education, improve her vocational skills, find a job, marry someone she wanted to marry and have a child when she and her husband were ready for it.[11]

Since that time, educators and health professionals have been advocating better sex education for teens and greater availability of contraceptives to combat the problem. Yet out-of-wedlock pregnancies and births grow at an alarming rate. Out-of-wedlock births have more than tripled since 1950 for women aged fifteen to twenty-five.[12] Why, in spite of vigorous educational activity and the greater availability of contraceptives, are we seeing this increase? There are several reasons.

First, the information given teens is not always good. A recently published "adolescent survival handbook" advised its readers not to take the pill because "you may want to have a child one day, and it seems almost insane to play such crazy games with the system that has to produce and protect it." The author suggests the use of the diaphragm instead. The method most frequently used by teenagers is withdrawal, the least reliable method.[13]

Many Christian parents are perplexed at sex education programs and contraceptives being proffered in a morally neutral atmosphere. It seems to them that we are assuming that our teens *are* going to have sexual intercourse. Statistics confirm the fact that even Christian teens are producing out-of-wedlock children. But this doesn't mean that sexual intercourse is the only way to handle sexual feelings, nor does it mean that old fashioned chastity is a relic of repressed religionists. After more than thirty years of sexual promiscuity, American singles are rediscovering chastity—a subject that will be developed further in chapter 11.

A second reason why teens are getting pregnant is that even though they know about contraceptives and find them readily available, they are not using them.[14] Teens have an incredible ability to believe that social ills such as alcoholism, traffic accidents, or unwanted pregnancy won't happen to them.

A third reason is that many girls don't know when they're fertile, in spite of a great emphasis on sex education. In one study only 20 percent of 184 teenage mothers knew when they were fertile.[15]

The inability to decrease the number of out-of-wedlock births among teenagers is due to our failure to recognize the psychosocial forces at work. In the same study cited above, the teenage girls were following in the footsteps of their own mothers, the grandmothers of the out-of-wedlock children. Of the 165 grandmothers in the group, 25 percent delivered a child before the age of fifteen and 82 percent before the age of twenty.

Unfortunately the policy of many schools is not to require compulsory education for pregnant mothers. The teenager who is not a good student and does not want a career may see motherhood as the solution to all her problems. She can leave school and get on with the one thing she *can* do—conceive and give birth to a child. She becomes economically disadvantaged through lack of education and the financial responsibility of a child and is locked into the "motherhood syndrome"—child bearing as her calling in life—which gives her a reason for existing. Empirical studies show that teenage mothers have more children than women who bear their first child at age twenty-one.[16]

Teenage mothers who go on to get an education avoid additional pregnancies and devote their energies to their education and raising the child they have. Such women don't seem to be locked into the "motherhood syndrome."

Advice for the Teen Mother and Parents

The teen mother and her parents who face the prospect of an out-of-wedlock birth must think about several issues.

First, don't be hasty to marry because of the pregnancy. The conception of a child is not sufficient grounds for marriage. If the young people are not right for each other, the problem of pregnancy would be compounded by an equally grave problem—an unwise marriage. If marriage would have been considered anyway, the couple should proceed with premarital counseling as though a child were not in the picture and be willing to give up the idea of marriage if counseling should contraindicate successful marriage.

Second, give serious consideration to placing the child for adoption. A young mother, now a college student, whose baby I helped place for adoption, talked to me about her feelings some four years later:

> It was hard to do [place the baby for adoption]. An indescribable feeling of giving up part of yourself. But I kept thinking, "What's best for my baby?" I couldn't see raising her without a father, and I didn't want to marry the father. I knew she would be at an economic disadvantage if I raised her. And it was important too that you had found Christian parents who could give her what I couldn't give—not just materially, but a mature mother and father and not a mother who is still a kid herself.

> I guess I was able to accept giving up my daughter because I recognized guilt games I was playing with myself, and I saw that I really had a little-girl mentality. You know, a little girl who didn't want her dolly taken from her. I had to grow up and realize that this helpless child was not a dolly to be played with or to have around for my own selfish reasons but a human being who deserved the best in life.

Third, if the child is kept by the mother she must be impressed with the importance of the child's care. The parents must not be quick to open their home to the mother, although ultimately this may be the only realistic solution. If living with her parents is the only solution, the mother should remember that she has the primary care of the child and that her parents are not built-in baby sitters.

In one study of fifty-one never-married mothers, half lived independently and half lived with parents. The accompanying table shows how the primary care of the child was handled in each situation.[17] Interestingly, there is only a 15-percent mean difference in primary-care responsibility between women living independently and with their parents.[18] Evidently the parents made sure that the mother would assume most of the primary care even though she was living with them.

	Percentage of Women Primarily Responsible for Child-rearing Tasks	
	Living With Parents	Living Independently
Task		
Feeding	80	87
Bathing	87	100
Dressing	87	87
Diapering	80	100
Walking	60	73
Playing	47	67
Taking child to pediatrician	93	93
Toilet-training	53	87
Doing laundry	73	93
Disciplining	67	93
Getting up at night	87	100

The problem with the living-at-home arrangement is that the young mother is not emotionally ready to settle down to the rigors and responsibilities of parenting. She wants to socialize and date. As she reverts to instincts normal for her age, more and more responsibility is left to the parents, usually by default. The parents, who have already raised children of their own, become angry and frustrated and feel trapped by new responsibilities at a time when they are looking forward to less demanding lives.

The stress on such a family is great and is one of the major reasons why adoption is suggested. If the child is white, the chances for adoption are good. If the child is black, the family may be consigned to keeping the child whether or not they want it, even though this does not help the child, the parent, or grandparent.

Illegitimacy and Welfare

It is easy to see how a black teenage parent quickly becomes enmeshed in illegitimacy and welfare dependency, particularly if she is not motivated to go to school. What is she good for? She can have babies. She's good at that. Her view of her mothering skills may not be realistic, but she can believe that she's a good mother—and could be a better mother if not economically disadvantaged. It is this belief that enables the trapped mother to have a sense of self-worth. Those who claim that women have illegitimate children in order to collect welfare don't understand the psychosocial motives of such women.

In addition to a self-worth motive, a woman may also have a problem with the Cinderella Complex, as discussed in chapter 2. She would like to have a man take care of her, even if she's not married to him. But given the reality that she probably won't be cared for by the child's father, she becomes a candidate for welfare. One researcher writes, "Even if one hesitates to say that conception is planned on the basis of economic considerations, decisions about what follows conception could certainly be open to economic influence."[19] This simply means that the mother who qualifies for Aid to Families with Dependent Children (AFDC) is going to take it if it's there. *But she probably would have gotten pregnant even if AFDC help were not available.* The researcher says that 30 percent of AFDC goes to such cases.[20] But the figure may go as high as 46 percent.[21]

We face a cruel social dilemma. Shall we not help the mothers of illegitimate children because they chose to have children out of wedlock? Even if we would agree with those who say these women deserve to face the consequences of illegitimate pregnancy, what about the innocent children? Shall we penalize them?

A far-reaching solution is beyond the scope of this book. It is hoped, however, that the informed Christian will, in his own sphere of influence, truly become the salt of the earth and have a positive influence on a decaying society. More will be said about the role of the Christian and the church in chapter 14.

The Never-Married Father

"Fathers are a biological necessity but a social accident."[22] Nowhere is this attitude more pronounced than in the case of the never-married father who is considered self-centered and irresponsible, a male who takes advantage of young women without thinking of the consequences of his behavior.

Don't Stereotype

Doubtless, some never-married fathers fit this description. But there are others willing to accept responsibility for a girl friend's pregnancy. Most never-married fathers report that they don't come forward because they feel left out; they feel that the agency or therapist is not interested in being helpful, or the girl's parents don't want them around. One seventeen-year-old revealed his true feelings as he awaited his girl friend's return from an abortion:

> I thought I was a much more liberated man and that I'd be able to walk in here, sit down, and say, "Here's an abortion," and that would be it. But now I'm here; I'm a wreck. I don't think anyone could depend on me in this situation. . . . I'm shaken. . . . I also feel that I was more experienced than my girl friend and should have tried to help more. . . . I really want to know what they will do for her . . . what I wanted to hear was this big elaborate story of how the doctor is there all the time. I was looking for reassurance. . . . How about me? Do they have something for me to lay [sic] on while I die?[23]

Though this young man's story is sad, it is still difficult not to stereotype the never-married father as irresponsible and dismiss him with little sympathy. When researchers report that most unwed fathers "are willing to accept responsibility regarding the girl's pregnancy,"[24] it doesn't square with the findings that 58.6 percent of AFDC cases in Texas are paternity cases and 80 percent of them are uncollectable.[25]

Yet other researchers maintain that never-married fathers "are generally interested in and financially support their children."[26] A report by North Carolina researchers says that "About 63 percent of all fathers were maintaining contact with their children five years after childbirth.''[27]

The task of the church, and the compassionate individual who wants to help, must be to deal with *persons* and not cases. There *are* never-married fathers who want to help. Be careful not to dismiss them with a stereotype.

Legal Status

Not only is it Christian and compassionate to consider each father on the merit of his own sense of responsibility, but there's a legal side as well. Never-married fathers have been accorded legal rights. In 1972 the U.S. Supreme Court ruled in *Stanley v. Illinois* that unmarried natural fathers are entitled to equal protection under the law and are also entitled to be involved in custody decisions concerning the child.[28] Family and friends of the unwed mother should be aware that the father must consent to adoption. Though the family may not want him around, they have a legal responsibility to get his release.

Never-married parents should be aware of some other important legal decisions that affect them:

- Frank Serpico, famous New York police crusader, won a suit against him by the mother of his child. He proved she was guilty of fraud and deceit when she claimed she was on a birth control pill, when in fact she was planning parenthood.

- The Supreme Court has ruled that only the woman can decide whether or not to terminate her pregnancy. The unmarried father has no say.

- A Texas court ruled that in spite of the above Supreme Court ruling on Serpico, a man is still responsible to take precautions or abstain from sex if he does not wish to run the risk of paternity liability.

- A California court ruled that a woman cannot contract with a man to impregnate her in exchange for the express agreement that he will not be financially liable. The contract is invalid and enforceable because it is based on "illicit consideration of meretricious sexual services."[29]

Who Speaks For The Child?

Teenage parents are ill-prepared for parenthood because of their immaturity. They have unrealistic expectations of child development and a general lack of experience with children. They tend to be impatient and intolerant and have a tendency toward child abuse.[30] They don't *intend* to abuse their children, but a combination of factors often triggers irrational behavior. Psychologically immature (and this is also true of older abusers), they have a low threshold of frustration. And when they feel the pressure of economic hardship, the child represents yet another burden. Ignorant of child development, they assume that the child's crying is only to annoy them, and out of anger and frustration they punish the child, often physically damaging him.

The most loving thing an immature, never-married parent can do is place the child for adoption. Sometimes the greatest expression of love is a willingness to let someone go. The abusing parent is also encouraged to join Parents Anonymous—a self-help group for abusive parents. The phone company's information service can provide a nationwide toll-free number to call for more information about Parents Anonymous.

The Never-Married Adoptive Parent

Adoption agencies usually place children with single persons only when a two-parent home cannot be found, but such adoptions are steadily increasing.[31] Moreover, contraception, illegal abortions, and a growing number of single mothers who keep their children are all reducing the number of children available for adoption. This is especially true of white infants. Hard-to-place children, who are older or mentally or physically handicapped, still need homes. It is believed that a single-parent family is preferable to the impermanence of foster care.[32]

Motives for Adoption

What motivates a man or a woman to adopt a child—often a problem child—and subject herself to the rigors of solo child-rearing, which often pushes the single parent to the brink of despair? Eighty-two single adoptive mothers, ranging in age from twenty-one to sixty-four years of age, were questioned in a study on this subject. Sixty-two of them had never married. Twelve of them earned less than $10,000 a year, and thirty-one earned between $10,000 and $15,000. Only nine earned more than $25,000. Why did they adopt? Ninety-five percent were motivated by fulfillment of their own needs. One mother commented:

> [I adopted] for precisely the same reason that couples want children—for the joy of my daughter's company. I like being part of a family.[33]

Another mother said:

> I had a stable job and could give a child many benefits. And I had love that needed to be given, and I needed to be needed. I wanted some purpose to my life other than my work and my cat.[34]

The needs of the adoptive children motivated thirty-five of the mothers. One mother, representative of this group, stated:

> [I adopted] because I continually saw children in my special education classes who lived in institutions or went from foster home to foster home. I decided that even as a single parent I could do more for the child.[35]

Adjustments

When asked what kind of adjustments they had to make to their new status, the mothers' answers were so varied that they were hard to classify. But some of the typical responses were:

- The lack of time that I had for myself was even greater than I had anticipated, so was the physical exhaustion and the twenty-four-hour-a-day-ness of the job.

- Financial adjustments.

- Learning to converse at mealtimes.

- The need to control my newly awakened temper.[36]

The young adoptive parent seems to feel the loss of a "normal" life rather quickly. An adoptive father said, "At twenty-one, I was running the dull treadmill of routine." He said that he wanted to be skiing with his friends or dating, but being a single parent introduced new complexities into what were otherwise normal activities for a twenty-one-year-old.[37]

Support Services

Asked what support services they used, the adoptive mothers in the study tried to provide male influence for their children and some belonged to support groups. Seventy-three percent found that relatives were helpful, but 48 percent preferred to rely on friends.[38]

In regard to counseling services or day-care services or adoption subsidies, most of the women were unresponsive, which may suggest that they did not feel a need for these. This is interesting in that most of them felt a financial burden. Their mean income was only $10,000 to $15,000 per year. The fact that the women were well-educated (three quarters had college or graduate degrees) and were single parents by choice probably enabled them to draw on their personal resources or find resources on their own when they couldn't cope.

Carolyn Loves Tony

One of the most touching stories of an adoptive single parent and child is that of Carolyn Koons and her son Tony. Carolyn, as Director of Azusa Pacific College's outreach ministries, was confronted with eight-year-old Tony's plight when she went to minister with her group in a prison in Mexicali, Mexico. Because of the providential moving of God and the love of this woman, Tony eventually became Antonio Hernandez Sanchez Garcia Koons. Tony and Carolyn had their struggles together, and Tony has emotional scars that have yet to heal. But the love and determination he and his mother share have enriched both their lives.[39]

Carolyn tells her story in her book *Tony: A Journey Together* (Harper & Row, 1984).

The stories of these adoptive parents indicate the importance of attitude in single parenting. The person who welcomes single parenting and is positive about it is most likely a successful single parent. This doesn't mean that there aren't times of discouragement and feelings of defeat. It means that the parent has sufficient physical and mental energy to bounce back and cope. Acceptance of the single-parent status and the responsibility to go it alone is all-important.

8

The Widowed Parent

Who hurts more—the divorced or the widowed? Whenever the two compare notes, this question surely will be asked.

One widow says, for example, "If any group suffers more than the others it is the widowed."[1] An irate divorcée replies that this "sweeping generalization is unsubstantiated" and ignores the individual case. What is more, she says, "the widow or widower *might* have had a beautiful marriage . . . they may have been very *successful* in their marriage. This can never be said of the divorced person. With the divorced person, there is always, *has* to be, a sense of failure, of not measuring up."[2] She suggests that perhaps each suffers equally, in their own way.

This divorcée is quite right. And suffering in their own way are approximately 2.2 million parents and children who have lost a spouse or parent in death and need special understanding and care.[3]

Shared Experiences

Though there are special differences in the needs of the widow and the widower, there are also experiences they have in common.

Grief

One common experience is grief. It is essential for the survivors and those who would help them to understand the dynamics of grief. The survivors need to know that there is nothing wrong with them when they go through the various stages of grief. Those wanting to comfort survivors need to know how to assist them through the grief experience.

Typically there are four phases the bereaved go through: shock and numbness; sadness, yearning, and searching; disorganization, despair, apathy, and loss of interest; and reorganization.

1. *Shock and numbness.* God has given mankind a fierce instinct to survive as well as a gracious provision to face death. This is true of both the dying and their survivors. Those who are about to die, whether suddenly or slowly, experience shock, a physiological numbness that dulls their senses and makes death bearable. People who are told they are going to die are often shocked and numbed with disbelief.

This "angel of mercy" also attends the survivors. The most common reaction of survivors to the news of death is a stunning, numbing disbelief. The mind is unable to grasp the reality and the pain of what's happening. This is even true in cases where death is expected. One father, who watched his thirteen-year-old daughter lie in a coma for two weeks, said when she died, "I just can't believe it. It doesn't seem real. I know what they said, but I don't feel anything."[4]

This phase of grief usually does not last long—a few hours to a few days. It should be remembered, however, that there's a sense in which this disbelief may occur for years after death. Perhaps not in its original, numbing shock, but it will be around for a while to ease the survivors through the experience.

It is important to see the value of initial shock. It is not something strange, but a merciful opiate to help the survivors. Family and friends may need to assure the survivors that their disbelief is normal and a part of the grieving process.

2. *Sadness, yearning, and searching.* As with all opiates, disbelief must be attenuated. God graciously moves the grief-stricken into a second phase as disbelief wears off—sadness,

yearning, and searching. Sometimes the grief-stricken, who as yet may not have shed tears, are suddenly wracked with deep sobs that come from a soul that is beginning to feel the agony.

Subjectively, it is horrible to experience and watch. The temptation is to do something, to say something, that will take the pain away. And yet the sobbing is a sign of healing. The mind and body once numbed by the opiate of shock, now begins to see and feel the world of reality and pain.

Those who counsel survivors become concerned when a year or more goes by with no indication of pain. This may suggest that the survivors are perpetuating the state of shock by denying the death. This is why it's important that those who want to help not be afraid to talk about the death. Many times family and friends are afraid of triggering an emotional outburst in the bereaved, so they avoid anything that may be a reminder of the loss. We must not be afraid to talk about the deceased, our feelings about the deceased, or the feelings of the bereaved. It is painful, but it is part of the healing process.

The process is much like what hospitals do with people who have undergone major surgery. They get the patient out of bed, and in spite of the patient's pain and protest, they begin to get him moving again. Someone put it well when he said, "Grief is the price we pay for being human."[5]

3. *Disorganization, despair, apathy, loss of interest.* There comes a point in the grief process where the tears flow less frequently. But as the tears dry, the bereaved feel no zest for life or interest in anything. Once again, this is a sign of progress, though it is important that the bereaved not get stuck at this or any stage. The agony that flooded every day with tears has crested. The tears now are only occasional. The sound of a door closing at five o'clock no longer excites the imagination that a dead husband has returned home.

The mind and body can't take the continued strain of the first two phases of grief. Disorganization is a period between the terrible shattering of our lives and reorganization where we have time to survey the wreckage in all of its reality.

Reorganization is not possible unless we accurately estimate the damage that has been done and count the cost of rebuilding. At the subjective level this is experienced as disorganization and despair. This in turn generates apathy and loss of interest—if we truly assess the magnitude of what has happened to us, it will seem *overwhelming*.

Yet God in His providence has put us together in such a way that if we *want* to recover, our minds will, quite apart from conscious effort, begin to make sense out of the chaos and organize for recovery even before we are aware of it.

Plastic surgeon Maxwell Maltz made an amazing discovery along this line years ago. He found that sometimes even though plastic surgery had restored a human face or body perfectly, the patient still felt ugly. He discovered that the mind is a goal-striving mechanism. If given the freedom to see success it will make us see and feel it. Moreover, without conscious effort on our part it will think of numerous reasons why success is possible. Conversely, if it is not given that freedom and is told that success is not possible, it will obediently accommodate us, help us feel defeated, and give us all the reasons why we should feel defeated.[6]

In the phase of disorganization and despair a solution is not important. A *desire* for a solution and a *disbelief* that God loves us and has our best interests at heart are all-important. Such desire and belief are used by God to free our minds to start organizing, albeit unconsciously, the disorganized mess.

Unfortunately there are those who refuse to allow the process to unfold. Belief in a gracious God and a desire for a solution to their staggering problems is rejected out of hand. It is beyond the scope of this chapter to delve into why people do this. It suffices to say that common to all cases like this is "the payoff." That is, whenever a person exhibits what may appear to be unproductive, even destructive, thinking and behavior, *they have a good reason for it.* There's some kind of payoff—a real or imagined benefit to behaving this way. These people can use professional help.

4. *Reorganization.* The last step in the grief process is reorganization.[7] At the subjective level it's an experience of new energy and positive attitude and is often expressed, "I'm going to make it." Psychologically it's the outcome of our desire for a solution and the belief that God has a wonderful plan

for our lives. Given the freedom to work on these concepts, the mind organizes all life's experiences around these propositions. We *rationally* see it. We know that the Bible is true and not mere platitude. And we *subjectively feel* it—"I'm going to make it."

There are no shortcuts to grief, though sometimes family and friends become concerned that the grief may be taking on pathological proportions. Grief *may be* pathological when these indicators are present:

- Increasing feelings of personal worthlessness
- Referring to the deceased in the present tense
- Subtle or open suicidal threats
- Antisocial behavior
- Excessive drinking or drug abuse
- Withdrawal or refusal to interact
- Impulsiveness
- Persistent psychosomatic illness
- Veneration of objects that remind of or link to the lost
- Preoccupation with the dead person
- Refusal to change the room or dispose of belongings
- Extreme or deep depression
- Resistance to counseling or help
- Stoic refusal to show emotion
- Intense busyness or hyperactivity
- Manifesting symptoms of the deceased's last illness[8]

The bereaved may show some of these signs briefly, but that does not indicate pathology.[9] Pathological grief is caused by denial, distortion, or delay of normal grief reactions. It is manifested by the indicators just mentioned in chronic proportions.[10]

Those who want to help the bereaved should remember that every situation is unique and that comparisons must not be drawn between different kinds of grief. The biggest need of the bereaved is to be listened to nonjudgmentally and nonanalytically.[11]

Other Common Problems

Widows and widowers share some other problems. Some of these are problems also faced by the divorced.

1. *Loneliness.* Every human being has an innate need to relate to someone else in a meaningful way. Relationships help us gain a sense of self-worth and feel a connection with society. The widowed are deprived of this in two ways. First, that significant-other who gave us much of our sense of worth is gone. Second, in a couple-oriented society the sense of connectedness is also gone. The widowed find themselves single in a couple-oriented society. No matter how hard couples may try to make the widowed person part of the group, he has the pervasive feeling that he's a "fifth wheel" and doesn't belong.

   The widowed person may be welcomed into the world of singles, but his instincts are not that of a single. For many years he has taken seriously the definition of a wedding ring as a band of metal around the wearer's finger that restricts circulation. It is difficult to adjust to the freedom of singlehood.

   The biggest mistake the lonely person can make is to look immediately for another person to fill that void. This is a mistake because he must make contact with himself before he can make contact with another person. In chapter 11 we will come back to the subject of loneliness from the standpoint of how it affects all single parents.

2. *The expectations of other people.* The widowed often receive a great deal of sympathy during the first few weeks of their loss. But then the attitude of friends seems to be, "You should be getting over this by now." The widowed feel that friends and family often are too impatient with them and aren't there in that critical period of bereavement, six to eight months after the loss.

3. *Greeting card mentality.* Those who attempt to comfort the bereaved often don't seem to know how to do it. They offer many platitudes. They can make Scripture sound trite. This is usually the case when the comforter and the grief-stricken

have not touched as human beings. We must remember that there are two dimensions to a Christian's life: the human and the spiritual. We are twice-born people with twofold needs. When we are born again we don't stop functioning as human beings; as regenerate creatures we continue to function as full-fledged, card-carrying human beings. Those who comfort bereaved Christians must relate to them both as human beings and as Christians because of our common identity in natural birth and the New Birth.

4. *Guilt.* It is common for the bereaved to feel guilty, though there may be no rational reason for it. Sometimes the guilt arises from the feeling that perhaps something could have been done to prevent the death. In other cases there is regret over "unfinished business" with the deceased—everything from unresolved marital conflicts to the feeling "I should have been more loving." God is in the business of forgiving the guilty. But when the guilty don't forgive themselves, they continue to feel unforgiven even though they are no longer guilty in God's eyes.

The feeling of guilt is an element of grief. If it is dwelt on and does not pass with time it may become pathological, and we need to find what the "payoff" is.

5. *Anger.* The bereaved often surprise themselves with irrational anger. The widow, unable to find an important legal document, may find herself fuming at her dead husband for leaving the paper work in chaos. The widower, frustrated at his inability to fix his daughter's hair, may be startled with anger at his wife for expecting him to know how to do it.

The expression of anger should be considered a normal part of the complex emotions that the bereaved go through. Of course, the anger is not rational. Feelings don't have to be rational. Feelings just are, for good or for bad. The more willing we are to accept them without judgment or analysis, the quicker we will get over them.

The Christian's high commitment to positive thinking sometimes makes him particularly hard on himself or on those he would comfort. He is quick to judge or analyze: "We shouldn't *feel* that way" or "Why are you feeling this way

when you know that Scripture says . . . ?'' Negative emotions
are not inconsistent with Christian commitment.

Special Concerns of Widow and Widower

Though a widow and a widower have many common needs and
face many of the same concerns, each has certain concerns more
perplexing to one than the other.

The Widow's Concerns

Of paramount importance to the widow is her financial security. This doesn't mean that her children are not important. But
her ability to care for herself and her children can be facilitated
greatly by a feeling of financial security.

In a traditional marriage the wife is often in the dark about her
financial situation. She trusts her husband to see that her needs
are taken care of. Even though he may have made adequate provision for her and she kept the books, she still needs to make the
transition from marriage to widowhood.

A helpful guide called ''What Do You Do Now?'' can be
obtained from the Life Insurance Marketing and Research Association, Inc., Hartford, CT 06141. It tells the widow all the things
she should do upon the death of her husband. Here is a list of
what they suggest:

1. *Funeral expenses.* Sometimes veterans or fraternal organizations offer a funeral allowance for the deceased members
   of the organization. She should contact any organizations her
   husband was a member of to see if she qualifies for any other
   allowances.

2. *Legal counsel.* It is hoped she and her husband have a will.
   If they don't, her assets will be disposed of in accordance
   with state law. Whether or not she has a will, she should
   contact an attorney to be sure all the legal formalities are
   properly carried out.

3. *Significant documents.* Search likely places to locate impor-

tant papers. Safe deposit boxes, briefcases, strong boxes, home and office desks, lockers, and safes should all be checked for important papers. She should keep *everything*. Sometimes auto clubs such as AAA offer life insurance as part of the membership package. Even though premiums have not been paid on an insurance policy, cash value may have kept it in force.

4. *Death certificate.* She should get at least six certified copies of the death certificate. She will need a number of copies in order to make claims for benefits due her.

5. *Life insurance.* She should contact her life insurance agent or home office. They will instruct her on how to go about making a claim.

6. *Social security.* She should contact the nearest social security office. If the deceased was covered under social security, she is due a lump sum benefit, which must be applied for. The amount was $255 in 1981. She should inquire about other survivor benefits.

7. *Civil service benefits.* If her spouse was in the civil service, she and her children may be eligible for some benefits.

8. *Veterans benefits.* She should contact the nearest Veterans Administration office if her spouse was a veteran. They will tell her what benefits, if any, she has coming.

9. *Business associates.* She should contact her husband's employer and/or business associates. Her husband may have accrued pay and allowances she is not aware of, particularly vacation pay and a pension plan. He may have been included in a group life insurance plan.

10. *Social service agencies.* She should contact social service and welfare agencies in case of emergency. She should check with the Red Cross and Salvation Army to see if they offer any help to widows.

11. *Current bills.* She should gather all current bills. Many installment loans are covered by credit life insurance, which pays the balance—usually up to five thousand dollars—in the event of the customer's death. Prompt request for release

should be made to each bank in which she and her husband have a joint account. This is necessary for her to withdraw funds. A bank usually stops payment on checks when the fact of death is published.

12. *Inheritance taxes.* She should consult her attorney or accountant to find out about her state inheritance and death taxes. *The World Almanac* also gives this information under "Taxes, State—Inheritance, Estate."

13. *Probate.* Probate is a procedure established by law for the orderly distribution of estates left by death. She should contact the clerk at the office of the probate judge to find out what steps to take.

14. *Fraud.* Widows are a common target for fraud and need to be cautious. Often someone will appear at her door claiming that her husband contracted for a product or service before he died. She should *not* pay this person. She should tell him, "Give me all the information you have, and I will have my attorney contact you."

The Widower's Concerns

A widower has most of the same concerns as a widow. But he has some that are particularly his own. A common problem the widower faces is the case of minor children. Unless his wife had a protracted illness, during which time he learned to care for house and children, he is suddenly faced with a task for which he may feel ill-prepared. He feels torn between the demands of his job and the worries of adequate child care, an experience many working custodial mothers face.

The widower often has an advantage, however. He has the sympathy and support (such as it is) of society. And he usually has adequate income to provide child care while he is at work.

This does not imply that he has an easy time of it. The demands of being breadwinner and solo parent leave him little time for himself. This can be physically and emotionally debilitating. All this occurs at a time when he is particularly vulnerable to the stress of grief.

The death of a spouse affects widowers harder than widows. Widowers do not live as long as married men. By contrast, there

s no difference in the longevity of unmarried and remarried widows.[12]

Widowers often attempt to escape loneliness and the stress of
single parenting by marrying again. But more than half of these
marriages end in divorce or abandonment.[13] The failure rate of
second marriages is 60 percent. For first marriages it is 50 percent.[14]

Many times the breakdown of the marriage is the result of poor
foresight. Not enough attention is given to the dynamics of the
stepfamily. Before any widower considers establishing a stepfam-
ly he should take the "Stepparent Test," found in *The Readymade Family*.[15]

Another reason for the failure of remarriage is that the widower
often remarries so he can have someone to take care of his children. That's a poor motive for marriage. Marriage should be
primarily for the widower. His children will eventually grow up
and leave home. Will marriage still look good to him then?

The Children of Sorrow

was thirteen years old when my baby sister died. She was six
months old. I remember my mother explaining to me that Susan
was born with "defective intestines." She couldn't digest her
food or eliminate properly. She was in and out of the hospital
until the day she died.

I can't remember the news of Susan's death—only the funeral.
The service was held in our church, and a little white casket stood
open in front of the pulpit. I couldn't see inside from where I
sat, but I remember being in a daze. It seems my mother and
older sister were there, but I can't remember my dad being there
in the pew with us.

There came a time in the service when everyone got up, and
my mother led the way to the casket with us children in tow. I
was stunned by what I saw—a little pale body all dressed in white
in a little white casket. In grief and tears I turned to my mother.
It's strange, but I can't remember Mom and Nan crying, though
I'm sure they did. I was in my own private world of grief, and
everything else was a haze.

The next time I had occasion to be near a casket was at age

twenty-seven while I was in seminary. My pastoral-care class
took a field trip to a funeral home. When we crowded into the
casket display room, I was struck with claustrophobia and panic
I had to get out! But I didn't want to embarrass myself in front
of my classmates. I silently screamed, "God, help me!" He answered with a sudden memory of Susan in her little white casket
That was exactly what I needed. It was as though He said
"There's nothing to be afraid of. Your panic has to do with an
event that occurred a long time ago. Today's experience just
brought back those feelings."

This was the first and only time that happened. As a pastor
conducted many funerals. Being able to separate the here and
now from the past helped me.

Children Look at Death

The point of this story is that if we are to help the children of
sorrow, we must understand how they look at death and react to
it.

1. *Their own kind of grief.* Children, even adolescents, handle
grief differently than adults do. They can't take too much at
one time. This is why it is not unusual for children to ask
what may seem like "inappropriate" questions when there's
a death—such as, "Can I still have my birthday party?" My
"daze" at Susan's funeral was from being overwhelmed by
it all. Children need a familiar routine, people, and events to
stay connected to reality.

   This is not to suggest that children should be kept away
from funerals. After the age of four, they should be allowed
to decide for themselves. But they should be told the type of
service that they will attend and that people will be crying and
that "Mommy's" or "Daddy's" body will be there in a casket. If the casket is open, don't force the child to see the body
let him know it's okay if he doesn't want to. The child should
be accompanied by an older person who is sensitive and not
intensely grief-stricken so the child can be taken out of the
service if necessary.[16]

2. *No sense of finality.* Children don't realize the finality of death
It is not unusual for a child to ask, "Will Daddy be back for

Christmas?'' The mother should hug the child and say, ''I know you wish Daddy would come back. It will be lonely without him on Christmas. But remembering the good times will help.''

At times like this parents often burst into tears. That's all right, and it's all right for the child to join in. It lends a sense of mutual support.

A child in a Christian family has a distinct advantage because of Christian education. The central message of Christianity is that the Son of God died to give us victory over sin and death. He rose from the dead to demonstrate that victory. A parent has an excellent opportunity to make Christianity practical for the child who has been taught this. From the human viewpoint death is final, but death is not permanent. A parent must be careful, however, not to confuse a child by leading him to think that Daddy will be coming through the door any minute. A strong educational program in church, in Sunday school, and at home will help the child understand the Christian view of death.

3. *Magical Thinking and Egocentricity.* In the magical world of the child, wishing makes anything possible. Children eventually outgrow their fantasies, but their fantasy world is important to their emotional development. It throws the world wide open to *any* possibility, and this stimulates curiosity and enhances their learning about life.

Egocentricity also plays a part. Children see everything that happens in life as somehow relating to them. This also enhances the learning process.

The effect of both these qualities must be considered when children face a death in the family. For example, they may wonder if they had any part in the death of the parent, particularly when they remember the parent's saying, ''You'll drive me to an early grave!'' or ''You'll be the death of me!'' Children need to be assured if there is any question in their minds.[17]

Not only do children think they may have caused the death, but they may also think something can be done to reverse the process and bring back the missing parent. Bargaining is a tool children often use with adults. It is not unusual for them to try to bargain with God to bring back the parent.

As a Christian child grows older and learns doctrine, he will understand that there is to be a reunion. However, the child tends to think in terms of the present and may become angry with God for not answering his prayers. The Christian parent must not scold the child for not relying on the promises of the Bible. Nonjudgmental, nonanalytical caring should be the parent's response.

4. *"Inappropriate" behavior.* Given the uniqueness of the child's worldview, what may otherwise appear as inappropriate behavior may seem very appropriate to him. Sometimes a child will say, "I don't care that Daddy (or Mommy) died." This is a common reaction to pain and fear. It is the child's way of saying, "I can't let myself think about it because it hurts too much. And I'm scared because I don't know what's going to happen to me. Will my other parent die too?"

Sometimes a child will have a temper tantrum or manifest other bad behavior. This may have its roots in depression or anger that the child is unable to articulate. Even adults irrationally lash out at others when they are deeply troubled by something else. Bad behavior is not to be excused, but it may be understood as a clumsy way of expressing otherwise inexpressible feelings.

Another caution: be alert to the "too good child." Sometimes a child will fantasize that if he's a very good boy, maybe Daddy (or Mommy) will come back. It is nice to have cooperative children in this time of deep distress, but don't overlook the child who has placed a terrible burden on himself.

Some Things to Remember About Children and Death

Here are some things to remember about children and death:

1. *If the parent knows he (or she) is going to die, it will help the child to discuss it.* This allows time for some desensitization and anticipatory mourning.

2. *Seeing a deteriorating parent can help a child adjust to the reality of death.* But remember that children can handle grief only in small portions.

3. *Children whose parents die as a result of accident or suicide will be more likely to have rescue fantasies than children whose parents die after a long illness.*

4. *A child should be reassured that his needs for food, shelter, and care will continue to be met.* Concern over these issues may hinder the grieving process.

5. *The death of one parent may make a child fearful about the death of the surviving parent or his own death.* Reassurances are helpful.

6. *Tell the child about the parent's death in terms he can understand.* Don't fabricate tales about the parent's being away on a trip.

7. *If the child attends the funeral, be sensitive to the amount of grief he can handle.*

8. *Let the child have a photograph or treasured possession of the deceased parent.* This helps the child through the grief process. The child who continually asks the same questions about the death is going through the process of desensitization.[18]

ㅅㅅㅅ 9
Who's Minding
the Children?

Should mothers work? This question is being raised again an
again with a growing national concern over who's minding th
children. One magazine raised this question in a feature articl
that said:

> Should mothers work? Americans still ask, including job-
> holders surveyed by the Public Agenda Foundation. . . .
> In fact, the majority of mothers do work and—as the survey
> also shows—most of the work force thinks that the care of
> their children is being neglected and something should be
> done about it.[1]

This kind of magazine article infuriates single parents and com
plicates that fury with a goading sense of guilt and failure. Afte
reading the article, one single mother said, "What a dumb ques
tion—'should mothers work?' These people need to know *I hav
no option*! I was deserted by my husband, and it's up to me t
take care of me and my daughter."

A single father said, "I'm envious of married working mother
who work because they choose it. I've *never* had a choice.
didn't have one when I was married, and I certainly have n
choice now that my wife is dead. Now I'm both breadwinner an
primary caregiver, and I'll tell you, it's tough!"

Single parents feel very sensitive about the issue of "the neglected kids at home." Those who formulate government programs and church ministries must be careful not to adopt a simplistic and cynical attitude that "these people ought to be at home taking care of their kids." *Some parents have no choice and need our help.*

Child Day-Care Options

"Day care" is a term used to describe the various types of arrangements parents make for child care while they are at work.

Types of Day Care

Approximately half of the children receiving day care received it in the caregiver's own home. This is called a "family day-care home." Some states do not require the licensing of these homes, which typically provide care for two or three neighbors plus the caregiver's children. A smaller portion of these children are cared for in their own homes by a baby sitter or a live-in housekeeper. Live-in help, however, is usually beyond the means of single parents.[2]

One-third of the day-care population is cared for by a family member such as an older sibling, a parent not at work, grandparent, aunt, or other relative. About half of these live in the child's home. Slightly more than half of the relatives babysit for free.

Surprisingly, only 16 percent of day-care children attend a child-care center, either profit or non profit. One reason for this low percentage is lack of availability; another is cost.[3]

Arranging for day care is not so simple as the statistics might suggest, however. Most parents must put together a "child-care package," using several types of day care in a given day. For example, a working parent may drop off the child at the home of a neighbor, who in turn takes his or her child and the other parent's child to a half-day nursery school. Then someone else is paid to take the child to a family day-care home, where another three or four hours of care is provided. This piecemeal arrangement may place the child with four to six types of day care in a given week.

If the child is sick or if one of the caregivers is not available
the parent has to make other arrangements or take a sick da
from work. Even if everything works, the child eventually out
grows the type of day care he started in, and new arrangement
must be made.

Every single parent or prospective single parent should obtai
the pamphlet called *A Parent's Guide to Day Care*.[4] The pam
phlet lists three main types of day care: in-home care, family da
care, and center-based care. It gives such helpful information a
finding day care, screening by phone, checking references, de
ciding what kind of care is needed, selecting the type of day car
most suitable for the child, and making day care work. It als
tells what to do about problems with the caregiver or problem
with the child's feelings and behavior, his health, safety, cloth
ing, schedule, day-care setting, nutrition, and day-care costs. Fi
nally, it offers thirteen pages of day-care resources.

What to Do About Day Care

In addition to getting the pamphlet just described, the singl
parent will need to take some other steps to find adequate da
care.

1. *Information and referral agencies.* Many localities have child
   care information and referral agencies (I & Rs) that can hel
   a single parent find the type of day care needed. The I & R
   may be run by a city, town, county, or private organization
   See the yellow pages under "Child-Care Referral" or call th
   city hall or county seat for information. The public librar
   often has such information.

   I & Rs keep lists of both licensed child-care facilities an
   in-home caregivers. They may even do preliminary screenin
   and match the child to a suitable caregiver. Sometimes sub
   sidies are available to income-eligible parents. Other I & R
   may help a parent arrange in-home "sharecare," where on
   caregiver takes care of several children and rotates among thei
   homes.

   Social-service or community-development agencies mak
   child-care referrals in some communities. You should chec
   the United Way, the YMCA, Red Cross, religious organiza

tions, and colleges and universities. When all else fails, write or call the agency in your state that supervises day-care agencies. They are listed in the back of the pamphlet, *A Parent's Guide to Day Care*.

Day-Care Centers. To get in touch with day-care centers or day-care home networks (groups of day-care mothers who work together), look in the yellow pages under "Child Care." This may not include centers run by religious organizations or school districts that are using schoolroom space.[5]

Other suggestions:

- Ask relatives, friends, neighbors, and co-workers
- Ask your pastor
- Ask your doctor, public health nurse, or public health clinic
- Check with local chapters of women's organizations, parents' groups, and child-care associations
- Talk to the parents of the day-care centers or homes being considered.

Advertising for day care. Advertising for day care can be done in different ways. One way is to place an ad in the newspaper and include the child's age, sex, kind of day care you want, hours needed per week, starting date, preferred location, and when and where to call.

Place ads on bulletin boards in churches, schools, community centers, student unions, dormitories, and supermarkets.

Parents will want to screen the people who respond. Here are some questions to ask a caregiver:

- Have you worked with children before, and what were their ages?
- What kinds of things do you like to do with children?
- Why do you like working with children?
- What other kinds of work experience have you had?
- Why did you leave your last job?
- Are you considering other kinds of work?
- Do you have the names of people you worked for before (references)?[6]

Listen to the questions the applicant asks you, and beware of people who talk only about the hours, pay, and amount of work required.

When you talk with family day-care providers you will want to know the following:

- What experience does the caregiver have?
- How long has the person been in the day-care business?
- How many other children are being cared for, and what are their ages?
- Do any of the children belong to the caregiver?
- What is the cost?
- References?[7]

When talking to day-care center directors find out:

- Is the center open year-round?
- Is it closed on public school holidays?
- What is the teacher-to-child ratio?
- What ages does the center accept?
- What hours of care are offered?
- What is the daily program of activities like?
- What meals are served?
- Will there be a vacancy when the child needs to be enrolled?
- What is the fee? Is there a sliding scale or a "scholarship" available for the needy?
- References?[8]

Before your child is enrolled, visit the center or family-care home during regular hours, preferably mid-morning. How is the staff interacting with the children? A quality atmosphere can't be faked. Trust your feelings. If you feel ill at ease, your child probably will also.[9]

Another indicator is your reception by the director. If your visit is discouraged, watch out. Also, don't overlook safety—equipment, health or workers, sanitation, building, and fire safety. Look for organization. Does it appear things are well-organized?

With respect to references on all of the above, listen to the person's tone of voice as well as to what is said. Does he or she ound slightly troubled or cautious or pause for a long time before nswering questions?[10]

When checking references, inquire exactly what service the aregiver provided. Ask whether they would use the caregiver gain and what they liked the most and least about the caregiver. t may be that the reference is just a friend and never did use the aregiver.

Be sure to check the current tax laws to see whether child-care an be deducted on your income tax return. A phone call to your ocal IRS office should give you that information.

When Adequate Day Care Is Not Available

t is possible that single parents may be unable to find adequate ay care, particularly those living in small towns or rural areas.)r, the single parent may be a Christian with specific require- nents for the spiritual guidance of her child. What does she do nen? There are a couple of possibilities, both of which require a)t of work and dedication on the parent's part. One option is to stablish her own business and become a family day-care caregiv- r at home. Another is to start a cooperative (co-op) day-care enter.

Either way you will learn the business inside and out. If you re going to take care of school-age children, become acquainted /ith the School-Age Child Care (SACC) Project, a national in-)rmation and technical assistance resource that promotes the de- elopment of programs and services for children ages five through welve, before and after school, and at such times when there is need for care and supervision. The project has published an ction manual that is a comprehensive how-to guide for parents nd community groups. It gives the basic steps of organizing and perating school-age child-care programs. Churches that are not sing their facilities on a full-time basis would find this an ex- ellent guide to providing a needed service to its own members nd community and at the same time make its building cost- ffective. For more information on the SACC Project, write to /ellesley College, Center for Research on Women, Wellesley, 4A 02181.

1. Do-It-Yourself Day Care

Before starting a day-care business at home consider the following:

a. Be sure you have the cooperation of your children and any other family member living in your home. Having a house full of children will affect everyone's routine. Your own children will need assurances that they won't be lost in the shuffle. One family day-care mother said that her daughter sometimes complains that the other children get more help on their art projects than she does.[11]

Another mother makes sure that her own child has her own private space when she needs it (usually her own room), private time alone with Mom, or a special chair.[12] She also points out that conflict sometimes arises over possessions. The caregiver's child must be taught to distinguish between what is his own in his room and what is available for all the children to use in the common play area.

Though overlap of family and business does create special problems, some family day-care mothers feel their children get the best of two worlds. They can be with Mom and yet benefit by social contact with other children.[13]

b. Draw up a budget. You will need to determine how much you will charge. This will depend on the cost of your operation (start up and running expenses) and how many children will be cared for. It is best to start modestly and grow. You will need equipment such as cots, high chairs, toys, and materials for activities. You don't have to make your home look like a nursery school. Even pots and pans can be used as toys.[14]

A license for a family day-care home may be required by the state. Standards of health and safety must be met, and items such as fire extinguishers, smoke alarms, electrical outlet caps, and a fenced-in play area should be included in your budget.

c. Other considerations. Additional insurance is necessary. Homeowners insurance will not cover a business in your home. Ask your insurance agent or local day-care association about special liability insurance for family day-care providers.[15]

If meals are to be provided, look into the Department of Agiculture's (USDA) Child Care Food Program. This is a reimbursement program in which the provider receives funds for each meal and snack served. Contact the nearest USDA regional office or more information.[16]

Consider the possibility of becoming affiliated with a day-care system. The advantage would be insurance coverage, some training, and help in filing taxes. But one of the advantages of being an independent operator is that you can be selective about the children you keep, and you can set your own hours.

Finally, be sure to keep track of business expenses for tax purposes. Also, to avoid misunderstanding with the parents you serve, draw up a contract for the parents to sign. It should include how much you are to be paid, when the payment is made, when the child arrives and leaves, and whether a sick child is permitted in the house. The contract should provide for extra charges for late pickup to discourage parents from being careless in this matter. Be sure to have emergency numbers for each child, and be aware of any medical problems a child may have.

2. Day-Care Co-Op

There are two differences between a co-op and a day-care business. A day-care business is run for profit, and the owner of the business is in charge—though responsibility may be delegated to hired workers. A co-op, on the other hand, is usually nonprofit and, since it requires the participation of the parents in its formation and operation, the parents exercise control. The need for cooperation can become a disadvantage; it can be frustrating to parents, already weary from the job of being single parents, to have to deal with other parents who are uncooperative and play out neurotic behavior in the organization.

Getting Started

Before attempting to start a co-op, get the following literature and study it so you will have an idea of what is required: the ACC Project "Action Manual" mentioned on page 121, and the Health and Human Services (HHS) pamphlet *A Parent's Guide to Day Care*, mentioned on page 118. To find out what federal funds are available for day-care centers, contact the Women's Bureau of the Department of Labor, Washington, D.C., and ask for the booklet they have compiled. Contact your State Department of Welfare to see what state funds are available. For licensing requirements check the list of "State Day-Care Agencies" in the back of the HHS pamphlet. Adequate information is essential if you intend to lead a cooperative effort.

Also, by taking leadership responsibility, you may become the logical candidate for a paid job as the co-op's director. Though your work may be similar to that of the owner of a day-care business, organizationally you would be hired by the parents who act as a board of directors and who have the final say about the operation of the co-op.

After getting your information together, start to promote the co-op idea. You will need about five to ten parents to begin. If there is a need for such a center, it shouldn't be difficult to get the project started.

Christian parents who wish to make the spiritual growth of their children a primary goal of the co-op have an excellent opportunity in working through their churches. Church facilities are often unused during the week and are already equipped to accommodate child care. When you approach your pastor with your suggestion, make it clear that you are not suggesting that he take the job. Tell him that you are willing to take leadership and organizational responsibility. You and the parents involved will be the workers.

Your First Organizational Meeting

When you have found enough interested parents, call an organizational meeting. Committees should be established to start the work. If you have done some preliminary research, you can pass on your findings to the various committees. They need information about licensing requirements, which will guide them in getting the license and in determining what the site and equipment committees must do to meet the licensing requirements. The licensing requirements may also specify the type of program that can be offered.

A funding committee should be formed. Funds will be needed

o renovate or supply the facility. Funds will be needed to operate or at least a month until the users begin to pay their way.

A budget needs to be set, by either the funding committee or a separate budget committee. This committee must determine what the day-to-day operation will cost—rent and utilities, salary for at least one full-time person, meals, and supplies. The SACC manual gives all the information needed.

Don't overlook the need for a summer program when the children are out of school. Consider coordinating the center's work with day camps or boarding camps. Churches often have camp facilities available that are not used to maximum capacity. Camping programs offer children a marvelous opportunity for physical, emotional, and spiritual growth.

Day Care: Good News and Bad News

Single parents who must work outside the home have no other choice but to seek some kind of day care for their children. But as loving parents they want to know the impact of day care on their children. Professional and popular literature can't seem to agree on an answer. One popular magazine carried an article titled "The Day-Care Child" that said:

> "What will day care do to my child?" Mothers ask, usually with anxiety. The answers are not always clear or conclusive, but the latest research suggests that good day care does not impede the development of the child—and may even enhance it.[17]

The same issue of this magazine ran another article titled "Now for the Bad News . . ." It asked:

> Is day care spawning a generation of ruffians? Some recent studies suggest that children who have been in center-based care since infancy may be significantly more aggressive than home-reared children. But their relationship, or lack of relationship, with the care-giver may be the cause.[18]

Before single parents become too alarmed, let me give some assurance. There is nothing wrong with the concept of day care having another person, or several people, take care of the child of a working parent. This has been done for centuries. The clan or the extended family was there to help out in the past. Grandparents, aunts, uncles, and older siblings shared in caregiving; it was not the task of the parent alone. With the demise of the clan and even the extended family in American culture, the task of child rearing fell on the nuclear family (husband, wife, sibling). And over the past thirty years, with the shattering of the nuclear family, child care has fallen on the shoulders of the single parent. *What a staggering responsibility* when we consider how far we have come from the care of the clan or extended family *to the care of one parent!*

Americans are socially and commercially innovative, however. The extended family has now become big business. The wealthy always had hired nannies and tutors in the past, but now child care is within the reach of practically everyone, though the quality differs. And that's the key issue. The idea of someone else parenting your child is not wrong. But will the child get *parent* quality care?

Standing In for Parents

Those who stand in for parents and seek to give parent-quality care must meet three primary needs in the lives of the children. The degree to which the caregiver gives these to the child is one indication of good care.

1. *Children need to be loved and to belong to a family.*[19] Even the infant in the crib needs to be picked up and loved. The warm touch of the caregiver communicates "belongingness." Sixteen infants in cribs and two caregivers is not parent-quality care—it's warehouse. The ratio should be at least one caregiver for every four babies.

2. *Children need specific information.*[20] They need to know colors, numbers, and words, and most important, how to gather information without help. This is essential to developing maturity, independence, and self-confidence in children. This means that younger children need to be in smaller group

so they may interact more with the adult caregivers. Five or six children per caregiver is the limit for toddlers.[21]

It is also important to have the *same* caregiver available for the children so that rules for social conduct may be set and followed consistently.

Those who supervise caregivers must enforce the rule that the caregivers don't socialize with each other during working hours. Their attention is to be devoted to the children. Even nap time is an occasion for the caregiver to observe the children and spot any troubled behavior patterns such as repeated failure to obey rules, disturbed sleep, or bed wetting.

3. *Children need rules for interacting with each other.*[22] In one study of children who had been in day care from ages six weeks to five years, their behavior showed fifteen times more aggressiveness than in a control group. Adequate adult interaction early in the child's life is essential for the child to learn kindness, nonaggression, and task persistence.[23] Parents or their surrogates who tell their children the rules of behavior at the time of an aggressive act and do so sternly in a one-on-one interaction ("We don't hit other people: it hurts them!") raise children who learn to show kindness as they grow older.[24]

What Can a Parent Do?

There are several things a concerned parent can do to reduce the negative effects of day care.

1. *Before enrolling the child, be sure that the ratio of caregivers is adequate for the child population: four babies per caregiver, five to six toddlers per caregiver, and with children over three, one caregiver per seven children.* Smaller groups permit more personal attention. Be sure the caregivers are devoted to the children and are supervised adequately so the children are getting the benefit of the care. Caregivers should be hired on a "review basis," which means that their employment depends on their passing a periodic review, the first one being no more than six weeks after employment.

2. *Be sure that quality day care is maintained after the child is*

enrolled. Is the caregiver/child ratio being maintained? Is there adequate supervision of the caregivers?

3. *When you are with your child, make your time count.* That is difficult with preschool children because of their limited attention span. Teaching a child of this age is "responsive," not "directive." This means that a parent takes advantage of situations that lead to learning experiences, whether conflict with another child or disappointment over the weather. Sometimes household tasks must be interrupted or suspended to capitalize on a teaching opportunity.

Television does not offer this kind of opportunity simply because the TV story moves on and a parent doesn't have time to stop and explain. It is important to explain things while children watch TV. When they see people on TV behaving in a criminal or antisocial manner *and do not understand the motives or consequences,* they are missing an important lesson. They may want to copy the behavior because it looks exciting without their understanding the consequences.

Reading with the child is a better activity. Talking about the pictures and story gives the parent an opportunity to connect these things to the child's everyday world.[25]

4. *Connect home and day care for the child.* Children have difficulty communicating what goes on during the day away from home. Even when they mention what goes on, they may leave out important details. The parent must know the program and caregivers well enough to be able to fill in vital information. By talking about the program and the caregivers by name, the parent is able to help the child's memory.

If the parent is close enough to the day-care facility to have lunch with the child, it might give more continuity of contact. The day-care provider's rules may discourage this, however.

The parent may also look for ways to become involved with the day-care center. The more the parent knows about the operation, the better he is able to connect day care and his own care of the child.[26]

5. *Finally, when parents get involved with the day-care center, they should work to make the atmosphere as caring as possible toward the children.* The physical plant and activities

should be as homelike as possible. Activities should stimulate interaction between the caregivers and the children. The mood of that interaction, even in discipline, should reflect loving concern.

Single parents should remember that the concept of surrogate parenting is not wrong. The question is, will the caregiver provide the necessary supervision, emotional security, and cognitive skills essential for the child's social and spiritual growth? Parents must insist on nothing less.

he Latchkey Child

ne "latchkey child"—the school-age child who lets himself into empty house after school—is a subject that fills both professonal and popular literature. A survey of recent magazines found e following articles:

"Lifetime of Fear: Legacy for Latchkey Children" *(Marriage and Divorce Today)*.
"When School Kids Come Home to an Empty House" *(U.S. News and World Report)*.
"Our Neglected Kids" *(U.S. News and World Report)*.
"Latchkey Children: How Much of a Problem?" *(Education Digest)*.
"The Lonely Life of 'Latchkey' Children, Say Two Experts, Is a National Disgrace" *(People)*.

ne phenomenon of latchkey children may be a national disgrace. is estimated that there are *ten million* such children in the United ates.[27] And perhaps those parents who selfishly indulge their sires for greater income or career ought to feel guilty. But what out the single parent who simply cannot find or afford adequate pervision for the school-age child? Certainly the public should ve some sympathy for them.

Rather than focus on the ills and evils of the problem, which ve been documented adequately in other literature, let us con- ler what can be done about the needs of the latchkey child.

Know Your Child's Limitations and Capabilities

More important than the child's chronological age is his degre
of maturity. This will determine how much responsibility yo
give him to follow the rules you lay down. *All* school childre
must have some responsible adult to turn to in an emergency o
time of trouble. *All* school children, including teenagers, are t
be accountable to the parent.

If the parent is not nearby, the other responsible adult shoul
be. The child is responsible and accountable to both of them
This will avert trouble in the teen years when a child active
pushes for more independence and less accountability.[28] The chi
needs to learn that even though people become independent adult
family members are always accountable to each other. That's th
nature of family life.

Make Sure the Home Is Safe and Secure

Does the home have smoke detectors? Is there a fire exti
guisher and a fire evacuation plan? Do the doors and window
have adequate locks, and do the children know how to use them
Are emergency phone numbers posted—police, fire, rescue squa
the parent's number, the number of a nearby responsible adult?

When There Is More Than One Child

Generally, leaving siblings together is preferred to leaving the
alone. Much depends on the children's ages, sex, and how we
they get along with each other. If an older child is left in char
of a younger child, will the older child abuse his position
authority? Will the younger child obey? An eleven-year-old ma
be capable of staying by himself for a couple of hours, but it
too much to ask him to supervise a younger child.

Though a parent should not be alarmed or alarm his childre
the possibility of sexual abuse between same- or opposite-s
siblings should not be ignored. How will the parent know? Th
general behavior of the children with each other and with frien
when the parent is around is one indicator. An attentive pare
who is not paranoid about this possibility will know if anythi
is amiss by how the children talk and behave. If there is susp
cion, *don't accuse!* Put it in terms of *your* problem. For examp

'When I come home and see . . . , or hear that . . . happened, 'm very disturbed. It makes me wonder if you're doing things hat you know I wouldn't approve of.'' The parent then makes it :lear what he does not want and what he does want. He can insist hat the children stay out of each other's bedrooms. Or, in the vent they share a room, to respect each other's privacy and ersonal belongings. An adult may need to be employed on a emporary basis to come into the house to monitor the children.

Physical or Emotional Problems

Children with physical problems such as severe asthma, hand-caps, or a tendency to act out emotional problems are not good andidates to be left alone. Or, if the child has experienced a rauma such as a stormy divorce or a death in the family, the arent may need to employ an adult to be with the child after chool.

Some Basic Rules

Parents often feel guilty about the latchkey situation and the ules that must be laid down in view of it. But rules must be stablished for the child's protection.

1. *The child should be sure to keep the door locked.* Install a solid security device, usually called a ''night latch,'' so the door can be opened a crack to respond to a caller but cannot be forced open. Night latches with chains are usually too flimsy and can be forced open.

2. *The child should call the parent as soon as he arrives home.*

3. *He should not let anyone in the house, not even friends.*

4. *He should not tell anyone he is home alone, especially people who call.* They can be told that the mother or father is not available and that the child will take a message.

5. *In case of a problem, the child should call the parent.*[30]

Organize In-Home Activities

Most children find it difficult to organize their own activities t home and quickly become bored. Assigning chores and setting

time for homework may be helpful, but after a day at school a
craft project set out the night before might be a pleasant change
of pace.[31]

Try to avoid using the TV as a baby sitter. A trip to the library
to check out some interesting books is one alternative. If the child
does not watch TV selectively, you may need to restrict its use.
If the set is small enough it can be locked in a closet. Another
alternative is to lock the plug. Most plugs have small holes in
the prongs. Get a small padlock that will fit the holes, and simply
keep it on the plug until you're ready to use it.

Record players (tape or disc) are good alternatives to TV. The
public library usually carries an assortment of entertainment or
instructional records or tapes for circulation.

A tape recorder also can be used to tape a message to your
child. You may simply tell him, "I love you," or make some
recordings from a joke book that is suited to his age group.

Spend Time With Each Child

If you have more than one child, spend time with each one
separately. Don't suppose that their companionship with each
other is enough.[32]

Come Home Immediately After Work

Save your routine errands to do with your child. It may mean
having to go out again and return to the store you passed on the
way home, but an extra fifteen minutes away from your child can
seem like an eternity to him.[33]

Call Frequently

The telephone is a lifeline to your child. Frequent calls reassure
both of you that the lines of communication are open and intact.
As much as your job will allow, let the child know that he is also
free to call you.[34]

Check Out School-Age Child Care

Some schools provide after-school programs for children. In
the absence of such programs, check the SACC manual mentioned earlier. It offers suggestions for latchkey children.[35]

Watch for Evidence of Acute Fear

Fear is usually the biggest hurdle for children at home alone. Some fear is to be expected. But acute fear may be evidenced by the following:

- When you arrive home, the TV or radio is playing loudly or both are playing at once.
- The phone line is constantly busy when you call.
- The child has recurring nightmares or other sleep disturbances.
- He appears depressed.
- He plays with fire (a serious symptom of fear and anxiety).

You may help by letting your child know that it's okay to talk about being lonely or afraid. He may be trying to spare you the burden of worry by keeping it all in. But above all, deal with *your own* fear and guilt. Our children take their cues from us.[36]

10

Other Single-Parent
Concerns

The two biggest concerns of single parents are how to reduce the trauma of a parent's loss and how to reduce the negative effect of a child's growing up without that parent. We have seen in this book that the answers to these concerns are complex. But two factors are essential to setting these concerns to rest:

1. *The* attitude *of the single parent is all-important.* If the parent's attitude is "We can make it," and he or she does not behave as though either parent or child is to be pitied, the child will most likely adopt the same attitude and *expect* to survive the rigors of a single-parent home.

2. *Even though one parent may be missing, loving parent substitutes can have a positive impact on the child.* But the parent substitute has to be ready to love the child as his own.

These are not the only concerns of single parents. This chapter deals with other single-parent concerns and what parents can do about them.

Single parents frequently express concern over symptoms of depression in their children—and the possibility of suicide. How concerned should they be, and what can be done about these concerns?

Depression

Though divorce does not always cause depression, the number of depressed children is higher in single-parent families. The statistics are only educated guesses, but it's believed that 5 to 10 percent of children from two-parent homes are depressed as compared with 30 to 50 percent of children in single-parent families.[1]

Signs of Depression

The symptoms of acute and chronic depression are similar. They may include severe impairment of the child's school performance, severely disturbed social adjustment, eating and sleeping problems, feelings of despair and helplessness and hopelessness, psychomotor retardation (such as slow speech response), and possibly suicidal ideas or threats. Children may also show a persistently sad affect (sad face), withdrawal, great agitation, aggressive behavior, and psychosomatic illness or complaint of illness when they really aren't sick.[2]

Unfortunately, when a home has lost a parent through death or divorce the remaining parent is often overwhelmed with his own feelings and is not in a position to recognize the onset of depression in the child. It is also easy to misinterpret the meaning of the child's behavior because the child may deny that he is hurting.[3]

Causes of Depression

Some parents find it difficult to understand why the child should be depressed, particularly when the parental fighting is over and the child is no longer subjected to a verbally or physically abusive parent. One reason a child experiences depression is that he is caught in a no-win situation. The custodial parent may be quite happy to be rid of the child's other parent. Divorce terminates the marriage, but divorce does not terminate the parent-child relationship, which the child hopes will go on. But how does the child show love and loyalty to both parents when they hate each other so?

Depression is a psychological reaction to an impossible dilemma. Giving up seems to be a sensible reaction. But a solution must be found to end the depression. Often the solution is to make the child feel understood. Nothing can be changed about the marriage, but a child who knows that the parent cares about his dilemma and will respect his need to love and be loyal to both parents has the best chance of getting over depression.

Some children are depressed because they feel they are the parent's caretaker. Some parents turn to their children when the spouse is gone and depend on them to provide companionship, conversation, and comfort. Some go so far as to say, "You're the man (or lady) of the house now." No, a thousand times no! A child is a child and must not be rushed into adulthood. *Childhood* is for children.

This is a particularly dangerous situation from the standpoint of recognizing the child's depression. He can't afford to show it because the single parent is counting on him.

But divorce may not be the only cause of depression. Self-esteem is especially important to children. Teenagers frequently suffer from low self-esteem, though they may attempt to cover it with aloofness or toughness. They lack self-esteem because they feel they are not doing well in a competitive society where parents have high expectations. They sometimes feel that they are in the way or a burden to the single parent.

What to Do About Depression

A necessary step, but a difficult one for divorced parents, is to agree that there is a problem. The custodial parent may resent the suggestion that there's a problem because it seems to reflect on parenting skills. The noncustodial parent may resent having to pay for a counselor or psychiatrist, another evidence of "extravagance."

But professional help may not be needed. The parents should first attempt to help the child themselves. Here are some dos and don'ts in dealing with a depressed child:

✔ *DO show your child that you are aware that he appears sad, forlorn, hurt, or dejected.* Try to identify the exact feeling and the degree of it and describe it to him as "You're feeling terribly sad today." Say it with a rising inflection so if he chooses to hear your statement as a question and wishes to respond, he will feel free to do so. The closer you are to expressing how he really feels, the more likely you will leave the impression that you're trying to understand him and are not judging or evaluating him.

✔ *DO encourage your child to express his feelings fully by not arguing with him over the appropriateness of his feelings.* For example, he may say, "I'm a big bother to you." Say to him, "You really feel I don't want you around, don't you. Tell me more about it. What is it I do that makes you feel that way?"

✔ *DO accept your child's dependency needs.* Your child is in a position were he is unable to cope. Because of your maturity you are able to help him explore options that he may not have thought of. Do so without forcing a solution on him. Say, for example, "Do you think it would help if you . . . ?" Or, be willing to be part of the solution. Don't just tell him that you're willing to help. Propose specific solutions, but leave them open so the child is able to assess their workability. Say, for example, "Would it help if I . . . ?" By approaching problem solving in this manner you are able to gain more information about the problem. You need to find out what's workable and unworkable, and why. It also shows the child how an adult goes about facing a seemingly insurmountable problem.

✔ *DO be sensitive to your child's feelings of low self-worth.* Depression is usually the result of loss or the inability to solve a problem and leaves the depressed person with a poor self-image. Self-reproach is a common response. The child feels guilty, ashamed, or weak because of his inability to cope. The parent is in a position to help the child appraise the situation more realistically and in a way that is less punishing.

For example, the child who feels responsible for the divorce or the death of a parent may feel that if he had been a better person, he wouldn't have driven the parent to divorce or death. The custodial parent may say, "Tell me what you would have done differently?" And, "How good do you think you would have had to be to have kept this from happening?" By encouraging the child to express the unreasonable burden he places on himself and by showing mild surprise, the parent is sending an important message that says, "I understand why you feel as you do, but it seems that you're being too hard on yourself." This message needs to be relayed subtly. If the parent were to say this, the child would not feel understood and reject the parent's perspective. But by *implying* it, he gives the child an opportunity to consider that maybe his position is a bit extreme, yet he doesn't have to defend it.

✔ *DON'T attempt to be reassuring.* Reassurances generally don't help, and they often come across as evidence that the parent doesn't understand. The child feels that if people really understood how badly he feels they wouldn't be so glib with reassurances.

Christian parents sometimes do this with Scripture—give assurances that go, "Don't you know that God cares and promises to take care of you? He tells us in the Bible that . . ." Scripture is appropriate, but the choice of Scripture and the timing has to be right. The Christian parent would be wise to start by having the same kind of understanding of depression the writer of Proverbs had when he said, "Hope deferred makes the heart sick, but a longing fulfilled is a tree of life." (Prov. 13:12).

In His earthly ministry, Jesus didn't start with a sermon. He ministered as the Son of Man to men to touch us in our pain and meet our needs. He ate with publicans and sinners and wept with the broken-hearted. He was angry over injustice and in every way identified with man in his pain and sorrow. He called Himself "Son of Man," and as such He established a place in the hearts of those He ministered to. He authenticated His divinity with miracles and proclaimed Himself, on the authority of Old Testament Scripture, the "Son of God," our Savior.

✔ *DON'T urge the child to "snap out of it" or "pull yourself together."* This has no more effect than reassurances. It can also make the parent appear insensitive. Again, the child will feel that the parent simply doesn't understand, that the parent wouldn't say these things if he really understood how hopeless the situation looked.

✔ *DON'T probe, examine, or ask questions about the cause of depression.* Karl Menninger once said, "You don't have to know how a fire started in order to put it out." The child will either not respond or give one-word answers. When someone's hurting, an analysis of why he hurts seems callous.

✓ *DON'T interpret.* For example, "You're depressed because you can't get your way." Even though there may be an element of truth in the statement, it will appear judgmental, and the child will be alienated even further.[4] Remember that the first task in dealing with a depressed person is understanding and caring—to stand with her in her pain and despair. Having dispelled her isolation by being there and having made a connection with her we are in a better position to pray and read Scripture with her.

Suicide

Parents often wonder if depression in their children will lead to suicide. For children ages ten to fourteen (there are no statistics for under the age of ten), the chances are remote; the most recent figures are 145 suicides a year in this age group numbering over 18 million. In the fifteen-to-nineteen age group the figure is significantly higher; there were 1,797 suicides in this age group numbering over 21 million. When the twenty-to-twenty-four age group is added to the fifteen-to-nineteen-year-olds (a total population of 42.5 million), the suicide rate soars to 5,525.[5] The figure is even more alarming when we realize that the incidence of adolescent suicide has risen 15 percent since 1960.[6]

Three times more boys than girls will be successful in their attempts at suicide. Girls will attempt it nine times more than boys. Half a million teenagers attempt it each year.[7] What can a parent do to avert a potential suicide? There are two things: first, dispel the myths of suicide, and second, effectively intervene.

Dispelling Myths of Suicide

Myth 1: Suicidal people want to die; there is nothing that can be done to help them.[8] False. Most people want to be stopped. A relatively small number carry out their plan with the lethal effectiveness or the secrecy required to prevent someone from stopping them. Usually the attempt either is not lethal or, if lethal means are employed, is carried out in such a way that the attempt will be discovered. Unfortunately suicide attempters are not always discovered, and they die when all they really wanted was to get someone to hear their cry for help.

Myth 2: Suicide occurs without warning. False. Most suicidal people hint at their intentions.[9]

Myth 3: Talking to someone about his suicidal feelings will cause him to commit suicide. False. Talking enables the potential suicide to air his feelings and gain the support needed to get through his difficult time.[10]

Myth 4: There is a typical person who commits suicide.[11] False. Suicide occurs among all classes of people. A Christian parent must not assume that because his child is a Christian and lives in a Christian home that suicide is out of the question. In fact, because the idea of suicide is so horrendous to the church, an attempt could be a very effective way of getting someone to hear a cry for help.

Myth 5: All suicidal people leave notes. False. Only 15 percent of those who are successful leave notes. Some suicidal people try to conceal self-destructive intent. Was the high-speed auto crash an accident? Why did the car hit the bridge abutment? Was the driver asleep, or . . . ? Some researchers believe that suicide statistics are for this reason 25 to 100 percent understated.[12]

Myth 6: Suicidal people are insane. False. Of those who actually kill themselves, an estimated one-third are insane. Of those who attempt, only one-tenth are considered insane.[13]

Myth 7: Those who attempt suicide won't try it again. False. It is easier the second time. If an attempter doesn't get help, the next try will be more lethal, with a greater probability of death.

Myth 8: Suicide is an inherited characteristic. False. Sometimes this is believed true because there was more than one suicide in a family. The reasons are not genetic. The emotional climate of the family is most likely the cause.

Myth 9: A person who suddenly becomes happy after a depression is unlikely to commit suicide. False. Sometimes severely depressed people suddenly appear happy because they have found a "solution" to their problems—suicide. It's only a matter of how and when.

Effective Intervention

Effective intervention requires observation and action. Parents, family, and friends should look for specific behaviors in depressed adolescents such as happiness after a long depression and what appears to be "getting his estate in order." Is he giving away prized possessions to friends? Does he seem to be saying good-by by going to teachers and friends and apologizing for behavior that has damaged relationships?

Is the adolescent a particularly sensitive person, does he find it difficult to control his impulses, or is he unable to verbalize anger? Is he prone to revenge and does he talk in terms of "You'll be sorry for what you have done to me" or, less cryptically, "You'll be sorry when I'm gone"?

Personality change can be an indicator. Is withdrawal, aggressiveness, or moodiness unlike him, and does the degree seem alarmingly chronic or acute?

Does he manifest somatic problems? These may include uncharacteristic physical illness, intestinal troubles, lack of energy, headaches, palpitations, blurred vision, or acute anxiety.[14]

Overt actions and statements should be taken seriously, such as expressions of hopelessness, extreme loneliness, or actual talk of suicide.[15]

Changes in relationships such as the loss of a parent or the end of a romance or a friendship are important indicators. This is especially true when the adolescent is left in a deep depression with acute feelings of worthlessness.

What can be done? What constitutes responsible action on the parent's part? Don't be afraid to voice your concerns. Remember, talking about the possibility of an adolescent's harming himself doesn't force him to do it. But express concern in a sensitive way. It is inappropriate to say, "You're not going to do anything stupid, are you?" Why *shouldn't* he do something "stupid" when that's how he feels about himself?

It is appropriate to say, "I have noticed that you have been deeply troubled lately, and I want you to know that I am very concerned. Would you help me understand what is happening?" When the adolescent tells you, *listen* with an understanding ear and don't try to correct his view of things. Your first task is to enter his world of pain. By being there as an understanding person you help carry that pain. Exploring what might be done about it may come later. Reminders of the hope that the Bible offers will be appropriate in due time. *But first, stand with him in his pain, and feel it as he feels it.*

It would be helpful to alert other significant adults about your concerns. These would include pastors, club leaders, coaches, and teachers.

Finally, counseling a potential suicide should be done only by trained professionals. If the adolescent does not respond to the parent's loving, caring, and understanding concern, professional help should be sought. This can be a positive message to the adolescent that you hear him and take him seriously.

School Performance

All parents have a concern for the performance of their children in school. Single parents were recently alarmed by news that made them even more concerned than other parents.

The Child Is From a "Broken Home"

In 1980 the National Association of Elementary School Principals (NAESP) gave reporters a news release titled, "Children From One-Parent Families at Risk in School, Major Study Shows." This release was based on a study (mentioned in chapter 1) by the Institute for the Development of Educational Activities (I/D/E/A). Though it has come under fire by other researchers and educators, a great deal of damage has already been done. One educator said that now when a teacher hears that a child is from a "broken home," warning lights go on, and the child is seen as a potential troublemaker—a perfect scenario for a self-fulfilling prophecy.[16]

The most important finding that resulted from a critique of the study was that single parenting was not the cause of the child's poor performance. A child coming from *any home*, single- or two-parent, that was economically and educationally disadvantaged showed poor performance ratings.[17] But because single-parent families tend to be low-income households headed by a mother with limited education, it was assumed by the researchers that the child's poor performance was due to his coming from a "broken home." Moreover, because the majority of single parents are women working in jobs with nonadjustable hours, they are often unable to attend parent-teacher conferences. This lack of contact between parent and teacher is usually blamed on an abnormal family pattern rather than economic reasons.[18]

Turned Off and Tuned Out—Why?

Single parents are concerned not only about their children being identified as problem children. They are also concerned about "under-achievers." These are students whose school performance is substantially below what is expected of them based on intelligence tests or educational assessment. They appear unmotivated, lazy, bored, and unresponsive. They simply will not do their work. Why is this?

1. *Fear of failure.* Many children lack self-confidence. It's bad enough to feel like a failure, let alone demonstrate it. Parents and teachers who have high expectations of a child are not an encouragement but actually make him more fearful. From his perspective they're inviting him to show them he's the failure he knows himself to be.[19]

2. *Rebellion.* Some children use schoolwork as an opportunity to rebel. They feel that their parents' values and their own are so different that they simply will not conform.

3. *Immaturity.* Some children, who through testing are shown to be capable, often do not have the maturity to connect any meaning or importance to what they study. Even if they do, it always seems remote.

   As a child I was interested in airplanes and flying. My parents tried to make me see that if I wanted to be a pilot I would have to do better in math. I remember seeing a remote connection between math and flying, but it was so remote that even thought I was interested in flying, math held no interest for me.

   When I graduated from high school (I barely passed), I wanted no more education. But after four years in the air force, at age twenty-one, I was ready for college. I was thirty-one when I graduated from seminary and forty-three when I completed a second master's degree and made a major career change. I often think that if I had started school when I was eight, instead of five, I probably would not have felt behind everyone else all the time.

4. *Hyperactive or just a boy?* Along the same line, parents should be careful that because a child, especially a boy, is very active, he is not labeled "hyperactive" by the parent or the teacher. "Hyperactivity" as a medical diagnosis is not simply activity that the observer may think excessive. It involves diagnostic criteria, difficult for a physician to assess, let alone a parent or teacher.[20]

When my oldest son was in third grade, his young teacher suggested he see the school psychologist because he was "hyperactive." My wife and I discovered that his "hyperactivity" was due to the fact that his desk was too small for him and, to get behind it, he had to prop it up on his legs. My son simply couldn't last the whole day wearing his desk.

Parents should also be aware of what psychologist Ronald LaTorre calls "the Feminized Classroom."[21] Elementary schools are important in the socialization of children. Predominantly staffed by women, often with an androgynous outlook on sex roles (men and women equally endowed with male and female traits), grade schools are a difficult environment for a boy to survive or thrive in.

LaTorre makes a startling allegation that the single mother will want to keep in mind as she follows her son's performance in elementary school. He says:

The feminized classroom, while exerting a slightly deleterious effect on all male children, is even more hazardous for the male child who enters elementary school with sexual identity confusion. If a boy's father is physically or emotionally absent, openly rejects his son, or presents a poor gender role model, the child is at a decided disadvantage in his attempt to resolve his sexual identity. The school mercilessly pounds its feminizing requirements into this child.

Such children can become so preoccupied with their familial problems that they cannot deal adequately with their academia. They may also need so much attention that their efforts to gain this attention (attaining high grades) may lead to unacceptable attention (punching other students or stealing).[22]

Exposure of the male child to males in other settings can help counteract the feminizing impact. Church and boys' club activities led by men are excellent sources for the male model.

How Parents Can Help

What can parents do to help motivate their children in school? Here are some suggestions:

1. *Use the progress-reporting system.* One effective way parents and teachers can cooperate is with the daily or weekly progress report. This is a special report card that lists all the student's courses on one side and across the top lists items of concern such as homework completed, next assignment, test scores, date of next test, and behavior problems. The student is responsible for having each teacher fill out a report, preferably each day at first. The child is to understand that no excuse will be accepted for failure to bring home the reports. Restriction of TV, phone privileges, or grounding may be used to enforce the rule.

   As the child begins to show improvement (after one or two weeks of daily reporting) the interval may be changed to weekly. Friday is a good day because it's the end of the week. Again, no excuse is accepted for failure to produce a report. For a free copy of a brochure on the periodic progress-report system, send a stamped, self-addressed envelope to Underachiever, Boys Town Center, Boys Town, NE 68010.[23] Another helpful publication is *Children of Divorce: 52 Ways to Help Your Child Learn,* available by writing to Children of Divorce, Illinois Education Association, 100 E. Edwards Street, Springfield, IL 62704.

2. *Make allowances for the loss of a parent.* Even if your child was not close to the absent parent, or even if the parent was abusive, the child still has some adjustments to make.[24]

3. *Age is important.* The child's ability to cope with loss depends on his at the time of loss. Small children may regress to bed-wetting or other infantile behavior. Children in the primary grades may fight and cry more than usual.[25]

4. *Let the school know your situation.* You need not give them details of the child's loss, but it is important for teachers to know what pressures are on the child. They may be able to take steps to reduce stress at school or head off behavioral problems before they get too severe.[26]

5. *Take advantage of school support services.* The school may have guidance counselors or psychologists who are available to help. Use their services.[27]

6. *Get to know your children's teachers and be aware of school activities for parents and teachers.* Single parents don't have much time for face-to-face contact, but a phone call during your lunch break may be all the contact you need. Or, you can leave a message for the teachers to call you at work or at home to discuss your child's needs. You can explain that as a single parent you find the phone to be the most efficient way to stay in touch.[28]

7. *Be aware of stereotypes.* Though teachers and administrators are becoming more sensitive to single-parent families, be aware of any stereotypes the teacher may have of your child: undisciplined, poor thing, unhappy, angry, revengeful—the list goes on. A stereotype in the mind of the teacher may put the child at a disadvantage in the classroom.

For other helpful resources, see *How to Help Your Children Survive and Thrive in Public School,*[29] and contact the Reading Is Fundamental (RIF) project. The RIF project operates on the principle that once children discover that reading is fun, they *will* read. RIF distributes books without charge and teaches parents how to motivate their children to read.[30]

Missing Parents And A Child's Gender Identity

Another major concern of single parents is the proper psycho-sexual development of the child. Every parent recognizes that gender identity is not established at birth.

A person may be born with a male or female anatomy, but gender identity is something that is learned. A child learns a gender *role*. Boys do certain things; girls do other things. A child also develops a gender-role *preference*. If a boy prefers to be like Daddy or a father figure who is a strong role model, he will adopt that role. He will feel comfortable with his maleness. He will then go on to develop gender *ability*. He masters those skills appropriate to gender-role expectation.[31] The entire learning process is called "sex typing."

Many feminists feel that society has gone too far in typing male and female—that we have made the differences too great. For example, traditionally the female is taught to be soft and nurturing while the male is taught to be tough and aggressive. Certain male and female gender abilities were developed on this basis and led to "male occupations" and "female occupations" that fit those abilities. Women's occupations involved nurturing or supportive work such as nursing or secretarial jobs, whereas men's occupations involved physical toughness or leadership such as fire-fighting, police work, or executive leadership.

As the feminist movement grew, women felt they should not be kept out of work traditionally considered men's. They felt discriminated against. "Sexism" became a battle cry, triggering as much emotion as "racism." As a consequence, feminist groups and individual women began to equate sex typing with sexism. It was felt that if we moved toward an androgynous society we would eliminate sex typing and thus stamp out sexism.[32]

But the push for an androgynous society will not relieve us of sex typing and job discrimination. What it has done, in fact, is to throw sex-typing into confusion, particularly for males who have a more difficult time differentiating themselves than females do.[33]

By eighteen months a child is aware of his gender identity.

After this age the task of the parent, or parent figure, is to strengthen and confirm that identity.

Between eighteen months and two or three years, a child learns what it means to be a member of that sex. There are certain dos and don'ts, certain behaviors that go along with that sex. Dress, hairstyle, and toys are all-important indicators.

As a child becomes aware of others around him, he begins to see differences between his mother and father. He also sees other role models who are similar to his parents. This further teaches him what it means to be male or female. By the age of four or five, little boys want to be like Daddy and girls like Mommy, or whoever the adult role model may be.[34]

When the child starts school, he begins to compare himself with his peers. His self-image begins to depend on how successfully he measures up to what his peers model as male or female behavior. This continues through adolescence. This is why the peer group is so important and why the child feels it is so important to conform to the peer group's dress and social codes. *His identity is at stake.*

A Parent's Role in the Child's Gender Identity

Even though children grow to rely on their peers for the *confirmation* of their sexual identity, the parents have the tremendous task of *establishing* it. The great fear of the single parent is that the child will not develop a proper gender identity with a parent absent.

Let me put the single parent's mind at ease. If it is simply a matter that one of the parents is absent, that is not a big problem. Children readily adopt another adult or several adults, opposite to the sex of the parent, as role models. As the child watches the parent relate healthily to persons of the opposite sex, he gathers much the same information he would gather by watching his mother and father interact in a healthy relationship. Obviously the child does not see the quality and quantity of interaction that he would see in a healthy two-parent relationship. But at least he is not being damaged by an unhealthy relationship between adult male and female role models.

The point is that children with troubled sexual identities are not merely the products of one-parent homes. They are the products of homes where they are caught between adult males and females who are providing *sick* models.

Many two-parent homes are destructive. Some parents may have stayed together "for the sake of the children" but thereby ruin the children.

After divorce, the pattern may continue. Even though there has been a divorce, a family still exists with two parents who have a profound effect on the child. The child's sexual identity depends on *how well the parents or parental figures relate, not on the intactness of the home.*

This is why we see troubled children from two-parent homes and well-adjusted children from single-parent homes. It should be noted, however, that a harmonious two-parent home is preferred. If that is not possible, then a harmonious one-parent home is the next best thing. The worst alternative, whether a two-parent or single-parent home, is for a child to be caught in a sick family relationship with his parents or parent figures.

Two types of family systems are particularly destructive to the sexual identity of children. They are called "pathogenic" families—families that produce sick people. These patterns may exist in either a two-parent or a single-parent home.

1. *The skewed family.* This family tends to produce males with gender-identity problems. It is characterized by a mother who sees her son as an extension of herself. She tries to live out her life through her son. The son is chosen, rather than the daughter, because the mother believes that as a male he will not be denied what she was denied as a female. Because she sees her son as an extension of herself, she is especially watchful over him and gives him little freedom. She is overprotective and dominant but at the same time cold and rejecting. She believes the child cannot survive by himself. So she must rule him to assure his survival and her fulfillment.[35]

She also affects the rest of the family. She expects them to want what she wants and feels. The husband may be childishly dependent on his wife, perhaps even competing with his son for his wife's attention. A very common reaction by such a husband is divorce—either emotional (he continues in the marriage) or legal (he leaves the marriage). In either case, the child becomes aware that the father is less than an ideal figure.

To be acceptable to the mother, the son must become different from his father. But he cannot solve the problem by separating from his mother. It becomes apparent that his mother needs him, and he feels he would destroy her if he did separate himself. At the same time he feels that something will happen to him if he doesn't.[36]

It is not difficult to see how the skewed family is hard on a male's sexual identity. The child is unable to establish independence and autonomy because "mother knows best," and he gets what she wants to give when she wants to give it. She clings, encouraging clinging in return, which is not characteristic of males in our society. All of this impairs the male's *separateness* from his mother. He needs to feel that he is physically different and separate. But by keeping the separation from occurring, the mother retards his growth as a separate sexual identity.[37]

Role modeling is another problem. The mother is often more assertive and tough-minded than the mothers of other families. The father tends to be passive and withdrawn, unlike the more aggressive fathers in other families. This tends to distort the child's sense of maleness and femaleness and thus he sees fewer differences between the two. That may be fine in a highly androgynous society. *But that's not where the child lives.* If he doesn't see much difference between the two sexes, it is unlikely that he will adopt gender-role behaviors that his peers consider male. Instead he may adopt role behaviors that his peers consider female.[38]

Some mothers may feel that it is unfair for a child to be exposed to a society that sex-types to the degree our society does, but *that's reality.* A mother does her son a favor by helping him fit the gender-role model that society expects. This doesn't mean that he can't learn to be caring and nurturing. But because aggressiveness, physical strength, and mental toughness are considered "male" behaviors, he had better develop these as well and not be subject to the ridicule of being "a mama's boy."

The single-custodial mother can avoid the sick pattern of the skewed family by choosing not to run down the father, by permitting her son his separateness, and by providing him with male role models that fit the societal norm.

The single-custodial father is unlikely to find himself in this situation since he is the custodial parent.

2. *The schismatic family.* This type of family is most difficult on the sexual development of the female. This family is split. In contrast to the skewed family where everyone gives in to mother, and the father is physically or emotionally absent, the schismatic family is marked by warfare between mother and father. Both parents vie for the love and loyalty of the child and openly undercut each other. The child is caught between conflicting demands.[39]

The mother is similar to the mother in the skewed family except she feels that the female child will get no further in life than she did. The mother is overprotective of the daughter, but rejects closeness and finds no satisfaction in the daughter.

The father is very different from the father of the skewed family who withdraws. The schismatic father remains very active—even after divorce—if for no other reason than to downgrade or destroy his ex-wife. He competes for the daughter's affection, is sometimes seductive, and offers the daughter love that the mother withholds. He makes it clear, however, that to have his love, the daughter must be unlike her mother, whom he rejects openly.

The danger to the female child is obvious. The mother is unhappy that the daughter is a female. She probably rejects any show of femininity on the daughter's part. This makes the daughter feel that she is not being what Mother wants her to be and that she should not be a woman. This is reinforced when the father instills the feeling that she *must* be different from Mother if she is to have his love.

This is terribly confusing for the daughter. Mother is to be the role model for the daughter, but she gets the message from Mother that being a woman is bad news. Moreover, Daddy, who ought to know what men like in a woman, is saying, "Be a woman, but not like your mother." The daughter is left to wonder, what on earth does it mean to be "a woman"?

The task for the single parent is evident. The father cannot—*must not*—derogate the mother. The mother must come to terms with her attitude about her own femininity and make her daughter feel okay about being a female.

Single parents should remember, as I have explained, that the absence of a parent from the household does not produce a child with impaired gender identity. What is important is how the absence of that parent is handled. Neither parent should be cut down by the other parent; the child should be permitted to have loyalties to both parents without being made to feel bad about it; and where the parents are not healthful role models, or a parent is missing, the children should be exposed to others who are good role models.

"This is a lonely world. We pump our own gas, get our money out of money machines. The man at the grocery store uses a computer sensor to ring up our groceries. We have been reduced to codes, numbers and letters."[1]

The speaker was Fred Ostern at the kickoff of the National Association of Single Persons. He was voicing what many other singles were saying: In spite of their image as "swingers," single life can be lonely.

Thirty-year-old Sara Parriott agreed. "When you're 21 you want to date for fun. By the time you're 24, it fails to meet your expectations. There's no mature approach to dating. There is only taking a mature approach to dating. I don't enjoy dating. It's just so exhausting.[2]

Is There Life After Death—Or Divorce?

For the newly singled person, this view of reality raises a tough question: Is there life after the death of a spouse or after divorce—particularly when you're a thirty-, forty-, or fifty-year-old

153

and back into the dating scene where the veterans say it's not fun, just exhausting?

As I talk to the newly singled, particularly women, I hear this question again and again. It comes as a shock to them that what they had fantasized during marriage—freedom to date again—is often a big disappointment. Jennifer, a twenty-seven-year-old business woman, says, "It's much easier to get an MBA than a good relationship." Her friend Lisa added, "Correction: 'than *any* relationship.' "[3]

A twenty-nine-year-old business woman from Chicago says, "Everything is so easy for men. All a man has to do is breathe, and women fall all over him. The competition in this city for the few good men is so intense that if you won't take whatever they care to dish out, someone else will."[4]

The Tyranny of Sex Ratios

Chicago is not the only city with the competition problem. Numerically speaking, there is a shortage of men in America today. The 1980 census reveals:

- There are just under 30 million single women for 21.5 million single men.
- There is a surplus in the 25–29 age group, but they're not quick to marry.
- In the 30–39 age group there are 102 women for every 100 men.
- In the 35–39 age group, there are 128 women for every 100 men.[5]

Since men tend to marry women who are four years younger, the biological clock ticks loudest for women over thirty-five.[6]

When women are in short supply, they are valued. Men are willing to marry and keep their commitments to remain married. Sex roles tend to complement each other, as in traditional marriages, and women gain economic mobility through marriage and the family. Sexual fidelity is stressed.[7]

When men are in short supply, the type of pattern we see today emerges. Women find it difficult to achieve economic mobility through marriage, adultery and divorce are common, remarriag is easier for men, and there is an increase in single-parent families headed by women. Sexual libertarianism replaces fidelity, and women, feeling devalued, attempt to rectify their situation by gaining economic and political power. Thus feminist movements flourish.[8]

There is no doubt that men are taking advantage of the situation. And they are quite shameless about it.

Beware of the Cad

One woman reports a case where her blind date came to pick her up with a second woman already tucked away in the back seat of his car. He explained that she was someone to talk to just in case the evening turned out to be "a drag." She was furious, but decided to go along after having spent two hours getting ready for the date. She figured she'd find some way to make him pay for what he did.[9]

It is not that women aren't being warned about the male exploiter. A typical warning was carried in the Parents Without Partners magazine *Single Parent*, in an article called "How to Spot a Cad." The article said that the Cad is usually a person who:

1. Has outstanding charm
2. May not like touching
3. Has a glib tongue
4. Is a name dropper
5. Has no local references
6. Has unexplained absences
7. Abuses drugs or alcohol
8. Can't be reached by phone
9. Has a flashy car or no car
10. Uses pat explanations
11. Sees *your* friends, not his
12. Uses a post-office box
13. Has financial troubles, always temporary
14. Never plans for the future[10]

Florence Nightingale Is Alive and Well

But more subtle than the Cad is "the Wounded Soldier" who makes a marvelous patient for "Florence Nightingale." In my counseling practice I have come to recognize a particular type of woman whom I call Florence Nightingale because she is so much like her namesake—the heroic nurse of the Crimean War. This is a woman who is selfless, loving, and nurturing and needs to be needed. She is not attracted to a strong, self-sufficient man— unless she sees beneath the strong facade a "Wounded Soldier." The Wounded Soldier can be a man who, though charming and loving, is a deeply troubled and needy person. He is often unable to hold a job, or is just on the brink of success and could make it *with the support of the right woman*—yes, Nurse Nightingale. Or, he may appear to be strong and self-sufficient, but is willing to reveal to Florence Nightingale those bloody bandages beneath his tailored jacket. She must promise, however, that if he does admit he is a Wounded Soldier, she will do *nothing, absolutely nothing,* to wound him further.

Some of these Wounded Soldiers may really have been wounded. They may not be aware of manipulation, but they nevertheless use their pitiful condition to get nurture, comfort, and generous doses of painkilling affection from Nurse Nightingale. There also are Wounded Soldiers who know perfectly well what they're doing.

But this Wounded Soldier manipulation would not work if it did not have an equally neurotic counterpart in Florence Nightingale—a woman who needs to be needed so badly that she literally gives her body and all that she has to make this man whole. She needs to know that this type of man can't afford to be healed. That would bring an end to her care giving. Nor can she afford to have it end. if he is able to take care of himself, then she is dispensable. She would have no alternative but to move on to the next Wounded Soldier.

The Option of Singleness

As we saw in chapter 1, about one-third of single men and women have no intention of marrying. But the majority of people on the dating scene are either actively seeking a new mate to marry or cohabit with, or would do so if they found Mr. or Ms.

Right. By "cohabit" I mean to live in a sexual relationship with another adult without the commitment of marriage.

It should be pointed out, however, that the single parent is much less likely to cohabit than the single without children.[11] A sampling of the general population, not just churchgoers, reveals that a sizable portion of respondents are against single parents cohabiting on moral grounds. They say: (1) living together out of wedlock is wrong, and (2) living together with a child in the house conveys a dangerous and unethical message to the child.[12]

What about the single who does not want to cohabit but has remarriage in mind? My advice is, *Please go slowly.* Remember, 50 percent of first marriages fail, but 60 percent of second marriages fail. Remarriage is *not* the only option for the formerly married who want to feel alive again. Singleness can be a live and healthy alternative—in spite of the high mortality rate among divorced and widowed men. Perhaps that mortality rate could be reduced if men were willing to accept singleness as a healthy option and would learn to take care of themselves as women do.

Cindee is an example of a single who believes singleness is a healthy option. She says, "I would like to see an organization that isn't pushing single parents to get married. Some single parents, like myself, are happy to be single. It seems to the world that this idea is hard to deal with." Another single put it, "Being single and being alone is deviant in our society."[13]

But the world is not alone in its opposition to singleness. The church has a hard time with the idea of singleness too. One single writes:

> We have a lot of good teaching here at Peninsula Bible Church about marriage being a picture of the Lord's love for the church, how marriage helps people become mature, etc. But because such strong statements are made about marriage, an imbalance is produced. I have even heard people say it's impossible to be a mature Christian unless one is married.[14]

If we are to value singleness as we should, several facts must be considered:

1. *Singleness is a gift.* The negative view of Bible-teaching churches is interesting, particularly in view of the fact that the Bible makes it clear that *singleness is a gift, and a gift to be prized.*

Jesus made this clear in His well-known treatise on divorce in Matthew 19:3–8. He said that Moses permitted divorce because of the hardness of the heart. The consequences of sin disrupted God's original design for marriage—marriage for life.

The disciples reacted to what they perceived to be marriage with no easy out and said that it was better, therefore, for a man not to marry (Matt. 19:10). Jesus pointed out that not everyone can do without marriage. Yet there are those who can, by nature and disposition, renounce marriage because it enables them to be more effective in the service of God (Matt 19:11).

The apostle Paul sounds the same note. He wishes that the unmarried and widowed would consider the example he was setting (1 Cor. 7:7–8). He was not married, though it is believed by some scholars that he had been married at one time. The single state he declares to be a *gift*. Men and women who cannot contain themselves sexually should marry (1 Cor. 7:9)

Paul clearly states that the purpose of this gift is to enable the Christian to serve God without the distraction of marriage (1 Cor. 7:32–35). Singleness is a gracious gift, to be preferred over marriage. How then can we view singleness as deviant or deficient?

One other observation should be made about Paul's teaching. He encourages the widowed to remain unmarried (1 Cor 7:8) and directs the divorced to do likewise (1 Cor. 7:10–11.)

I pointed this out because the widowed and divorced sometimes say, "When you've been married and have been used to having sexual relations, it's difficult to have it ended suddenly." Paul recognizes this and makes allowances for it. It is better to marry than to burn with passion (1 Cor. 7:8). It is important to remember, however, that those who have been happily married for a long time often find that, though sexual relations are enjoyable, it can't begin to measure up to the intimacy that's found in the friendship and companionship of marriage. That kind of intimacy is nurtured over time and can't be quickly replaced. A mature marriage, like wine and cheese, needs time to mellow.

The widowed are to remarry if passion is a problem. In fact, Paul urges remarriage for young widows in 1 Timothy 5. He advises the church not to put the younger widows on the roll of those supported by the church. He recognizes that it is difficult for a young widow to maintain the decorum and purity that befit the single Christian; so rather than put her in the position of burning with passion, he advises that she remarry (1 Cor. 7:8; 1 Tim. 5:14).

2. *Friendship is important.* Man is a social creature and needs social contact. One form of social contact is friendship. Friendships are a viable alternative to those who have their passions under control. It should be acknowledged, however, that opposite-sex friendships can be difficult to maintain on a friendship level. *Both* people must want friendship and no more.

The apostle Paul, recognizing the danger of friendship becoming more than that, tells the churches that younger men are to be treated as brothers and younger women as sisters, "with absolute purity" (1 Tim. 5:1–2). Even though *he* may have a brother-sister relationship in mind, does *she*? How can you tell the difference between friendship and an intimate relationship that makes people hear wedding bells? Consider the following questions:

- When the two of you are together, is your focus primarily on each other rather than your mutual interests?

- Do you enjoy spending a great deal of time alone with this person and resent the intrusion of a third party?

- Do you feel driven to this person for some unspoken need or for emotional support and affirmation?

- Are there questions in your mind about the expectations you have of each other?

- Have you spent much time imagining or fantasizing about being married to this person?

- Is your focus on how the relationship benefits you rather than him or her?

- Is it hard to see this person and treat him just as you would your brother or sister?

If your answers to the above are yes, then you have more than friendship on your mind. It should be remembered that friendship is *about* something other than the two people who are involved with each other. They are shoulder to shoulder looking ahead at their common interest rather than face to face. Moreover, friendship is not exclusive. Friends are willing to invite a third or fourth person into the circle. Intimates are jealous of their time together. Finally, friendship is an appreciative-love not a need-love. That is to say, we appreciate our friends, but in terms of affirmation and affection we don't *need* them. Intimates we need for our emotional survival.[16]

Overcoming Loneliness

Trying to overcome loneliness by jumping into a new relationship is no solution. When two people do it to each other, the relationship is doomed to failure. It is unlikely that two people who feel incapable of making successful lives for themselves are going to make a successful life for each other. "But," the single insists, "I have so much love to give and no one to give it to." That may be true, unless he considers *himself* a nobody. And that's a large part of the problem of loneliness. As the old song goes, "You're nobody 'til somebody loves you."

Love Yourself

It is incredible, in an age described as the "Me Generation," populated by allegedly narcissistic men and women, that people have such a tough time loving themselves. Even Christians who know that they are accepted by God (Rom. 15:7) have this problem. Why is this?

A large part of the problem is that many of us were raised by parents who were afraid that we might become conceited if we liked ourselves too much. As children we learn to play the selfffacing game, and we quickly discover that if we look miserable enough, miraculously we get what we want—an ego boost. Many of us grow up mastering the fine art of being the poor soul and tragically adopt it as a life script.

Sometimes it helps to see humor in this kind of behavior. At least one writer thinks so. She wrote a hilarious piece titled, "Indulge Yourself! Get Into The Joys of Self-Pity." She advises, "You'll get little mileage out of suffering in quiet despair. The trick is to put on a heart-rending, flamboyant display of the post-divorce blues."[17] She then lists seven ways to accomplish this. My favorite is the last one on her list:

> Let others strive for the preppie look or the Venice style. Your body and your clothing should make a statement about you, and in your case, that statement should whine, "POOR ME!" Since it is difficult to pity a lithe, tanned and vital person, physical fitness is definitely out. Throw away your vitamins and stop running. (Shuffling is OK.) If you are forced to venture out into the sunshine, wear a sun block so you won't lose your deathly pallor and have to begin on it all over again.
>
> If a starvation diet isn't your cup of bouillon gorge yourself on junk food. Eschew vegetables in favor of chocolate-covered marshmallows, imitation potato chips, cream-filled cupcakes. The combination of obesity, late blooming acne and constipation will conspire to make you pitiable beyond belief.[18]

It's difficult to play the self-hate game when we know we are playing it. The benefits of acting as though we love ourselves, even though we may not feel it, set in motion the internal machinery that actually results in our feeling self-love. People who have overcome loneliness have learned to like the company they keep—themselves.

Keep Busy

It may sound foolish to tell a single parent to keep busy in light of all the demands made on him. But feeling those demands and doing something about them are not the same.

Cindee, the mother who wishes to remain single whom I referred to earlier, says, "Sure I get lonely, but it makes me work harder." She directs a lot of that hard work toward doing something about her problems. "I miss having a husband when the car breaks down. I'm not mechanically inclined. So I'm going to take a 'Women, Know Your Car' course at the local college."

Cindee also deals with her loneliness by keeping active with her children. "Once a month I have what I call kids' night. It's marked on the calendar. The kids look at the calendar and await the day. On kids' night Mom has to put her stuff away and do kid things all night—including supper." She says they all enjoy it.

Keeping busy means getting in touch with what we like to do, too—something we're not always free to do in marriage. Another single mother says that she was raised with the idea that middle-aged women just didn't go out by themselves. But she couldn't find friends to go to the places she liked or when she could go. She said that the answer came one evening as she was reading the newspaper:

> I wished aloud that I could attend a play at a local college, but there was no one to go with. "Well," I answered myself, "you are a mature, liberated woman. Who says you can't go alone?" So I called for a reservation and bravely asked for a single seat. Since no one seemed shocked or even interested in my solo entrance into the lobby, I relaxed and had a delightful time. I enjoyed a witty performance and was pleased with myself for having broken out of an old restrictive pattern.[19]

Try a Support Group

Many lonely singles find a great deal of help meeting with others in support groups where everyone is having similar experiences. But be sure that the group is compatible to you, particularly your value system.

Support groups are not for everyone. Sherry, a single parent with an eight-year-old daughter, writes:

> Initially I went to single-parents groups. But they turned

out to be more gripe sessions (oh, let's feel sorry for the way the world treats single parents) and I found them counter-productive and a waste of my time. I was aware of what was going against us. I was interested in things that work to solve some of these problems. Once I got me together—got over the guilt (what have I done to my kid?) and realized that I could either continue on a downhill course or go upward—we got along OK.

Make Many Friends

Rather than jump into another dating relationship right away, develop a number of friends. Remember, one of the tests of friendship is that friends are not exclusive. Opposite-sex friendships are possible, but be honest with yourself and each other if you see the friendship turning into an intimate relationship. Is that what you both really want?

Multiple friendships provide enjoyable contacts with others without the commitments that intimacy demands. Go slowly in making commitments. You have commitment enough with a child to raise.

Give Yourself Time to Grow

Single parents need to go slowly in establishing new relationships because they need time to grow and learn from their loss. For the widowed this involves learning to become an individual again and functioning as such—a difficult task when one has been accustomed to functioning as a twosome. The divorced person must face this task, and one more. Does he really understand what went wrong? Does he understand *his* part in the demise of the marriage—if nothing else, that he made a poor choice to begin with.

I'm not talking about wallowing in failure. The task is to understand what went wrong so it isn't repeated. Perhaps the marriage was a "Wounded Soldier/Florence Nightingale" marriage. Or, perhaps it was a "Deaf and Dumb" marriage where he never listened and she never spoke loudly enough. Maybe it was a "Bulldozer/Swamp" marriage in which he was an energetic, roaring bulldozer and she consistently defeated him by miring him in her swamp of passivity. We are not to be concerned with what our spouses did wrong. We need to know what *we* did to interact destructively with our spouses. This self-knowledge may preserve us from a disastrous second marriage.

What does this have to do with loneliness? It puts us in touch with ourselves, the person we know the least and are most guilty of ignoring. The lonely person is basically a person who is out of touch with himself, not other people.

Understand Your Loss

One reason why people have a difficult time with loneliness is that they don't realize the many factors that contribute to it. They feel alone or adrift—alienated from society. They suppose that a meaningful connection with another person is the answer. This is not so. The alienation we feel in loneliness is really the result of multiple losses that cannot be replaced by a new person.

1. *Loss of understanding.* You have moved from the known to the unknown. Your marriage may not have been happy, but at least you knew what you faced.[20]

   Even though your marriage was filled with conflict, you had a pretty good idea of the unresolved issues. You could almost predict the next argument. Bad as the marriage was, you *knew* where you were going and what would happen.

   Now you're adrift on the sea of uncertainty. What will happen to you in your single state? What problems may suddenly arise? You feel you need someone because you don't have the faintest idea where you are. You naively suppose that someone else will be able to navigate these unfamiliar waters better than you. The kind of relationship that develops out of this is *two* lost people adrift on the sea of uncertainty, *neither of* them knowing where they are and where to go. It is best to *get your bearings first* before you invite someone else aboard.

2. *Loss of the valued familiar.* Another reason for a feeling of detachment and alienation is the loss of valued relationships, activities, and surroundings associated with your married way of life.[21] Friends that both you and your spouse cultivated turn out not to be your friends but your spouse's friends. Or, they don't know what to do with your new status as singles, so they cultivate neither of you. No longer are things done as a

family. You may have lost your home and familiar possessions. Things are not the same.

One of the most important things a newly single person can do is establish a new home and make it his—with his own possessions. Sometimes singles, particularly men, make the mistake of putting up with temporary housing until they find someone else to marry and make a home with. Having a home of our own with our own identity reflected in it lessens the feeling of alienation and the temptation to dispel it by finding someone else. It decreases our loneliness by putting us in touch with *ourselves*.

3. *Loss of power.* A third reason for a feeling of detachment and alienation is a loss of power.[22] As a single you often find yourself less able to get what you want. Single women are ripped off on a regular basis at auto repair shops: for example, wheel alignment is prescribed for worn tires that only need proper inflation.

Formerly married men often feel a loss of power in the church. They couldn't make their marriage work. Therefore the church may either forbid membership or positions of leadership—a decision based on qualifications for elders and deacons (1 Tim. 3:4, 12).

The result is grief, helplessness, and alienation. The man feels, ''I don't fit in.'' The woman at the auto repair shop feels, ''I need someone to care for me and watch out for my interests.'' But does she *really* need someone to take care of her? She can learn to take care of herself. Does he need to feel as though he's on the shelf? Perhaps church policy keeps him from being an elder or deacon, but he can be useful in some other significant field of service.

4. *Loss of acceptance.* A fourth loss is the loss of acceptance.[23] At the feeling level the new single feels cut off from society. The social role as parent is different. The parent and child may bear the social stigma of ''broken home''—the place where ''problem children'' are found. The parent's social life is different. Though friends may want to help, they often don't know what to do. If they accept the divorced parent into the social circle, it means excluding the former spouse; they don't mean to exclude anyone, but they don't know what to do with

the divorced spouse either. It may mean developing a new circle of friends. A new feeling of acceptance can help dispel the feeling of loneliness.

5. *Loss of confidence.* A fifth loss is the loss of confidence. Our ability to feel part of society rests in part on our skills to meet life's demands.[24] Self-confidence enables us to face people in the business and social world and helps us interact freely.

   Now you're single. Will you make it on your own? Failure and inadequacy make us feel apart from the rest of the couple-oriented world that appears to be succeeding.

   The answer to the question "Will you make it on your own?" largely depends on the mental picture you create. This gets back to psychocybernetics. Do you choose to see yourself succeeding as a single parent, or failing? We can choose to mull over past failures and anticipate future failures, or we can choose to put them out of mind.

   Many times so-called spiritual problems are not spiritual problems at all or a lack of fellowship with God. The real problem is poor mental hygiene. It is significant that the apostle Paul teaches us that if the God of peace is to be with us, then *we must think about things* that are true, noble, right, pure, lovely, and admirable and *put into practice* what the apostle taught (Phil. 4:8–9)

6. *Loss of identity.* The final loss is the loss of identity. Your old definition of personhood, that of a married person, has been left behind.[25] Social identity has to do with who we are connected or not connected to, what we do and with whom. The loss of a spouse drastically alters our social identity. It throws us and others into confusion as to our new identity as a single parent. Friends want to be helpful, but they don't know how to relate to us in our new role. It is new to us too; as a consequence, we feel isolated and alienated from society—a major component of loneliness.

   We must learn to accept this new identity. We must ignore the stereotypes and establish ourselves in our new identity as successful singles. The children need it too. If the parent acts as though a single-parent home is pathological, the children will regard it so. They will also feel isolated and alienated from "normal" society.

The single parent may ask, "Where do I start?" The answer is that you have already begun. You are recognizing what needs to be done by reading this book. But remember, transition after a loss takes time. Two years is not an excessive amount of time. In the case of a spouse's death, the transition may take as long as five years. The transition can be a time of growing happiness if you will accept the task and take pride in your growth as it comes—and it will.[26]

When Single Parents Date

Most single parents eventually begin dating. It is important, therefore, to be aware of the pleasures and pitfalls for you and your children.

Dating Too Soon

The widowed or divorced parent is often pushed by family and friends to get back into the social stream and start dating. It is felt that this will help ease the loss.

We have already considered the issue of dating too soon from the standpoint of retarding an individual's personal growth. We must also look at it from the children's point of view.

There is no right time for every single parent to begin dating. The reactions of children vary. Some children are relieved that Mom or Dad has someone to occupy them. Other children become resentful that the remaining parent's attentions are taken by someone else. This resentment can turn to fear if the child, who had one parent leave home, thinks that he may also lose the remaining parent.

Children usually let their parents know when they are unhappy about dating. It's not unusual for a child to be rude to the parent's date. One ten-year-old boy made it a habit of asking his mother's dates, shortly after their arrival, when they were going home. He was even more direct when the mother left the room and told the date, "Why don't you go home—we don't need you here."[27]

It's important for the parent to take the child aside privately and let him know that rudeness is not acceptable behavior. He doesn't have to like someone to be polite.[28]

Other children take the passive approach. They sulk or pout. It is important that the child say what he is unhappy about and not get his way by sulking. The parent should not plead with him to tell what the problem is. The parent only reinforces his passive-aggressive manipulation.

Whatever the child's reaction, it is important that you both talk openly about his feelings. Don't tell him he shouldn't feel as he does. Hear and understand his feelings, and let him know that you do understand his feelings. It may be that by talking about it you will discover how you can make your child feel secure while you continue to date.

Children As Matchmakers

Sometimes children can be embarrassingly helpful once they understand what dating is about. They may even fantasize getting the parent together with a favorite schoolteacher or Boy Scout leader.

Tommy, a fourth-grader, who missed having a male adult in his life, tried to match his mother with his teacher. He tried to get his mom to be an adult helper on class trips time after time, often embellishing the teacher's general request for volunteers. When his mother didn't respond, Tommy asked her why she didn't invite Mr. Blank to dinner. Mother handled it very well. She told Tommy that she appreciated his interest in her life and that she was glad he had found such a good friend in Mr. Blank. But, she told Tommy, friendships don't happen because someone wishes they would happen.[29]

When a child's matchmaking efforts are embarrassing, don't get angry or laugh. The child is trying to meet his needs in what seems to him a socially acceptable manner. It is not something to be angry at or to ridicule.

You Say You Have a Child?

One of the difficulties of returning to the dating scene is that some dates are very interested in the single parent but don't enjoy children. If your interest in dating is just for a good time, it *may* work—if that's what both you and your date have in mind. If you're looking for a new mate, forget this person. Should you marry him, your children would be a constant source of resentment on his part.

When Your Children Disapprove

Sometimes children will make negative comments about a date. It is unwise to defend the date, however. It will make the children feel that you are siding with a stranger against them and that this stranger's feelings are valued above their own.

Regard their feelings carefully and respectfully. Let them know that you understand and care how they feel. You will keep their feelings in mind when you consider having future dates. But they need to know that the decision, though thoughtfully made, is your decision. Remember, one of these days your children will be grown up and making plans of their own. They need to know that you have a right to think of a companion for yourself, as they will be finding companions for themselves.

Too Serious Too Soon

Sometimes single parents get too serious too soon with their dates. They raise unnecessary hopes or fears in the children that wedding bells are about to ring.

It is best to keep your display of affection a private matter. If your child likes your date, he may fantasize marriage only to be disappointed later when you break up. The child has already lost one parent. Don't make him lose a stepparent even before there's a wedding by raising false hopes. Or, if your child doesn't like your date, he may worry unnecessarily that you will marry. He may even resort to bad behavior to drive away the date. Do not discuss the subject of marriage with your children until it appears to you that marriage is feasible and it has been a matter of serious discussion between you and the prospective spouse.

Also, before you talk to the children, take "the Stepparent Test," found in *The Readymade Family*, chapters 2 and 3.[30] It will help the two of you objectively assess the workability of a stepfamily.

When you do talk to the children, take them aside privately and tell them that you have been thinking about marrying Mr. or Ms. X. You're not asking them for permission to marry; this is your decision. But before you make up your mind, you want to know how they feel.

After talking with them, let them know that you appreciate their opinion, even though it may be negative, and that you'll let them know when you decide what you're going to do about marriage.

Daters Anonymous

Some single parents feel very strongly that their dating lives and their lives with their children ought to be kept separate. Some go as far as to keep their dates away from home and children. They feel that this approach to dating relieves many of the problems with the children just mentioned. One mother said that it is strange to think that just because *she* is going to be involved with someone that her son has to be involved too. She kept her son, Jimmy, and boyfriend, Guy, apart. She said, "I don't want Jimmy to become involved with Guy and then have Guy leave and have Jimmy experience what might have been a greater loss than he is able to deal with."[31]

Another woman said that she dated a man for three years. She and the children grew to love him, and then he was gone. She said she simply couldn't let that continue to happen to the children. "So now when I date," she says, "I rarely have the man pick me up. And if he does, it's just an introduction. . . . I don't get the men involved in any family stuff."[32]

Other parents feel that separating dating life and family life keeps a date from getting to the parent's heart through the children—using them as pawns.

Single fathers seem to be less concerned about separating dating and family life. One divorced single father with the custody of two teenage daughters said that his children know every woman he went out with. When the father and his new steady broke up, he said that he and his daughters would talk about it. He said, "It helped them understand that just because two people like each other, they may not be able to get along.[33] It should be noted, however, that this involved teenagers, who were in a better position to understand than younger children.

If it is possible, a parent should keep his dating life and family life separate. Children look and long for permanence. They think of adult relationships as permanent and something secure that they can wrap themselves in. It is too much to ask of a child to suffer the loss of a parent and then endure a succession of losses of adults whom they have come to love and emulate as role models.

The phenomenon of widespread single-parent dating is too recent to give us any sociological perspective. But my intuition tells me that the parent is wise who keeps his dating and family lives separate.

Sex And The Single Parent

After thirty years, the Paul Reveres of the sexual revolution are beginning to lose their enthusiasm for spreading the word. Its proponents have begun to have second thoughts about the whole thing. This growing disenchantment with the sexual revolution is illustrated by the remarks of two single parents. One said, "The first guy I go out with expects sex on the first date!" Another said, "I always thought that sex and love went together. Now just saying, 'Hello,' seems to be enough of a relationship for sex."[34]

Is Celibacy an Alternative?

One of the most telling evidences that the sexual revolution is faltering is the growing popularity of celibacy. This may not be new to Christians who have been committed to it prior to marriage, but it is novel to those who view morality as something you decide on for yourself and not read about in the Bible.

Consider, for example, Nancy Friday, who wrote *My Secret Garden: Woman's Sexual Fantasies* and other books about the sexual lives of men and women. In an interview she was asked, "Why has celibacy become an increasingly attractive option for some single women today?" She replied, "Sex is so easy to find nowadays, but it's intimacy that certain people miss. . . . They choose celibacy rather than settling for relationships that are not emotionally fulfilling."[35]

Friday added that most women, even those raised by feminist

mothers, ''understand the kind of seduction, the loss of self, that comes with sexual intimacy.''[36] Sexual relations, she points out, stir up primitive emotions that sweep a woman away. But women today who are learning to take care of themselves ''perform best when alone; a man may throw them off course.''[37] She sees celibacy as ''a period of self-enrichment and growth.''[38]

It comes as welcome news to traditionalists and the church that celibacy is actually becoming ''chic.'' Says Friday, ''. . . it is a highly *approved,* if not encouraged alternative for women. For example, in studies I have done in the past few years on university campuses, a surprising number of male college graduates said they actually *preferred* a virgin bride.''[39]

Given the swing of the social pendulum and historic precedent, I would not be surprised if the next fifty years are marked by a resurgence of Victorianism. The neo-Victorian in my fantasy takes a great deal of pride in not smoking and drinking, eats health food, works out at the gym (or spa if affordable), and is almost religiously committed to celibacy.

Why is the sexual revolution sputtering? Though men and women may scorn biblical morality as outdated, they can't escape the fact that they live in a world that was designed and is operated by the God of the Bible. The wisdom of Scripture says again and again that if man does the smart thing and follows the Creator's pattern, he will enjoy life and health. If he doesn't, he'll get hurt. This message is powerfully stated in the first two chapters of Proverbs, which deal with human sexuality. The prologue sets the tone: ''The fear of the LORD is the beginning of knowledge, but fools despise wisdom and discipline'' (Prov. 1:7).

The public has been waking up to the reality of the foolhardy behavior and the lack of discipline that have been weakening and demoralizing the individual. We have seen living proof in our time of what the apostle Paul had in mind when he warned the Corinthians to flee sexual immorality: ''All other sins a man commits are outside his body, but he who sins sexually sins against his own body'' (1 Cor. 6:18). People may scoff at the idea that a future day of reckoning is coming for sinners, but they cannot scoff at the idea that the day of reckoning is right now for those who think they can have casual sex. They may reject theological realities, but they cannot reject the psychological reality of the loss of self that comes with sex without commitment. Nancy

Friday describes this loss very well when she says, "There is a great desire [for the woman] to 'melt' into a man, especially after sex. You can be very self-contained and up front and independent, but lovemaking has a way of throwing you back in time and opening you up to all those early primitive emotions."[40]

The words *melt* and *primitive emotions* are interesting when related to Genesis 2, where it is said of Adam and Eve that the two became "one flesh." There is a psychological sense in which sexual intercourse produces a "one-flesh" feeling—the "melting" that Nancy Friday speaks of. Sex outside the marriage demands, however, that the two who have melted into a one-flesh union physically and psychologically be torn apart and separated again. That tearing produces an agony that takes a terrible emotional and physical toll. It is the price one pays in this life for sin against the body.

But I Can't Be Celibate

Perhaps some singles will say impatiently, "Yes, yes, I know all that. But I can't be celibate. I *need* someone." Obviously this person falls into the category of those who don't have the gift of celibacy and should marry rather than burn with passion (1 Cor. 7:9). It should be remembered, however, that just because a person may have been married does not necessarily mean that he does not have the gift of celibacy. The fact that the widowed are encouraged to remain unmarried suggests that they may have this gift (1 Cor. 7:8).

Single women may not be satisfied with this answer. They may say, "That's nice that Paul suggests we marry rather than burn with passion. What suggestions does he have for finding an available man?"

It is really not fair to put Paul on the spot. He had a solution in that day that is not available today. He suggested that the girl's father should arrange for a marriage. The footnote in the New International Version is correct when it reads:

> If anyone thinks he is not treating his daughter properly, and if she is getting along in years, and he feels she ought to marry, he should do as he wants. He is not sinning. He should let her get married (1 Cor. 7:36).

In those days the woman had the advantage of a social custom we don't have today—arranged marriages. Today we have problems because some women who want to marry can't find the right man. What makes it worse, marriage customs and morality are in chaos.

First of all, if a man can get sex from a woman without marriage, he may well do it.

Second, our marriage customs are in chaos. Dating and marriage are a highly individualistic matter. Today men and women no longer have the support of society and family—support systems that could be called on to make the right match. If modern men and women want the freedom to choose a spouse for themselves and don't want the interference of matchmakers, they will also have to accept the consequences of that choice—singleness. The return of the arranged marriage might be what our troubled society needs.

Let's get back to the single woman who wants to marry, but can't find a suitable man. What does an available woman do? I go into this in detail in my book *But I Didn't Want a Divorce*, particularly in chapters 8 through 10. This much should be said here: The problem of celibacy is not simply the lack of sexual intercourse. I point out in my book on divorce that some singles feel comfortable with masturbation as a substitute. But the issue is larger than sex. It has to do with a *spiritual union* and *psychological intimacy* with a person. But this may be sublimated outside of marriage through involvement with others.

My sister is single (never married) and a missionary to the inner city. One day I was talking to her about feelings of mortality. I told her that having four sons and grandchildren are a great comfort. Though I will face death, I will continue to live on earth through the progeny I have left behind as a result of my biological and spiritual fathering.

She made me see that even though she is not a biological parent, she too will leave behind a great spiritual progeny whom she has parented in her lifetime of work in the inner city. It is possible to have both a *spiritual union* and a *psychological intimacy* outside a marriage without having sexual intimacy.

ᚴᚴᚴ 12

Your Child From One to Twelve

Parenting is the only major occupation affecting children that requires no training or license. That's a sobering thought.

A crash course in parenting—especially single-parenting—can't be given in two chapters, but perhaps this chapter and the next will encourage parents to read books and take courses that will improve their parenting skills.

The plan of these two chapters is suggested by the biblical proverb that says, "Train a child in the way he should go, and when he is old he will not turn from it" (Prov. 22:6). The words "in the way he should go" don't mean "as a God-fearing child," though that is included in training. The "way" has reference to instruction that is suitable to his age and recognizes age-group characteristics.[1]

Christian parents are vitally interested in the Christian education of their children. But we must not fail in the socialization of our children, which gives them the skills essential to living successfully in the society in which they are growing up. This chapter and the next give a brief sketch of what we should expect in the development of our children and what we can do to facilitate it. The subject is discussed in broad terms, and parents will find that each child differs slightly. Parents need not be concerned about minor departures from "the norm." Children develop at different rates and manifest the characteristics of each age group to greater or lesser degrees than others their age. It would not be right to say that your child is not a typical five-or ten-year-old because he hasn't achieved the equilibrium characteristic of those ages. Perhaps he will reach it closer to six or eleven.

From One to Six

Between the ages of one and six a child changes more than at any time in his life. These are called the "preschool years."

The Preschool Child

Few children walk by age one. But by six a child is able to handle his Big Wheels or tricycle with ease.

He leaves infancy when he starts walking. He is then called a "toddler" and makes his first move toward independence. He is no longer a baby. He is quite self-absorbed. Before the age of three he becomes less self-absorbed and begins to notice people and things. He also romps carefree through an imaginary world. Between five and six he begins wanting to learn to do things right. Elementary school is designed to build on this drive.[2]

Parents should be sure, however, that their child is ready to enter elementary school. Both social and intellectual growth may be facilitated by giving a child another year or two before he is regimented in school. Many schools have, in addition to kindergarten, a "pre-first grade" level. *Don't rush your child's childhood.* One of the big pressures of the single-parent home is that children are expected go grow up too fast.

It is also important to remember that young preschool children do better with a substitute mother at home than in day-care center where they may stay up to eleven hours a day.[3] A good nursery school that runs from nine to noon is good for threes and fours. But they should be picked up by the home-based caregiver and given as much of a home environment as possible.

If your preschooler must be in a day-care center, insist on an atmosphere that is as homelike as possible and insist that the child is cared for by the same nurturing caregiver each day.

From One to Three

By age one your child has made a good start in learning something about being a loved and loving human being. The physical touch of cuddling and rocking and the gentle sounds of voices all awaken his senses to the fact that there are some special people who care very much about him. He learns that he can even encourage loving responses by crying or cooing.

Parents sometimes worry that playing with and cuddling a baby too much will "spoil" him. Don't worry about that. Reality demands that there will be times when a baby must be left to cry simply because the parent has to tend to other children or other duties. But don't withhold cuddling and playing with the baby for fear of spoiling him. A baby's selfhood is very tender and will experience enough frustrations in the course of living without fearful parents adding to them.[4]

1. *The first birthday.* By his first birthday your baby will have grown half again his birth length and tripled his birth weight. By now he can use his fingers and thumb to pick up small objects, he tastes everything first to see if he considers it edible, he crawls and maybe even walks a little, and he has a few words in his vocabulary like "mama" and "dada" along with sounds that stand for other words. He understands more words than he can say. He is waking and sleeping according to a pattern by now. He will usually sleep through the night and take one or two naps during the day; his meals have been reduced from six to three; and he now chews, though he may still need to suck. He may drink from both a cup and bottle. He knows his mother and father or parent substitute, but may be very leery of strangers. Though he can spend a half-hour alone with playthings, she's more interested in people than things. Patty-cake and peekaboo and even roughhousing on the floor are sources of endless delight. The playful mood of people conveys to him a safe, relaxed atmosphere that offers him a sense of security. Likewise, he knows when someone is upset with him or just upset.[5]

The single parent under great stress cannot conceal these feelings from the child. It is best for a parent to deal with the stress before tending the child or he may make the child distressed also.

2. *The toddler.* The toddler is a contradiction. He is independent, even bossy, but he may show greater dependency on his primary caregiver than he showed as a baby. He is beginning to feel separate from the primary caregiver, yet he realizes that this person is the source of his security.

It is not unusual for the single parent to experience the heartbreak of the toddler's calling the day-care worker "mama" and preferring her to his own mother. This is a sign that the primary caregiver has done her job well. The child has developed a sense of security in this person.

Now that the child is walking, his world is enlarged—and it is a time when his curiosity abounds. The combination is nerve-wracking. When the child charges off in four directions at once and seems to have more hands than an octopus, he's not being bad. To chastise him for doing what comes naturally inhibits normal development. This does not mean the child should be permitted to do as he pleases. *Child-proof* your child's living and play area. Fence off doors and furnish the living space the child uses in such a way that he can develop his motor skills and satisfy his curiosity.

Spanking need not be the first method in disciplining a toddler. If his living area has been child-proofed, he doesn't need to be told "no" constantly. If he is doing something he shouldn't, he can sometimes be distracted with a more suitable activity. When he is doing what you want him to do, reinforce it with praise.[6]

Spanking should be used as a last resort, and only when the child challenges your authority as a parent. The independence of the "terrible two" is a time of testing to see just how independent he is. Parents must learn that there is no conflict between rules and a free spirit. A child can be as free as he wants just as long as he stays within the boundaries set by parental rules. Make those boundaries as wide as your adult discretion permits. But the child will always have boundaries.

Sleeping and eating habits may change, and the child may not eat or sleep as much as the parent thinks he should. If the child is getting *plenty* of physical exercise and fresh air, he will probably eat and sleep well.

Thumbsucking is usually given up by age three or three and a half. Some children persist long past four.[7] Some psychologists object to putting bad-tasting medicine or other devices on a child's thumb, because they may make him feel unloved.[8] But something may be needed if the child is damaging his teeth. Usually, however, a contented child gives up sucking when he is three.[9]

Toilet training begins during this time. Some parents succeed by putting the child on the potty at the time he usually has his bowel movement. He soon connects the idea of a bowel movement and sitting on the potty. Realistically, however, most children don't learn bladder control until they walk. An attentive parent learns after a while what facial expressions or behaviors indicate bowel or bladder distress. Toilet training is very time consuming, but whenever distress is shown, put he child on the potty.

Single parents need to coordinate this activity with the day-care provider. Compare notes, and make sure that you both know all the signs the child gives when he needs the potty. Needless to say, don't attempt to force the child or scold him when he fails. Let him see you empty his pants into the potty, and it will help him get the connection that it goes in the potty, not his pants.

Talking is another skill that develops at this time. Children love to play with sounds, so have patience with all the noises they make. It's part of learning to speak. When the child does volunteer a word, assist him by repeating it and pronouncing it correctly and identifying the object he is referring to. A delighted response by parent or caregiver encourages the child in the development of this skill. Don't use baby talk when talking to your child. It may sound cute, but it doesn't help him learn to speak correctly.

Three- and Four-Year-Olds.

Now that he has learned to eat, dress, and go to the toilet, a child may seem to relapse. He may have been very careful about these things, but now he's too busy with new and more important things—too busy sometimes to go to the toilet before he wets himself a little. It helps to give the child a little more independence at this point—he will usually reward this with his cooperation. The growing awareness of the child requires that attention be given to the following:

1. *Fathers become important.* To this point the primary caregiver has occupied all the child's attention; this person is usually the mother or another woman. Now the child becomes interested in the other significant adult—the father or father figure. If his father sees him infrequently, it is important that he be exposed to another male role model. This is important for both girls and boys. Both learn what a man is like, and should be, from a good role model. Children also watch the interactions of men and women to learn what is expected of each in their relations with each other.[10]

2. *When parents disagree.* By the time they are three or four, children are able to abide by different sets of rules.[11] It should not be difficult for a child to abide by different rules in the custodial and noncustodial homes. It is important that the religious and moral sensibilities of the child be respected.

   The child becomes troubled when either or both parents cut each other down or attempt to get him to give up his loyalty to the other parent. Parents who can work together in setting and enforcing rules, sharing information, and encouraging the child stand the best chance of keeping the three- and four-year-old in good mental health. If this is not possible, then the child should be exposed to a surrogate, such as a teacher or club leader, who is willing to share with the parent what he learns about her child and is willing to assist in setting and enforcing rules. Remember, "stand-in" parents are okay.

3. *Brothers and sisters quarrel.* It is important that parents don't try to become judge and jury in sibling quarrels. Children must learn to settle their own differences, and this is facilitated by not doing it for them. If they begin to quarrel, let them know that you don't care to hear the quarreling and that they will be separated if they don't settle their differences. Being the social creatures they are, children don't like separation for any length of time; they soon learn to accommodate each other

rather than be separated. However, if they verbally or physically abuse each other, the situation is not to be tolerated—it doesn't matter who started it.

4. *Jealousy in families.* Jealousy occurs when a child feels left out or hasn't gotten what is due him. It often occurs with the arrival of a new baby who seems to be getting all the parent's attention. A child may show displeasure to the baby directly by annoying it or indirectly by reverting to childish behavior himself, such as wetting. It is important that the parent not see this as "bad" behavior but rather the child's clumsy attempt to protest being displaced. Preparing the child beforehand for the baby's arrival is important. When the baby is brought home, talk to the older sibling about his feelings of having a new baby in the house. Listen to his feelings nonjudgmentally and nonanalytically, and assure him you understand and will not let his fears become fact.

There is also the constant struggle to be "treated equally." The slice of pie can't be smaller; the glass of milk must be the same amount; the candy must be counted out piece by piece. Parents burden themselves unnecessarily by trying to treat everyone equally. There are times when some children are more deserving than others. The issue of equality and fairness is usually due to insecurity. It is the child's way of assuring himself that he is loved just as much as the others. A parent's time would be better spent on activities that are designed to demonstrate love and warmth.

There will always be children who will protest that they are coming up on the short end no matter how much they get. When that is the case, it is best for the parent to say calmly, "That's all you get," and go on with other business. If the child then throws a tantrum, fairness is no longer the issue; the tantrum is. The message and discipline must convince the child that tantrums are not a good way to express unhappiness. The message must be, "You may be unhappy if you wish, but you may not throw a tantrum."

5. *Conscience.* Conscience is a capability that every human being is born with but requires instruction for proper development and function (Rom. 2:14—15). By the age of three a child knows what the parent expects. Conscience develops most

readily in an atmosphere of patience where the parent is quick to praise or reward.[12] Willful or persistent disobedience that runs contrary to the rules the parent has laid down may require discipline. But this should come only as a last resort. It is far better for the child to obey the parent out of love—as Jesus told us, if we love Him we will keep His commandments (John 14:15).

There is an important link between the socialization of the child's conscience and his spiritual life. Children develop their feelings about God, His expectations of them, and His dealings with them from their experiences with their parents. The parent who commands the obedience of the child through fear will probably raise a child who has an unhealthy fear of God and has difficulty with the Christian life. Conversely, the child raised by a patient, loving parent, who teaches that obedience is a sign of love and family loyalty, will most likely have fewer problems in living an obedient and joyful Christian life.

6. *Telling the truth.* Three- and four-year-olds live in a magic world of pretend. All kinds of marvelous things happen simply by wishing. When it comes to telling the truth, wishing plays an important part. For example, a dish is broken or cookies are missing, and mother asks, "Who did it?" Little brother says that sister did it. Little brother really did it, but he wishes so hard it was his sister's fault that he almost convinces himself. Parents can help their children tell the truth if they don't make it unnecessarily painful for them to do so. The incidents just mentioned don't require an inquisition. They require the parent to say, "I don't know who broke the dish (or took the cookies). I'm just sorry that someone is not telling me the truth," and let it go at that. The child soon learns that there is something more important than broken or missing things and that is telling the truth. When the child tells the truth, it should be reinforced with a loving response.

Again, a spiritual principle is at stake here and can be taught. Lying creates a breach of family fellowship. Confessing the truth restores that fellowship (1 John 1:6—7). Children must understand that their lies put up a wall of distrust. The only way that wall can be taken down is by telling the truth. As children learn the rewards of confession in family life they will be inclined to carry it over into their spiritual lives. They will understand that when they sin, God doesn't want them to whip themselves physically or mentally. He just wants them to say about their behavior what He says—that it was wrong. The word *confess* in the Greek New Testament means "to say the same thing as." When we confess our sin we say the same thing about it that God says—it was *sin*.

7. *Learning about sex.* When a child first starts to talk he wants to know "what is that?" He builds his vocabulary with the names of things. The child of four and a half moves from asking "what?" to asking "why?" All questions are legitimate as far as he is concerned—everything from, "Why does our hair stay on our head?" to "How did that baby get inside you?" We need not be concerned that we react to sexual questions differently from others. In fact, when we react in a way that indicates the child has touched on an important subject it will help him distinguish between questions that are frivolous and those that deserve serious attention.

Children are naturally curious, and that curiosity should be rewarded with straightforward, simple answers. There is no need to give them a course in sex education. Just answer their questions as they come up. This is "responsive" teaching.

Children will also explore themselves by sight and touch. This is part of the learning process. As they listen to your explanation of "why" and watch how you handle your own sexuality they will learn that our sexuality is a very private part of ourselves. They see you close the bathroom door when you shower and not walk around the house nude. They realize by this that sexuality is something private.

Five-Year-Olds

The five-year-old may look like a little grown-up person. But he still needs his rest—if not a nap, a rest period during the day and ten hours of sleep at night.[13]

1. *Which hand to use?* By age five most children show their preference for right- or left-handedness. If the child is unable to decide or seems awkward, consult your pediatrician to test

which is better for him. Once it is decided, encourage him to use that hand.

2. *Still farsighted.* The five-year-old is still farsighted and for this reason is not ready for close work. He can't cope with small print or printing letters without strain. This is another reason why some parents and educators prefer to start children in the first grade at age six or seven.

3. *Sex-role identity.* Children at this age love to mimic what they consider behavior appropriate to their sex role. A boy may swagger into the house and heave a big sigh over his chores. A girl may play little mother to her dolls.

    It is important that the parent watch the child act out the sex role. The parent will learn from the child's behavior how the child perceives the adults of his or her sex. Good adult role models continue to be important to the five-year-old. If the opposite-sex parent is absent, expose the child to other role models.

4. *He wants rules.* The five-year-old wants to do things right and understands the need for rules. In fact, some children may go overboard with each other and become overbearing. This is part of the child's socialization. He needs to learn that rules were made for people and not people for rules. That is, rules are not an end in themselves. They are created to give us order and predictability.

    Some children become tattlers at this age. They may be so bound by rules that they are overly afraid of the consequences of breaking them. Their fear may lead them to tattling. Or they may use tattling to make sure the rules still are in force.[1]

From Six to Ten

In this period of the child's life, called middle childhood, he is making an important shift from the family to the outside world. It can be a difficult time for him. Until now he was loved by his family simply for being, and that was sufficient for his self-concept to thrive. Now his self-concept comes from the reaction of ociety at large and is based mostly not on who he is, *but on what he can do.*[15]

For this reason, the developmental task at this age is mastery of skills in school and in his peer group. "You don't know how to do anything" is an incredibly painful slur to a child in middle childhood. An impatient adult who says, "Here, let me do that," conveys the same message.

The mastery of skills involves both the subject matter at school and group activities that involve throwing, catching, jumping rope, and other physical coordination. He is also learning the psychological skills of dealing with people in the larger world. Now it is important what *other people* think of him, not just what his family thinks, and how he can win the approval of others.

In the middle years the child also begins to see his parents more realistically. The child may even tell the parent about the flaws he sees. This may be especially difficult for the single parent who already feels inadequate and is worried about damage that may have been done to the child. Accept criticism as a sign of growth in your child. He is trying to break away from the dependency of earlier years; seeing the parent more realistically helps the process.

His peer group begins to become important at this age. It is *imperative* that the parent begin to know who the child chooses for friends and to monitor friendships to be sure they are wholesome. A parent must prohibit any friendship that is considered unwholesome. More is said on this in the preadolescent discussion on page 190.

The child still needs home and male and female parent models. Just being there, accessible to the child, is often enough to make him feel your support. Now is the time to correct any mistakes made in the child's earlier years. If either parent has not been close to the child, this is the time to get close—before adolescence, when he begins to make his major break from home.

When Your Child Starts School

Though your child may have been in nursery school, starting elementary school is a milestone in his life. The National Institute of Mental Health puts out an excellent brochure with some pointers for parents. It says:

1. *Recognize that the day your child first goes off to school
   an important event.* Make sure it is a positive experience.
   is his first major separation from the secure and familiar worl
   of home and family into a new world of friendship, learnin
   and adventure—a world that parents can never again sha
   entirely. Your loving support and understanding are impo
   tant.

2. *The first school day can determine the child's attitude towar
   school, positively or negatively, for the rest of his scho
   years.* Learning to like school and liking to learn are close
   related.

3. *Take an active interest in what your child tells you abo
   school when he comes home.* Be a good listener, and gi
   him an opportunity to say how he feels about school and t
   people there.

4. *Don't complain about the school in front of your child.*
   things need to be changed, get to know your child's teach
   and try to find out how you can help.

5. *Praise your child for good work he has done in school, ev
   though he might have gotten four out of five answers wron
   You can be glad that he did get one of them right. The po
   is, what is your focus with your child—what he does rig
   or what he does wrong?

6. *Learning to cope with frustration at school is one of t
   developmental tasks he must master.* Don't be the kind
   parent who feels that your role in life is to make things ea
   for your child. Your role is to help him cope, not to ma
   things easier.

7. *Avoid comparing your child and his school experience
   how his brothers and sisters did when they began school.*
   can be helpful, however, if the child knows that what he
   facing in school is not something he alone experiences.

8. *The first report card offers an opportunity to talk about
   feelings regarding school.* If he hasn't done as well as
   would like to, reassure him in some way that he is still i
   portant to you and that you still love him.

9. *Give your child plenty of time at home to do what he wants to do.* School is hard work for a young child.

0. *You will be spending less time together as your child becomes more and more involved in school.* Be sure to set aside special times for each other.

1. *Quarrels with friends should be handled as you would handle sibling quarreling.* Unless children are harming themselves or each other, it is best to let them work out their own problems.

2. *Think of yourself as supporting and helping your child's development and not protecting him from the world about which he has much to learn.* [16]

The Six-Year-Old

The child at five is usually a delight. He is in a state of equilibrium. But the equilibrium begins to break up at six. [17] Conflicts with the primary parental caregiver are to be expected. The child is attempting to break away from dependency on home and family and learn how to cope with the larger world. The break will not be smooth, but recognize that the child is not trying to be bad. He is trying to break away, but still needs the assurance that the parent is there.

When the primary caregiver is Mother, the breakaway will enhance the position of Father, since Father is not a symbol of dependency. If the father is absent or not sufficiently involved with the child, a suitable male role model should be provided.

Learning new skills at school and coping with the larger world of his peer group puts a lot of pressure on a child. The parent must give the child an opportunity to unwind after a hard day at school. The single parent may not be wholly sympathetic, however. He may think, "Hey, kid. You don't know what a hard day means!" But remember, he's just six.

The Seven-Year-Old

Age six was a time of action. Age seven is a time of reflection. What may appear to be withdrawal or moodiness may be a child's contemplation of the lessons he's learning about life. He is gen-

erally more relaxed and cooperative, thrives on praise, but
terribly sensitive to criticism.[18]

Respect the child's need to do nothing but think. He is actual]
working to understand the meaning of life's experiences. Whe
he is reflective, a parent sometimes worries that it might be
sign of depression and may try to snap him out of it. Give hi
time. The child will most likely move on to other activities ar
join the human race again.

The seven-year-old usually has a good time at school. He ha
had a year of experience and is in the second grade. He need
praise from the teachers, and even a physical touch. The teacher
acceptance or nonacceptance of the child is important to his sel
image.[19]

This is the age of the clique and ganging up on someone ar
taunting him with, "Cry, baby, cry." Children begin to lear
how to make themselves feel bigger by making someone else fe
smaller. To gang up on someone makes them feel that they a
on the inside while the other one is on the outside. This does n
excuse the behavior; it only points out that children of this ag
are not trying to be cruel or bad when they do this. But they a
adopting poor tactics to enhance their own self-worth. Often th
displeasure of an adult over this behavior, along with an expl:
nation of why, provides a good learning opportunity. Christi:
parents should treat such behavior merely as a spiritual problen
It is true that it is not nice to treat people this way. But th
motives need to be understood to correct such a problem.

The Eight-Year-Old

Age six is a time of action, age seven a time of reflection, an
now age eight is again a time of action. It is as though the eigh
year-old is going to try out the theories about life he contemplate
at seven. The seven-year-old likes to play alone. The eight-yea
old abhors being alone and attacks life with gusto; he become
demanding of attention, from his mother or a caregiver awa
from home.

Three traits characterize the eight-year-old: speediness, expa:
siveness, and "evaluativeness." He is physically quick and ofte
impatient. He is exploring new worlds and often is an avid co
lector. He evaluates what happens to him and what he causes

appen. This is part of his preparation for adulthood, and he may even expect to be treated like an adult.[20]

He tends to dramatize and exaggerate and express a bravado that makes him appear quite self-sufficient. This may carry over into being unmoved by scolding or disappointment. He is experimenting with the "I can't be hurt" defensive system.

It comes as a surprise to some parents when the eight-year-old bursts into tears with little provocation. Fathers in particular must not tell their sons, "You're too old to be crying." In fact, this is an excellent opportunity to begin the development of a warm, sensitive male by putting your arms around him and saying, "I understand. I feel like crying too." Real men *do* cry.

It is important that the parent not encourage the "I can't be hurt" attitude. Mothers often do this when they throw up their hands in despair and say, "I don't know what I'm going to do with you." Whether or not the child appears to be responsive to discipline and control, do it anyway. And insist on *respectful* compliance.

This brings me to the subject of spanking. The Bible makes it very clear that spanking is appropriate (Prov. 13:24; 22:15; 23:13; 6:3; 29:15; Eph. 6:1–4). It is important to remember that, historically, striking or other corporal punishment was used as a display of *authority*. Striking should not be done in anger. What spanking means is, "I'm in charge here." Corporal punishment is the badge of that authority. When we require our children to respectfully comply, we are asking them to have a proper attitude toward authority.

This is essential to the socialization of the child. These are the principles of civilized society and government. The child learns them first at home. Moreover, the single mother raising a son should get him under control now. The teen years are a difficult time to start.

Here are some other facts about the eight-year-old: in school, his teacher is less important and peer group more important; he is hungry for facts, though his interests may sometimes seem frivolous; he definitely prefers boys because girls are "stupid" or "silly"; his self-confidence is greater; he is more choosy about friends and doesn't feel he must please everyone; he often finds a special friend of the same sex, an important development in social skills; his interest in children's books and magazines offer

an opportunity for further intellectual growth; he displays an ir
terest in horror stories, which—if they are not excessively viole
or gory and have the benefit of parental explanation—help hir
set to rest questions about this aspect of life. It is better to de:
with this in books rather than in TV or movies, because time
needed for parental commentary.

The Nine-Year-Old

Age nine is an extension of age eight, with the exception tha
the nine-year-old is more self-motivated, and individuality begir
to stand out. His particular interests and skills begin to show.[21]

Nine-year-olds respond best if treated with respect—taking int
account their preferences and eccentricities. Parents should re
member, however, that respect is to be *mutual*. The child is a
an age when he is learning to give and take with his peer grou
He should learn it at home also.

Friends are the focus of his attention.[22] His preparation fc
adolescence and adulthood depends on his ability to become les
dependent on parents and more skilled at dealing successfull
with his peers.

Gangs, clubs, and "secret societies" are important in deve
oping these skills. What a parent may consider useless or id
chatter is the way a nine-year-old tests out his ideas on peers an
learns how to express doubts and worries and discover that *othe
feel the same way*. Thus the peer group begins to become th
primary support group.

Boys and girls express great disdain for each other at this ag
It is an excellent cover for a growing interest in the opposite se>
A nine-year-old girl put it this way: "Boys are loathesome cre:
tures. I enjoy watching them."[23]

Here are some other facts about the nine-year-old: reading di:
abilities will become evident at this age; self-motivation applie
only to a child's own interests and not to bathing, brushing teetl
and doing chores—all of which will require reminders. He begir
to develop selective deafness; he can hear the bell of the ic
cream wagon five blocks away, but not be aware of being calle
by a parent from the next room.

All this requires much patience from parents. The child is nc
trying to be difficult; life is just too full of more important thing

than personal hygiene and chores. He is developing a sense of fairness; his spiritual development can be facilitated by capitalizing on the child's growing understanding of truth, honesty, property rights, and personal rights. Some nine-year-olds are worriers, and a parent can be most helpful, not by rushing in with premature assurances but rather by listening with an understanding, caring ear.

The Ten-Year-Old

Enjoy your ten-year-old while you can because afterward you will encounter the stormy, rebellious preadolescent of eleven. The ten-year-old, like the five-year-old, is at a stage of equilibrium. The lessons he has learned so far he now is applying. When he has learned his lessons well he will feel a great deal of self-assurance and be a very enjoyable person. He will sometimes have an outburst of anger, but it's usually toward his peers or younger siblings.

The major problem with ten-year-olds is their relationship to younger siblings who "bug" them or are otherwise obnoxious. A child of ten usually doesn't start trouble with the younger sibling but is baited until he explodes. A wise parent can avoid this by stepping in and separating them before the war begins. The ten-year-old's sense of fairness should be respected here, particularly if he didn't do anything wrong. The younger sibling should probably be the one who is isolated, perhaps even sent to his own room to play.

Though ten is a good year, don't expect the child to take care of clothes and keep his room straight. A parent can save himself and the child a lot of grief by keeping the bedroom door closed and having the child do a general cleanup once a week.

This is a good age to teach the child something about the consequences of his own behavior. If his clothes aren't washed because he didn't put them in the laundry hamper, or if he can't find a shoe because it's under a ton of debris in his room, he has only himself to blame. The parent should be very matter-of-fact and not accept responsibility for the child's distress.

It is also important not to lecture the ten-year-old. News items on drugs, alcohol, or substance abuse and other social problems will have greater impact if the parent doesn't give an "instant replay"[24]

Finally, the subject of sex is of interest, though boys may appear very casual about it and girls may seem embarrassed. This is a good time to browse through your bookstore for a child's book on the subject of sex. Christian bookstores stock books that deal with both the physical and the moral aspects. By browsing you will find the book most suited to your child. Don't worry about the child's embarrassment or indifference when you give him the book. Boys and girls feel it necessary to hide their growing interest in sex. Respect it.

Preadolescence—Eleven and Twelve

Preadolescence, as the word suggests, prepares a child for adolescence. Though some children pass through preadolescence with little difficulty, this stage often appears in the home suddenly like a monster out of a science-fiction movie. The loving, compliant ten-year-old has become, at eleven, a creature we hardly recognize. What has happened?

Perhaps I can best describe it in terms of a clay likeness the child has been making of himself for ten years. At age ten he seemed to be satisfied with what he saw and was happy other adults were pleased. But suddenly he becomes surly, and SMASH! He destroys what he has made, and with great energy and agitation he takes the raw materials and mashes them all together so he can start all over and remake himself.

The horrid behavior of the preadolescent is the process of breaking up what was suitable for childhood but is unsuitable for adolescence. The child decides to become his own person and not a replica of what adults expect. Therefore, whatever adults approve, he disapproves. What they disapprove, he approves.

The parent must see preadolescence as a period of reorganization. Even though there is much resistance and rebellion, remember that the child has spent ten years collecting good raw material. It is still there. The parent must give the preadolescent enough room to reorganize, usually along the lines of his peer group, but at the same time set limits. Moreover, the child must learn how to disagree without being disagreeable.

Parents must be careful they don't let themselves be caught in ie game of "bait and hook." Your child knows exactly how to et to you. Don't let him bait you and hook you into an uproar. 'es, there will be disagreement; but there need not be uncon- ollable tumult.

It is important that the parent be even more vigilant about omething he should have been doing since the child was six— amely, exercising veto power over friends. Some children say, 'My parents aren't going to choose my friends." The parent's :ply should be, "I agree. I won't choose your friends. But you an be certain that I will veto any friendships that I think are nwholesome. And if we can't agree on which friends are good or you, I guess you will have to entertain yourself."

Don't make the mistake of making everything an issue with ie preadolescent. Some conflicts can be avoided. If we insist on nd get respect from him and control of his friends and activities, ther things will take care of themselves, such as school grades, aste in music, table manners, grooming, and general considera- on for the rest of the family.

Parents should also remember that the preadolescent's behavior not pure cussedness. Great physical changes are taking place boys and girls that spark emotions they don't plan on and are inexplicable to them as they are to the parent.

By now girls should be prepared for menstruation and be shown ow to provide for sanitary needs. This may happen as early as welve. Boys should be aware that in the next few years they will experiencing "wet dreams." This will probably happen in eir fourteenth year, though there are individual differences. A ood book on sex, geared to the child's age, would be helpful. irls will show more interest in heterosexual sex than boys. Boys' sdain for girls continues, but it's a cover for developing inter- t. The parent should be settled in his own mind how he feels out masturbation. I discuss the subject in chapter 10 of *But I idn't Want a Divorce*.[25]

The twelve-year-old differs from the eleven-year-old in that he beginning to level out and put into practice lessons he has arned by trial and error. As with other stages of development, e child goes through periods of disequilibrium and equilibrium. welve tends to be a mellowed version of eleven.[26]

Points to Ponder About Preadolescents

Here are some pointers in dealing with preadolescents.[27]

1. *Obnoxious behavior is temporary.* Be patient. Eleven-year olds eventually make it to twelve.

2. *Avoid parental counter-hysterics.* We need to remember that it is the child going through a phase, not ourselves. We ought to be the stable ones when the preadolescent "crazies" hit.

3. *Don't make every issue a matter of controversy.* Let some things go by, such as choice of music, TV programs, clothes and the appearance of his room.

4. *Look behind the preadolescent's provocative behavior to learn the real message.* Rebellion doesn't mean he hates his parents. It may mean that he's afraid that he will look like a "nerd" to his peers if he's too compliant.

5. *Drain off some of the preadolescent's energy by encouraging vigorous activity, preferably outdoors.* It is remarkable how compliant he can be when he's exhausted.

6. *Respect his need for being treated as an adult.* He is very sensitive to being categorized as a child.

7. *Don't take the preadolescent's rebellion personally.* It is not you but the adult world he's against. And don't panic. The world is not about to be taken over by preadolescents. After a while they discover that they don't have to attack the system in order to be different.

8. *Take matters in stride.* It's all part of being the parent of a adolescent.

⅍⅍⅍ 13

Your Adolescent From Thirteen to Twenty-one

We saw in the last chapter that age-group characteristics are behaviors that are typical to the developmental stage of a child. It is important for parents to understand that psychologists can only speak in terms of a range of behaviors and an approximate age. A child or adolescent may be a year or more "off the mark" in manifesting the emotional characteristics of his age group and perhaps even two or more years in physical development. In sexual development, for example, some children blossom early and some later.

A parent should not say, "My Suzie isn't a typical fourteen-year-old girl. She isn't easy to get along with at all." Parents should remember that "easy" and "difficult" are relative to the individual child and not necessarily to other fourteen-year-olds. If fourteen is tough, it just means that thirteen and fifteen are tougher.

The purpose of this discussion of age-group characteristics is to help parents understand and read their teens better. Most teens are not trying to be bad. Their behavior is their way of coping with the new pressures and pleasures they find as they grow up. Parents sometimes take a teenager's belligerence personally. Wounded parents should remember that *all* adults are on your teen's blacklist.

The adolescent years are roughly from thirteen to twenty-one.

195

The task of the adolescent is to form a separate ego identity. He continually asks himself the question, "Who am I?" The answer to that question depends on his achieving *independence*. He is moving from the dependency of childhood to the independency of adulthood. This is difficult in highly industrialized and complex societies because many social and intellectual skills must be mastered before the adolescent can make it on his own. The process is immensely frustrating for both the teen and his parent. For every three steps forward, it seems the teen takes two steps backward. There is continual tension between dependence on the parent and wanting to be an independent person.[1]

From Thirteen to Fifteen

Adolescence is generally divided into two stages: early adolescence (thirteen to fifteen) and late adolescence (sixteen to twenty-one). The task of all adolescents is the same—to achieve separate ego identity and to answer the question, "Who am I?" The early adolescent handles this question with respect to the family and peer group, and the late adolescent with respect to the world at large.

This task comes at a time when teens' feelings and bodies are changing as a result of the onset of puberty. The teen emotionally and physically is not the same person he was at ten, when he enjoyed equilibrium in his life. He habitually compares himself to other teens his age to see if he fits in, and he is extremely sensitive to any suggestion or evidence that he is different.

Early adolescence is the period of "revolt and conform." In his bid to achieve ego identity through separation from parents, the teenager is in a state of revolt. His need to fit in with his peers makes him feel the pressure to conform to the dress code, special rules, and structure of that group.

The revolt-and-conform phenomenon results in thought and behavior patterns that parents find difficult to deal with, particularly the repudiation of family and family values and what appears to be a mindless conformity to the peer group. Some parents say "I'm losing my teenager." In a sense, this is true and also normal and natural. What the parent is losing the teen *to* is another matter. The wise parent will make the breakaway as easy as possible and attempt to influence only the *direction* the teen is taking. The more certain the teen is that the parent accepts the breakaway, the less inclined he will be to fight the parent for freedom of choice at every point.

Christian parents, particularly the very strict, often feel that their teens are "drifting from the Lord." This creates a great deal of tension in the household, particularly if the parent thinks that a Christian teen should behave as a Christian adult.

Nevertheless, the teen must make the breakaway not only as a human person but also as a spiritual person. If he is a professing Christian, he must make his faith and the expression of it *his own* and not a mere reflection of the parent's faith.

The parent who makes every issue a "spiritual" issue is liable to impair the teen's spiritual life. The teen may react to what he feels is a stifling experience. For example, if the music he listens to is not "Christian," if the way he eats is "not honoring to the Lord," if the way he dresses is "a poor testimony," if all the TV shows he watches are "of the Devil," he is likely—to use *his* vernacular—to "ditch" the Christian life.

The Bible makes it clear that there is room for differences in the way the Christian life is lived. There were those who did not observe holy days and those who did; there were those who ate meat from idolatrous sacrifices and those who did not. They were to respect each other in matters of Christian liberty and not to judge (Rom. 14—15; 1 Cor. 8—10).

The single parent, particularly the single mother, faces a mammoth task in raising a teen. If she has been a good parent and her relationship with her child has been particularly rewarding, she may find it difficult to "lose" him. She may be tempted to obstruct the breakaway because the teen has become such a great companion. Don't put the teen in the terrible psychological bind of having to deny the need to achieve an ego identity of his own because he can't handle the guilt of leaving you alone.

The Thirteen-Year-Old

Remember the pattern of development we have seen thus far: equilibrium, disequilibrium, equilibrium. This can be terribly frustrating to parents. Just about the time the teen seems to be leveling out and returning to the human race, he's out of sorts

again. The ages of twelve through fourteen are a good example
of disequilibrium. At twelve, the preadolescent has mellowed a
bit and is used to the idea of being neither a child nor a teenager.
Then comes thirteen. Everything unravels again. The thirteen-
year-old is in a state of disequilibrium, trying to find out how to
achieve his own ego identity and separateness from family.

The thirteen-year-old prefers to be alone in his room and may
appear to be sullen and depressed. But all those "wasted hours"
in the room listening to music or just "messing around" are work
hours. He is trying to figure out this business of being a teenager.
The parent should respect the teen's need to be alone and not
pry. Only if there's evidence of acute or chronic depression is
some kind of intervention needed. A parent must learn what is
normal teen isolation and what is abnormal. If a parent is in
doubt, he should consult a professional therapist.

The Fourteen-Year-Old

The fourteen-year-old achieves a measure of equilibrium. The
difficulties of age thirteen begin to pay off, and at fourteen things
start going better.

Friendships, the gang, and socialization become very important. At this age a girl may be defined as "one young female
connected to another by a telephone line." A wise parent will set
rules for phone use by which the needs of both the teen and the
parent are respected.

Because they are emotionally and physically ahead of boys,
girls often want to date older boys who are more compatible
physically and emotionally. Parents should discourage this. Also,
group dating rather than pairing off should be encouraged.

Though interested in girls, boys will tend to conceal this feeling. In time they will show interest. Let them take their time,
and don't suggest that something may be wrong with them for
not showing more interest. Privately they probably already have
a lot of interest in "girlie" magazines, fantasy life, and masturbation. But confronted with a real live girl, they may feel very
awkward.

The Fifteen-Year-Old

Whatever happened to the fourteen-year-old who began to make peace with his parents and himself? Remember, equilibrium and disequilibrium.

Fifteen is a transition between early and late adolescence. Just as the teenager was getting the hang of things, he experiences a new growth spurt, a new body image (generally negative), and more intense sexual desires. Moreover, he realizes that one of these days he has to choose a vocation and become a full-fledged, self-supporting adult. How on earth can he do that when he doesn't have the faintest idea what vocation he may like?

It may be helpful to give the fifteen-year-old some vocational guidance and talk about the possibility of college. For more on vocational testing and college see *Everything You Need to Know About College*.[2] But don't suggest college as the only option. The teen's personality may be more suited to skilled labor. My oldest and youngest sons opted for college, whereas my two middle sons, with some college, opted for the welder-pipefitter trade.

Be prepared for a fierce bid for independence. The fifteen-year-old may resist all attempts to place restrictions on his behavior no matter how reasonable they may be. He may be hostile and sullen, but again, don't take it personally. His rising spirit of independence is nature's way of pushing him out of the nest.

The frustrating thing for parents is that the fifteen-year-old seems to want the best of both lives. He wants all the amenities of homelife and parental support and all the benefits of adult independence. The hard part is finding the balance between the two—how to facilitate the breakaway from home without making the teen feel frightened or unloved, and how to make him feel welcome at home without turning him into a disrespectful, self-seeking monster who makes the parent feel taken for granted—or worse, physically abuses the parent. More will be said about the abusive teen later in this chapter.

Parents need to be particularly on guard against being baited by the fifteen-year-old's provocative remarks such as, ''This family is hopelessly old-fashioned.'' The best approach is to take a nondefensive tell-me-about-it approach. You may be steaming inside and want to put him in his place, but you will be much more successful by responding, ''I understand how you feel, and one of these days you will be on your own and can do things your way." The statement should not be delivered in a threatening way. It acknowledges that the parent's and teen's goals are the same—for him to achieve his own identity and independence. But at the same time the parent refuses to be baited.

The Christian parent should remember that if the teen isn't successful in precipitating a heated debate on everyday matters, he may debate in the sensitive area of faith or morals. For example, he may say, "What's wrong with believing in Darwin's theory of evolution?" or "I don't see anything wrong with having sex before marriage." The parent must then decide whether these are honest attempts to have the Christian view articulated or whether this is a game of bait and hook. The parent will know the first minute or two into the conversation.

One approach is to answer calmly and intelligently, and if your teen is trying to get you upset, smile and say, "I'm wondering if the purpose of this conversation is to get Mom in an uproar." Proceed with the discussion if it generates more light than heat. Otherwise, drop it

When the parent assures the teen that his breakaway from home will not be impeded, it may help the teen feel less of a need for belligerence. It also gives the parent an opportunity to let the teen know that with adult privilege comes adult responsibility.

This is perhaps the trickiest part of all. The teen is already fearful that he may not make it as an adult, and we don't want to increase that fear. But he needs to be reminded that he can't have the best of both lives—financial support by parent and adult freedom. But don't despair; the fifteen-year-old has a way of becoming sixteen, where we again see a return to equilibrium.

From Sixteen to Twenty-One

Less is known about the period of development called "late adolescence" than the earlier stages. In my practice of family therapy I am discovering more and more families where young men as old as twenty-five and twenty-eight are still living at home, emotionally and, to a large degree, financially dependent on their parents. Chronologically they are no longer adolescents, but their lifestyle, behavior, and dependence are still very much like that of a late adolescent.

The Sixteen-Year-Old

Sixteen is a time of new equilibrium. The sixteen-year-old feels less need to prove his independence by flaunting it.[3]

Though American society does not have a "rite of passage"—a ceremony in which the youth becomes an adult—this is the age when a teenager may legally work for wages outside the home and get a driver's license. These two achievements help the sixteen-year-old feel a sense of moving toward adulthood.

It is important, however, that the parent and teen come to some agreement over what he will do with his newfound privileges and responsibilities. How will his money be spent? It's time that he begin to provide for his own needs. Both girls and boys may be required to pay for their own auto insurance, or at least the amount of the increase in premium on the parent's policy. They may be expected to buy some of their own clothes or begin to save for college or for a place of their own if they are not going to attend college. They should also provide for their own spending money. All this helps them understand what you mean when you say, "With adult privilege comes adult responsibility." If the teen chooses not to work and provide for license, insurance, and gasoline, then he can do without the adult privilege of driving.

It is seldom that a sixteen-year-old *must* drive. If he chooses not to work and have spending money, the parent should not dole it out. Either the teen does without money to spend as he wishes, or he accepts the responsibility to earn it. These are some ways a parent can help the teen achieve independence.

Seventeen to Twenty-one

This is a difficult time for the teenager. He will soon graduate from high school but still may not know what he wants to do vocationally.

It often helps the teen to find himself by going to work full-time and becoming self-supporting. Sometimes this is achieved by going into military service, an attractive option for both men and women. In my home we told our boys from their early teens that the only way they could continue to live at home after high school was if they attended school full time. If they chose not to further their education or learn a trade, they could stay at home long enough to build a financial reserve for moving out.

Some parents might protest, "Do you really expect a high school graduate to be able to get a job that will pay enough to support him?" My answer is yes. It may not support him in the style to which he has become accustomed in his parent's home, but he can *survive*.

This may seem like cruel and unusual treatment for one's own flesh and blood, but there's a good reason for it. Parents often cripple their teens by making things too easy for them and shielding them from the harsh realities of life. The teen who does not want to learn a skilled trade or go to college needs to know what it's like to try to live on an unskilled laborer's wages. One of the biggest motivators to go back to school is to get tired of living in a grubby room or group house and having to ride a bus everywhere.

Certainly the loving parent will take care of an adult child who is unable to care for himself. Children do this for their parents. But if young men and women are able-bodied, they should be required to make it on their own—either by going on with further schooling or facing the consequences of their unwillingness to accept adult responsibility.

Earlier I mentioned twenty-five- and twenty-eight-year-olds who still live at home. Those whom I see in my practice are pathetic. They have a pride and belligerence about being independent adults, but they also display a childlike fear of facing the world.

The late adolescent may manifest an unrealistic confidence about going out on his own, but his spirit of independence is a gift of God. If he really knew how tough it is, he'd never want to leave home. The further he gets beyond age twenty-one, the more he realizes how tough life is and how realistic his parents are. If he has not achieved breakaway by the end of late adolescence, around twenty-one, he begins to rethink the whole matter of "independence." His parents, sensing his fear, often conspire with him to make it possible for him to retain the illusion of being an "independent adult," all the while knowing he is still very dependent emotionally and economically.

The effect is what I call "atrophy of the psyche." The person is much like the young eagle who, when not pushed from the nest at the appropriate time to try his wings, becomes fearful of trying. Having lost the moment of "insane boldness," to try to fly on his own when he's never tried before, he now folds his wings and dies a little bit every day from the atrophy that sets into his fearful soul. Parents, in the name of love, may conspire with him to make excuses why he should stay in the nest.

Out-of-control Teens

Marge appeared in my office sporting a badly blackened eye. I knew that she had made an appointment to talk about her fifteen-year-old son, Craig, so I suspected the black eye had something to do with him.

"Yes," she admitted, "Craig gave me this eye Saturday night when I told him that he was grounded and was not going out. He just laughed in my face. When he headed for the door, I stood in his way, and he shoved me. When I shoved him back, he hauled off and punched me and walked out the door."

I asked if she went to the police to get a warrant for his arrest. No, she hadn't. "If I were to do that," she objected, "can you imagine how bad things would get then?"

Norma was more fortunate. Her thirteen-year-old daughter, Melissa, only verbally abused her. "Bitch" was Melissa's favorite name for her mother. Norma had come to see me because Melissa was a chronic runaway and truant. Melissa wouldn't run far. Whenever she and her mother had a blowup, she'd find friends to stay with and might drop out of sight for a day or several days.

A great number of these "power-drunk" teens are coming from single-parent homes, usually headed by mothers who have no support in managing their teenagers. These teens, even girls, are often bigger and physically stronger than their mothers.

One Connecticut therapist says of the parents, "Many seem to be intimidated by their kids. They often preset very rigid values, while at the same time being too permissive in the behavior they allow their children."[4]

What's a Mother to Do?

Intimidated mothers seeking therapy are fearful. They explain that if they have the teen arrested for assault, "Things will get worse." But how much worse can things get? Moreover, by doing nothing about it, they are doing the worst thing they can do. They reinforce the teens' belief that the parents and courts are powerless to control them.

If the police seem reluctant to take seriously domestic disputes, even assault, it is because they have learned by experience that more often than not there is no follow-through. Either the mother doesn't press charges or, if she does, she drops the matter before it comes to court.

All states have some provision in juvenile law for a teenager out of control, although the method of enforcement may vary from state to state. The state usually has a family court system that hears the cases and decides whether the teen is enough of a problem to be institutionalized, sent to a foster home, or sent home under the eye of the court.

Family Court Judge Alexander Strange II of Michigan has found it helpful to make it plain to both parents and children that parents have rights too and that the court will assist them in making reasonable rules. Judge Strange says, "Sometimes a statement about parental rights is a revelation to the parents as well as the kids who believe they can do anything."[5] But the parent must take the initiative and be determined to take no more abuse from the child.

What a Counselor Cannot Do

Sometimes a mother in desperation will consult a counselor. It may be a psychiatrist, psychologist, social worker, or family therapist. The desperate parent hopes that by some magic of psychotherapy the therapist can "fix" the child.

Sometimes the child will agree to therapy and may spend many hours with the therapist talking about "problems." But often it is a sham. The teen strings the parent and therapist along, saying what he thinks they want him to say, but nothing is changed.

The experienced therapist will quickly recognize this pattern and take a new direction in therapy. The benefit of *family* therapy is that the teen is not treated as "the indicated patient." It is the family as a system that is sick. The need is not only for the teen to accept limits to his behavior but also for the parent to set limits and do whatever is legally permissible to accomplish the task of controlling the teen. A therapist cannot "fix" a troubled teen. Nor can he do what the parent must do—be courageous enough to set limits and be willing to go to court if necessary. It often helps the parent to know that the therapist is going to be supportive, and it helps the teen to know that Mom or Dad is being coached to be firmer. But in the final analysis, only the parent can do what is necessary. If a parent goes into therapy, he should go with the purpose of getting *family* therapy and with the resolve that he must be willing to take a tough approach to the problem.

Sometimes the question is raised, "Should the noncustodial parent be included?" Yes, if the parent will be cooperative and not use the occasion to show "what a rotten parent the custodial parent is." The therapist has to make this decision.

Toughlove and Teens

A lot has been written in recent years about the organization called "Toughlove," founded by professional counselors David and Phyllis York. The Yorks, parents of three daughters, founded the organization after a traumatic episode in 1976. Police came to their home with shotguns and a warrant for their eighteen-year-old daughter, who was charged with holding up a cocaine dealer. It struck the Yorks that something had to be done about their daughter who was out of control.[6]

The Triumph of Toughlove

As a result of their experience, the Yorks founded the organization. The idea is basically this: parents, in dealing with teens who are constantly in trouble, will find that understanding and forgiveness don't work. These are important qualities in dealing with teens generally, but have no effect on those who are out of control. Toughlove parents are encouraged to draw the line on unacceptable behavior and back it up by restricting the use of car and phone and refusing to bail out the teen if he gets in trouble with the school authorities or police. If the teen consistently breaks curfew, the parent may lock him out of the house and post on the front door the names of other Toughlove parents who are willing to take in the offender until he is willing to live by the rules. A teen with a drug habit may come home to find his bags packed and advised to get into a drug rehabilitation program or to find another place to live.

Family therapists use variations of this technique in counseling troubled teens and their families. The teen usually complains that his freedom is being encroached upon by the parent and that, if he had somewhere to go, he'd leave so fast that "all they'd see is my dust." The therapist, taking the teen at his word, should say, "I may just be able to help you."

In conference with the parents he should point out that the teen is out of control and should be told that they will agree to his making his break from home. The parents may object that terrible things may happen to their teen out there in the cruel world. I point out that it is unlikely that anything is going to happen which has not already happened or will happen with the teen living at home out of control—even sex, drugs, and alcohol. All the parent is being asked to do is employ the Al-Anon technique of refusing to pick up the mess that the teen makes of his life. The parent refuses, in Al-Anon terms, to be an "enabler." The message clearly is this: "We love you, but there's nothing we can do. We therefore give you your freedom."

In thirty-five years of parenting and twenty-five years of family therapy, I have yet to see this approach fail—if the parents are really serious. It creates a therapeutic paradox. Given the freedom to do what he has been insisting on, the teen now has an opportunity to take a second look and decide whether this is really what he wants. Invariably he decides that home and parent aren't so bad after all. If he does choose to leave, he usually decides to return home—and obey the rules. The exception is the older teen who is ready to make the break from home anyway.

David York recalls his work with seriously troubled youths in California in 1970. He said, "I started out being this nice therapist: 'let me listen; let me daddy you guys.' And what really needs to happen is to grab these kids and say, 'You really can't do that. You've got to follow the rules here, and if you don't, we're going to call the police and have you locked up!' "

Susan, a Toughlove mother, said, "It's just old-fashioned discipline, where the parents run the home and there's cooperation among the family members." Susan had turned in her son Jeff, seventeen, to the police after he admitted he burglarized a home to support his drug habit. He was put in a rehabilitation program and is now back home and attending Narcotics and Alcoholics Anonymous.

Judy, age fourteen, ran away twice before her parents joined Toughlove. One of the other parents in the group became Judy's advocate and negotiated a contract between Judy and her parents: no drugs, alcohol, or cigarettes in the house; chores are done; an allowance is given; privacy in her room is guaranteed. The advocate calls periodically to see how the contract is working out.

Judy's response was positive: "Toughlove helped my parents understand what I was going through, and I could understand what they were going through. We can talk now, and we really get along."[7]

Phyllis York says that the typical Toughlove teen is caught up in dependence-independence games with the parents. "Drugs, alcohol, all that whole life-style is nothing but a false kind of independence, while these teens really have been caught in a state of dependence. They do not feel that they have the skills to deal with life on their own."[8] Parents interested in the book *Toughlove* and in starting a Toughlove group should write to P.O. Box 70, Sellersville, PA 18960.

Why Toughlove Works

The reason why Toughlove works is that it is based on the principles of family and social behavior that God has laid down in His creation. These principles were established both in government and in the family after the Noahic flood described in Genesis 6—9.

The Book of Genesis makes it clear that God destroyed the human race by flood because of its wickedness (Gen. 6:11–13). After the flood waters receded, God reestablished the human race through Noah's family, promising not to destroy the earth again by flood. But man was to accept the responsibility to govern himself, going so far as to protect human life by executing the death penalty on murderers (Gen. 9:6). The apostle Paul's words echo this sentiment by reminding us that governmental authority is "an agent of wrath to bring punishment on the wrongdoer." (Rom. 13:4).

The family was another line of defense against evil in society. In fact, a child who assaulted his mother or father *had to be* put to death under Old Testament law (Exod. 21:15). Talk about Toughlove! There weren't any abusive children in those days—at least any who lived to tell about it!

The apostle Paul again takes up this theme when he warns children to obey and honor their parents "that it may go well with you and that you may enjoy long life on the earth" (Eph. 6:3). This warning is based on the doctrine of "sin unto death." The person who willfully persists in sin is in danger of having his life taken from him by God (1 John 5:16). The government did not execute the death penalty on abusive children in Paul's day, but children were in danger of being dealt with directly by God. This is undoubtedly what Paul has in mind in Ephesians 6.

All this may be too much for the fainthearted parent to accept. He may cite the statistics of child abuse and say, "I don't want to be a child abuser." Toughlove is in no way child abuse. I suspect that the parent who throws up the child-abuse argument is really a fearful parent who wants to avoid confrontation. This parent is running a serious risk of damaging the teen far more by permitting *him* to be the abuser—whether physically or verbally.

Talking With Teens

Not all teenagers need the Toughlove approach. Some might communicate better if encouraged by the example of parents. This is not to minimize how difficult it is to have meaningful conversations with teens. It is true that at certain stages of development our teens are in states of equilibrium and are enjoyable, but the teen years are often a time of withdrawal and explosive anger—states of disequilibrium. How is it possible for a parent to have any meaningful contact with a teen at those times?

Two Principles of Communication

Parents must observe two principles of communication if they are to succeed.[9]

1. *The first task of communication is understanding, not agreement.* When we talk with our teens, we usually have a point of view that we want them to adopt as their own. The "talk" assumes more of a lecture or sermon than an exchange of information. Any resistance from the teen, verbal or nonverbal, makes us push the issue harder and we become more confrontational.

   When the teen resists what we are saying, he needs assurance that he doesn't need to see it our way, but we would like him to understand where we're coming from. In turn, we would like to know where he's coming from.

   Such a conversation might go this way: "Craig, I'd like to talk with you about something. May I have a few minutes with you?

   "Something has been bothering me that I've been wanting to talk about. When you came home the past few Saturday nights, I've smelled alcohol."

   At this point the teen may roll his eyes as if to say, "Here we go again," or become defensive and say, "I haven't been drinking anything!"

   The parent should continue low-keyed: "Please just hear me out. I'd merely like you to understand where I'm coming from. I worry a great deal about this, so much so that it's starting to interfere with my concentration at work. I understand that you say you're not drinking. I want to believe that. The reason I'm bringing this up is that I need something from you. I need to feel secure in knowing that when you're out with your friends you're not drinking. Can you help me?"

   The teen may continue to deny that he drinks with his friends, or he may accuse you of hassling him, or he may give you nothing but stony silence. But by approaching him in this manner, with an "I" message rather than a "you" message, you are creating the best atmosphere for communication. An "I" message reveals where you are and expresses the problem in terms of your own doubts and fears. A "you" message is accusatory and expresses the problem in terms of how bad the other person is—which leads to the second principle of communication.

2. *All communication is to be nonattacking and nondefensive.* By sending an "I" message rather than a "you" message, the conversation will sound less attacking. Try not to evaluate, judge, or present evidence that you are right. Simply express your feelings about the matter.

When the teen replies, try not to be defensive. Hear and understand what he is saying, and don't tell him that he's wrong. He is giving his perception of the matter, no matter how distorted you think it may be. He needs to know that he is heard and understood. Sometimes that is the solution—a feeling of being heard and understood. When we feel this way and live together in a spirit of good will, we feel that the person who *does* understand will be more considerate of our feelings.

Some Dos and Don'ts in Communicating

There is no guarantee that if you follow the two principles I have explained, everything will be fine. It is important to observe some other dos and don'ts when communicating with teens.

✔ *DO accept restlessness and discontent.* Remember that your teen is going through the most difficult period in his life. This is the period of breakaway where he's caught between feelings of dependence and independence. He is also unsure about who he is. He is very concerned about his self-image and whether or not he fits into his peer group. His apparent discontent with his family and his need to be with his peers are nothing personal.

✔ *DO differentiate between acceptance and approval.* We may accept a given situation or point of view without necessarily approving of it. For example, we may accept the fact that our teen has a particular taste in music without approving of it. The message of the songs may run contrary to our value system and what we have taught our teen, and we don't approve, but it's something that we can let go by.

✔ *DO be aware of the "hassle-factor"—learn that we must*

decide what is really important and not be on the teenager's back all the time about everything. Every human being has a limit to how much hassle he can take. If we can get a respectful attitude and maintain veto power over our teen's friends and activities, the rest will come in due time.

✔ *DO be aware of words that hurt, particularly those that call attention to the teen's personal flaws.* Remember that this is a time in the teen's life when he is terribly unsure about his self-image. Parents will often say thoughtless things like, "What? You've outgrown your jeans already? If you don't stop eating, you're going to be a blimp!" Or, "Quit squeezing those pimples on your face. It's already a mess!"

✔ *DON'T be too understanding.* While it is important for us to understand our teen's problems, his behavior still may be totally unacceptable. He may need to be understood. But you have a need for peace of mind and order in the house. Respect and rights are a two-way street. Parent and teen owe them to each other.

✔ *DON'T emulate his language or conduct.* Some parents, trying to get close to their teens, talk and act like teenagers. This only embarrasses your teen and his friends. You will always be a parent, which is a breed apart. You will get much further if you accept that role and fulfill it in a mature and sensitive way.

✔ *DON'T invite dependence.* Remember your teen is trying to break away. Let him make as many of his own choices as you can, if they are not permanently damaging and can be reversed. A bad choice may help the teen realize that he really doesn't know everything and that his judgment is still immature. Let him know that there are other options. But if he insists, let him learn from his mistake.

✔ *DON'T hurry to correct facts.* As pointed out earlier, the first task of communication is understanding, not agreement. The "facts" as the teen represents them are true as far as he is concerned. Correcting the facts too quickly will leave the impression that we're not listening.

When we express our own point of view we can say, "It's interesting that you see the situation as you do. I'm coming from somewhere else." Then you can explain how you see it with the attitude, "I'm here and you're there," rather than "I'm right and you're wrong."

✓ *DON'T, as a general rule, invade a teenager's privacy.* This is a general rule, and a good one because privacy is part of breaking away. But if you have reason to suspect drug or alcohol dependency or criminal behavior, then you may need evidence in order to take aggressive action. But this is only *a last resort.* Also, distinguish between substance *dependency* and *experimentation.* Most teenagers experiment. You will soon become aware of dependency if that is a problem. If you doubt whether you can recognize it, get some literature on alcohol and drug abuse and study it. You can get such literature from your local police department, library, or public school system.

✓ *DON'T preach or use clichés and platitudes.* Christian parents are some of the worst offenders. It is true that we have a value system that we cannot compromise, but preaching to our children is not an effective way to get them to hear. Leave the preaching to the preacher.

An example of a platitude is, "A person won't become an alcoholic if he refuses to take that first drink." That statement is true enough, but it is a platitude because there is far more to the issue of drinking and alcoholism than simply not taking the first drink. When our answers to problems are simplistic, we leave the impression that we're really out of touch with the world our teen lives in. He feels, "How can they help if they don't understand?"

✓ *DON'T label your teen.* A mother will make thoughtless remarks such as, "You're just like your father." Now "father" is her ex-husband, whom she has no use for and lets her son know it in no uncertain terms. When we label we may help our child decide who he is, and he may try to live up to that label.

✓ *DON'T send double messages.* "Have a good time," Mother says to her daughter as she's about to leave for her date, but she does it in such a way as to send a second message. "It's going to be quiet and lonely here tonight without you." This is one way parents manipulate their teens. They can get what they want without running the risk of asking for it and having the request denied. Or, if Mother is accused of being possessive, she can always say, "Didn't I tell you to go out and have a good time?" The teen may reply, "Yes, and you managed to do it in such a way that if I did I'd feel like a rat."

✔ *DON'T play the prophet.* The prophet says such things as, "You'll never amount to anything." This is similar to labeling, but it's a prophecy. We may encourage the teenager to fulfill that prophecy. If we must play the prophet, then let's prophesy good news: "You're going to turn out to be one fantastic woman!"

🧍🧍🧍 14

What the Church Can Do to Help

Not too many years ago the mainstay of the evangelical church was the two-parent family with two children where the father was the breadwinner and the mother was the homemaker. Today only 6 percent of American households fit this description. Ministry in the eighties and nineties must take into account the tremendous changes in the American family if we are to reach people where they are and not where they used to be.

One of these great changes, as we have seen in this book, is the single-parent explosion. It is being felt in our churches. One Chicago church reports that singles make up 60 percent of its membership.[1] Though many churches are ministering to singles in general, the specific needs of single parents must be identified.

Greater Awareness Needed

Ministry to singles is a relatively new venture in the church. Ministry to single parents is even newer. The church that wants to minister effectively to *all* its people must be aware of significant differences among them and seek to meet their various needs.

"Wed and Misled"

Singles have been doing a good job of getting the message to the church that they have felt treated as stepchildren—or worse. They are very sensitive, for example, to the names given to singles groups in the church. One group, made up of couples and singles, was called "Pairs and Spares." One of the singles objected and said that a "spare" is by definition something you keep on the shelf until needed—superfluous. Singles already sense enough of this without having a label to go along with it. This single suggested some other names for singles groups that might be equally insulting, such as "Riced and Iced" or "Wed and Misled."[2] Churches are beginning to realize that the differences between married couples and singles are great and that those differences need to be recognized. These differences are not too noticeable in corporate worship and Bible study groups. But they are conspicuous in fellowship groups, workshops, and seminars.

The debate over whether singles ought to be "mainstreamed" (made part of the larger church fellowship) or ministered to separately is answered by determining what type of ministry we're talking about. They ought to be mainstreamed in programs where differences are of little consequence, such as corporate worship. But in social life and family-life education, they have different needs than two-parent families. For example, sex and the single person, being whole as a single person, the single person's identity are topics that need to be targeted especially to the nonmarried.

Just as single people have needs that differ from married people, single parents with dependent children have needs that differ from other singles such as the never-married or the formerly married who never had children or whose children are out of the nest. *To ignore the differences within the singles ministry can make ministry to singles in general and single parents in particular ineffective.*

Sixty-Year-Old-Divorcees Welcome

A case in point is a singles group highlighted by the *Single i* newsletter. The report, evidently prepared by one of the group's leaders, said, "As to age, we're composed of people from post-high school up to 45, with most being in the 20 to 30 range.

We're about half college, half career type persons, *and the sixty year old divorcee is invited and welcome as well*"[3] [italics mine]. I'll bet she feels welcome! This group is doing to the poor old divorcee what couples have been accused of doing to singles for years—treating her as a fifth wheel. But this is to be expected when we fail to recognize important differences among singles themselves. My guess is that the singles group described above is made up mainly of never-marrieds and a few younger divorcees. The majority of those in the group would probably marry if the right person came along.

This points up another important difference among singles. There are some singles who enjoy their singleness and have no intention of marrying, and there are others who want marriage and are aggressively pursuing it. Where this tension exists, the group suffers. On the surface their Bible studies and social life are very compatible, but there is a certain amount of tension. In terms of interpersonal psychology, there is a *hidden agenda*. The group's members simply don't face the fact that the group is made up of these disparate elements, and they need to deal with it head-on.

It is important to recognize, therefore, that single parents have needs that differ from other singles. The single parent with custody is more than likely a woman between twenty and forty who is struggling financially, needs adequate day care for her child, and needs relief from the dual burden of being breadwinner and parent. To group her together with other singles may meet some social needs but not specific single-parent needs. Unless the church recognizes the great differences among its singles, its ministry is going to be ineffective.

Assessing The Needs of Single Parents

Before the church can minister effectively to single parents, their needs must be assessed. Many of their needs can be anticipated by their status—whether they are divorced with custody or without custody, widowed, or never married—and other criteria such as age, sex, and income. After identifying the needs, we can determine how much can be met by mainstreaming and how much must be met by a separate program for single parents.

How to Make an Assessment.

Every church has singles. What do we look for when making an assessment? How are we able to meet the needs of a group made up of never-married young people who wish to marry and single parents with dependent children who don't wish to marry again?

As a data base I will use the "New Friends Directory" published in the Fall 1983 issue of *Solo* magazine. The directory offers information on 108 singles—66 women and 42 men.

The magazine states that the purpose of the directory, in which readers advertise, is to help people make Christ-centered *friendships*. Though they realize that the directory may result in date- or mate-finding opportunities, that is not the purpose. The magazine offers its readers an opportunity to:

- Share common interests
- Encourage and build up one another
- Dialogue on ideas/opinions
- Give advice
- Provide prayer support
- Meet people across the country or around the world
- Locate vacation/traveling companions
- Build relationships with like-minded Christians
- Promote Christian growth in another believer

These are all objectives worthy of a singles group in a church. If this were such a group, what could be said about the group as a whole, and what common needs are represented that a church might meet? Are any single-parent needs revealed? An assessment reveals several outstanding facts about this group.

1. *Interest in dates and mates. Solo* says its goal is to facilitate friendship, which involves common interests and Christian commitment, but the overwhelming interest of the group is dating and mating. Of the sixty-six women who responded, only three stated that their sole interest is a pen pal and not dating or marriage. These woman were aged eighteen, nineteen, and thirty. One woman, who did not give her age, said

she wanted to be an "intercessor"—just wants to pray for singles and their needs.

Of the 42 men in the group, 3 stated they want pen pals only. One was age twenty-one, one was incarcerated and did not give his age, and one (no age given) was interested in corresponding with either men or women.

I do not criticize *Solo* or the friends directory when I point out that the prime interest is dating or mating. In fact, the magazine is providing a valuable service. The point is that a singles group may *state* that its objectives are Christian fellowship, friendship, and mutual edification in the faith. But the opportunity to find a suitable date or mate is irresistible. This opportunity may be both bane and blessing. It is a bane to those who want just want friendship but find that the "friend" is always pushing for more. It is a blessing to those who want an opportunity to find a Christian mate.

Singles groups might remind their members that some do not wish to marry (or remarry). To push for marriage when only friendship is wanted shows insensitivity and can lead to divisiveness in the group.

2. *Status of the women.* Of the 66 women who replied, 4 were widows, 12 were divorced, 24 were never married, and 26 did not state why they were single. The majority of the "n/s" (not stated) group were probably never-marrieds with a few more divorcees. Only 3 divorced and 1 n/s woman stated they have dependent children.

The addition of the men to the equation didn't change the single-parent-with-custody picture. One widower had several adopted children and 2 other men wanted to marry and have children. One stated he wanted no children.

If this group is evaluated from the standpoint of ministry to the single-*custodial* parent, the need is minimal numerically. Of 108 people, only 5 said they were custodial parents. However, a ministry to parents without custody may be needed. Nine divorced women and 6 divorced men said nothing about children; they may not have any or may not be custodians. Also, a number of men and women who are n/s may be divorced parents without custody. If this were a profile of a church group, a query in the church bulletin would be in or der. It would state that plans are being made for workshops for parents without custody, and ask those who are interested to give the church office their names and addresses.

3. *Status of the men.* Of the 42 men who replied, 1 was a widower (with several adopted children), 6 were divorced, 16 were never married, and 19 did not state why they were single (n/s). I suspect that most of the n/s group of men were never married, but with a higher proportion of divorced than among the women.

4. *Age groupings of respondents.* The average age of all the women was 36. Of the men, the average was 34. Most of the women who stated an age preference for a mate were willing to consider a man anywhere from 1 to 9 years younger than they and anywhere from 4 to 17 years older. The biggest surprise was their interest in younger men.

Most of the men who expressed an age preference for a mate stayed with tradition. They were looking for women considerably younger than they, in one case up to 34 years younger. Three men would consider women 2, 3, and 6 years older than they. Perhaps they are signaling a break in the tradition of the older man seeking a younger woman.

Summary of Assessment

The information given by this group enables us to make an educated guess about the kind of program they would need if they were a church group. Most have marriage in mind. The group would look for social opportunities to get to know each other as potential mates rather than mere friends. Bible studies, aside from generally good spiritual growth opportunities, would need to include the subject of singleness versus marriage. Workshops and seminars would need to include the same. Some in the group would marry (or remarry) and may need direction in preparation for marriage. Others would not marry, though they want to, and would need to consider singleness from both the biblical and psychological viewpoints—particularly singleness that they don't want. The burning question for these people would be, "What do you do when you don't want to be single?" One of the answers would be to advertise in *Solo*.

The need of a *program* for single-custodial parents in this group appears to be minimal. A program for parents without custody may be needed; this possibility would be explored if this were a church group. Individual needs are expressed, such as the custodial mother with a ten-year-old-son "whose father has forsaken him." This would be dealt with through individual pastoral care or on a "Big Brother" basis rather than through a program.

The need for a program for widows is not evident, though ministry to the person widowed for just one-and-a-half years might be met by the other widows. Each widow would be contacted individually to determine personal needs.

This group is perhaps less typical than a cross section of a local church. But it illustrates that evaluation begins with who is in the group and what their needs are. Program is dictated by need.

The church should not be shortsighted, however. What about the needs of unsaved and unchurched single parents? The church has an excellent opportunity to reach them through its educational program, and if it does not have a day-care center, one might be started as an outreach to single parents. Most church facilities are under-used yet are equipped for day care. A day-care program would not only meet needs but also help pay the mortgage.

An efficient way of reaching out to the community is by newspaper and telephone. The United Methodist Church has enjoyed great success in reaching singles through newspaper ads. Samples can be found in appendix D.[4] The only change I would suggest is that the church's phone number be included in the ads.

When singles call the church, they should be given information on the church's ministry to singles, and their name and address should be obtained for a singles mailing. If the church has no singles program, it can organize a get-acquainted activity and advertise it in the newspaper. Remember to include parents without custody. How about bold-print copy that reads LONG DISTANCE PARENT and says something about the difficulty of being a parent without custody, particularly when the child is far away? The ad could announce a seminar in the church for noncustodial parents. Another might read SATURDAY FATHER AND SON, a takeoff on the Barry Manilow song. It would be geared toward the noncustodial parent who sees the child only on weekends. Again, this could be used to introduce a seminar for parents without custody.

At these get-togethers or seminars, registration cards should be given to the attendees. The cards should ask for name, address, phone number, age, single status (divorced, widowed, never married), ages of dependent children, whether the parent is custodial or noncustodial, and what needs the single parent has. Offer suggestions such as day care, adequate housing, AFDC information, Big Brother/Sister program, effective parenting education, single-parent support group, divorce recovery group, loss and grief support group or seminar, and other needs.

Another need the church can fulfill is an after-school program for latchkey children. This would be for children of single parents and children who have two working parents.

A questionnaire could be included in the church bulletin to assess the needs. See appendix E for a sample.[5]

Churches Successful With Singles

Some churches are successful with their single ministries while other ministries die. Why is this?

Six Mistakes to Avoid

Churches that are successful avoid six mistakes common to churches that fail.

1. *Lack of support and understanding by the senior pastor, church staff, and congregation at large.* Encouragement for the ministry must come from the top down. If the senior pastor doesn't take it seriously, why should anyone else?[6] This doesn't mean that he must be involved actively or even directly promote it. He can use singles in general or single parents in particular in a positive way in his sermon illustrations. He can set aside a particular Sunday to recognize single parents. Does he view singles as whole people with lives and gifts of their own, or are they just in a holding pattern waiting to get married? Are single parents, particularly divorcees, an

embarrassment, or are they capable of being adequate parents with the support of the church as an extended family?

2. *Lack of money because through lack of vision a singles ministry was not included in the budget.* An adequate singles program requires money.[7] As pointed out earlier, a day-care center in the church facility is one way to fund a program for single parents. Seminars, workshops, and groups that use marriage and family therapists and psychologists as leaders and facilitators can be operated on a pay-as-you-go basis. A modest registration fee could be charged to cover the speaker's expenses with a little money from the budget to cover any shortfall.

3. *Fad.* If a church is attempting to run a singles program because everyone has one, it is bound to fail.[8] We don't start with a program; we start with a need and build a program to meet that need. The need may already exist in the church. It definitely exists in most communities, and your community can be reached by some imaginative, aggressive promotion.

4. *Lack of leadership.* Leaders are difficult to find. Good ones take responsibility and initiative with little prodding from the top. Leaders also require training. A leadership retreat is one way to develop leaders.[9] Many men are discouraged from attending programs because too many women occupy leadership roles. Leadership needs to be divided between men and women.[10]

5. *Lack of a balanced program.* A once-a-month potluck and a Sunday morning singles class is not a complete or balanced program. A balanced program includes Bible teaching, small group discussions, a wide variety of social events, retreats, conferences, and specialty seminars. Give your leaders a chance to use new and innovative ideas.[11]

6. *Lack of a long-range program.* Many groups have no idea what they are going to do more than two weeks in advance. If professionals or well-known speakers are going to participate effectively, they need to know in advance what is going to be done.[12] A program that meets needs must have a plan of execution.

Some Pointers on Programming

A solid program has "four prongs of ministry," according to Jim Smoke, singles' pastor at First Presbyterian Church in Hollywood, California.

First, it must have a biblical base. It must rest on solid biblical teaching that is integrated into everyday life and experience.[13] Bible study ought to be geared to the special needs of singles. Opportunity for Bible study on the wider aspects of the Christian life is available in the church at large; but the singles' Bible studies should be addressing issues pertinent to various aspects of single life.

Second, the program should include small groups such as prayer groups that focus on the special needs of the singles in that group, and sharing or support groups where singles can voice their concerns to those who are in tune with singles' needs.

Third, social structure is important. Christian singles often feel a lack of attachment. Most of them have no family nearby with whom they can enjoy social life and affirmation. The church, particularly the singles group, becomes their extended family. Activities on weekends and holidays are especially important.[14] Aloneness is keenly felt at these times.

Finally, it should provide educational workshops and seminars to deal with practical needs.[15] For the single parent these practical needs may include single-parenting skills, how to be a long-distance parent (for parents without custody), child-care skills for young single mothers, car care for single women—the list goes on. Ask single parents to express what subjects they would like offered in workshops.

Single parents can be mainstreamed with other singles in some social activities and some workshops. Support groups and Bible studies need to be geared to their special needs. A special resource center, perhaps the church library, could amass information needed by single parents, such as how to apply for food stamps, how to apply for Aid to Families with Dependent Children, where to find low-cost housing that accepts children, clinics that give low-cost medical and dental care, and recommended day-care facilities, both home-based and center-based. An information packet could be developed for every new single parent coming into the church along with the name of the deacon or elder who will give oversight.

Because of the mobility of singles, singles groups have a high turnover rate—from 30 to 80 percent annually.[16] Therefore flexibility is important.

Developing qualified leaders is another need. They are often chosen on the basis of availability and popularity.[17]

"Leadership is no accident," says Jim Smoke. "It is trained. Your leaders need to be a closely knit team to have an effective ministry and program. A clear definition of 'who does what' will give you clear sailing for months ahead. If people cannot do their jobs, offer to let them out and replace them with people who can."[18]

Smoke recommends selecting new leaders every six months and holding weekend training seminars each time a new group is installed.

Highlights of Two Successful Churches

Single Point Ministries in the Detroit metropolitan area is part of the ministry of Ward Presbyterian Church of Livonia, Michigan. Started around 1978, Single Point developed a wide variety of activities for singles. It is based on a nucleus of fifty-five singles who lead various aspects of the ministry, which now reaches more than a thousand single adults.[19]

Each week eight to ten small groups meet to study the Bible or a contemporary Christian book. The meetings are led by single adults in homes. A bimonthly Friday night meeting includes a 6:30 supper followed by a program at 8:00. It is geared to reach out to new single adults. Meetings feature a variety of personalities and activities such as drama, music, and a message pertinent to singles.[20]

The ministry is divided into four specific groups: young single adults, singles thirty and up, "New Beginnings" for widows and widowers, and a single-parents ministry.[21]

Trips and tours form another important part of the ministry. Trips are planned to points of interest that cover just a day or weekend. Every September these include a journey to the Shakespeare Festival in Stratford, Ontario.[22]

Another successful ministry is at the St. Stephens Church of

God in Christ in San Diego, California. The philosophy of the singles ministry there is that the church should minister to the total person—the human nature as well as the spiritual nature—a good philosophy in view of the fact that we are twice-born people.[23]

The church does not have one singles' pastor. All the pastors rotate responsibilities, and much of the leadership comes from the group itself.[24]

Small prayer groups, potluck dinners in homes around the city, weekly educational activities, and a full calendar of social events typify what goes on at St. Stephens.[25] Two major retreats are held each year. One is in San Diego, the other out of town. "Mini-conferences" are held on such subjects as divorce recovery, single parenthood, and relating as men and women. Because San Diego is a Navy town, many married women in the church are "single" for six to nine months while their husbands are at sea. Programs are available to help them as "single parents."

Four Programs for Single Parents and Their Children

It has been stated several times in this chapter that program is based on need. Here are some programs, based on need, that can be helpful to single parents and their children. This is not an exhaustive list; rather, these are mentioned to give churches and their leadership some ideas of what can be done for single parents with different methods of organization and leadership.

The "single-parents group" relies on grass-roots organization. The "Christian big brothers and big sisters" program requires more professional direction, as does the "communication workshop." The "widowed group" may use a combination of grass-roots organization with a professional facilitator, or both organization and facilitation from the grass roots.

These groups were chosen as examples because they express the essence of biblical Christianity. "Religion that God our Father accepts as pure and faultless is this: to look after orphans and widows in their distress and to keep oneself from being polluted by the world" (James 1:27).

Single-Parents Group

One of the strengths of the New Testament church was hom
grown leadership. The apostle Paul told Titus that older wom
ought to train younger women to be good homemakers and mode
of Christian maturity (Titus 2:4). It doesn't take a college
seminary education to do that. It takes emotional and spiritu
maturity.

Single-parents groups are designed to provide emotional su
port, an idea-sharing network, and the sharing of experience
successful single parents.[26] It may involve everything from hc
to give a newborn baby a bath to how to handle a troubleson
teenager. It may also provide a sharing of child-sitting servic
or other support services essential to the single parent. T
strengths of such a group are a common task and familiarity wi
the needs of single parents. By banding together in a network a
becoming acquainted, the single parents are able to draw frc
each other's strengths on a regular or as-needed basis. For e
ample, what do single parents do when they must go to wor
but their child is sick and the day-caregiver does not accept si
children? A single-parent network can offer great assistance.

1. *Where to start?* If you are a single parent, don't shy aw
   from taking a leadership role. Parent groups are easy to st
   and quite spontaneous once a core of charter members is e
   tablished. The local church is an excellent place to begin. C
   permission to advertise in the worship bulletin, in the chur
   paper, and on bulletin boards that you are interested in heari
   from single parents who want to start a group. Those w
   respond will help make the decision as to the focus of t
   group. If they are chiefly women with small children, t
   focus of the group will be on their needs. Remember, *nee
   dictates program.* Three parents are enough to get started.
   you talk with others about the group, you will be surpris
   how well-known it becomes.

2. *The first meeting.* In the beginning when the group is sma
   the parents usually meet in each other's homes. Rotati
   meeting places may help all to alleviate the burdens of
   sponsibility.

   As the group grows, get permission to use the church fac

ities. A meeting room is needed as well as child care for parents who are unable to find sitters for their children. A small contribution by each parent may pay for the services of a child-caregiver who uses the church facilities.

The purpose of the first meeting is to assess the needs of the group and to explore ways of helping each other. The appeal of this kind of group is that no one formula needs to be followed, and it allows for the maximum creativity of all the participants with a minimum of external leadership.

Time of the meetings and their frequency will depend on the members' schedules. Since most single parents work during daytime hours, the meetings most likely will be held in the evenings. But the group decides what is best.

At the first meeting each person should be given opportunities to say why she or he is there, to relate personal experiences and problems of adjusting to single parenting, to express expectations regarding the group, and to indicate in what direction she or he would like to see the group go. It is important that all express their needs and hopes.[27]

Common interest soon becomes evident. For some, just talking with other single parents is enough. Others will want a more formal structure with programs and rotating discussion leaders or facilitators. Others may want to study certain subjects or invite professionals to conduct workshops. Some will want to use the group as a clearing house for information about all the support services for single parents in the community. The group will take form as needs are defined.[28]

This kind of definition is essential early in the group's formation. Many groups put together a statement of purpose to guide their activities and alert new members to what the group is about. Such statements are best left broad and open-ended. A general emphasis on mutual support and self-help is best.[29]

3. *Leadership.* After the first meeting, someone must take leadership if there is to be a second meeting. Usually the person who organized the first meeting will help the group plan for and organize the second meeting. Titles are unnecessary at this point. This person is simply a "facilitator." Permit the organization to emerge in a way that fits the personality of the group and the personalities of the people in it. Organization

that is too rigid too soon can inhibit the spontaneity of the group and limit the direction of its growth.

Group discussions are important during the first few meetings. Remember that all participants need to be heard from if the group is to develop into an organization that meets needs.

The discussion group will need someone to keep track of the time and place of the meetings and to see that meetings convene and end on time and provide opportunities for *all* to speak. Some members may be more verbal and tend to monopolize the time if permitted. The less verbal ones will not speak unless encouraged.

It may help to have rotating facilitators—a different person made responsible each week.[30]

Rather than construct a formal organization, let leaders emerge as needed. One organization operated on the premise "If you come with an idea, leave with a job." Usually the person who suggests an idea will be willing to follow through with the organization's support. Some groups use the term "coordinator" to describe the person taking a particular responsibility."[31]

4. *How big should the group be?* A group that depends on the interaction of all of its members should not exceed twenty. When the membership increases beyond that, the group should be divided into smaller units. They can be grouped according to location of the members and be facilitated by an experienced single-parent member. Limiting the size of the group permits a closer bond and does away with the tendency of timid members to hold back and not participate.

If more than one group is established, a coordinator can be appointed to link the groups through newsletter and periodic get-togethers for inspiration, social interaction, and idea sharing. Sometimes groups grow large enough to federate and gain media recognition for funding and attracting prominent professionals as speakers or advisers. One such federation is the Childbirth and Parent Education Association (CPEA) of Madison, Wisconsin. It attracts parents from a countywide area through a variety of smaller group programs.[32]

Or, the single-parents group could fashion itself after Family Focus, Inc., of Evanston, Illinois. They have a drop-in center where parents can stop and talk with other parents or participate in educational and recreational activities.[33]

Another group that is providing a useful service is the Buckeye Singles Council. This organization acts as a clearing house for all singles activities in the Columbus, Ohio, area. They publish an excellent directory.[34]

Your ability to fill your special needs is limitless. Perhaps your group would like to start a baby-sitting co-op or a child-rearing discussion group based on certain literature. How about a clothing or toy exchange, a toddler play group, or a baby-sitting pool to hire baby sitters so the group can enjoy an outing together?

Whatever you decide, there are other groups around the nation anxious to share their experiences. Appendix F entitled "More Resources for Self-Help Groups" will give your group additional ideas.

5. *Funding*. Foundation grants are usually not available to small groups. But don't overlook other ways to raise money: a bake sale, a parking lot sale featuring children's clothes and toys, or a fashion show featuring maternity wear or children's wear.

The simplest way to spread the word is through the church's internal information channels such as the worship bulletin, church newsletter, and bulletin boards. It helps to advertise in your community with mimeographed fliers. Local newspapers will often include such events in their community calendar. Generally a 10-percent response can be expected on publicity of this type. You will have to estimate what to charge at your fund raiser to cover your costs. Sometimes local businessmen will donate to a worthy cause such as a single-parents group. Finally, modest dues may be needed. It is hoped that the church will catch the vision of a single-parents group and budget money for it. But don't let lack of church budget support discourage you. If the church will let the group use the facilities, that's a valuable contribution.

6. *Opportunities unlimited*. Parents groups that learn to organize without professional leaders can inspire and educate the church to the possibilities of other groups such as divorce recovery and bereaved singles (for widows and widowers). Senior pastors, their staffs, and church officers are always pleased to see

initiative come from the congregation. Generally the staff have more ideas than they can put into service, so instead of ideas they want people who have a need and are motivated to do something about it with a little help and encouragement.

Christian Big Brothers and Big Sisters

A program modeled after the eighty-year-old Big Brothers/Big Sisters of America could become Christian Big Brothers and Big Sisters (CBB/BS).

There is a growing need for adult Christian role models to befriend children in single-parent families. The church needs to encourage its members, both male and female, to help fill this need by participating as Big Brothers or Big Sisters.

A concerned and frustrated single mother seeking a male role model for her son underscores this need in the following letter:

> I just got off the phone with Big Brothers/Big Sisters of America. I was told that if I was a single parent (I am) and my son was seven years old (he will be in June) that I could fill out an application for a Big Brother and then face a wait of anywhere from six months to six years. You see, they have a shortage of Big Brothers.
>
> A shortage? How could there be so many upstanding, caring, understanding Christian men in this world and there be a shortage of men who want to put a little happiness and friendship into the life of a boy who, at no fault of his own, has no father to speak of?
>
> My question is: Why should I have to go to Big Brothers to find a companion for my son? Because I can't find anyone in my church or place of employment who wants to make time for him. . . . Is it that they are so busy with their own lives that they have no time for anyone else? . . .[35]

Christian Big Brothers and Big Sisters (CBB/BS) differs in its organization from a single-parent group in that it requires more attention from the pastoral staff or outside professionals who may be hired to start it up and then act as supervisors or advisers. I differs from the secular program in that it subscribes to a particular value system. The Christian Big Brothers and Sisters are screened to determine whether they are born-again Christians and are mature enough in the faith not only to share a salvation message with a youngster, but also to model the Christian life. They are also screened to determine *balance*—they know how to model wholesome human growth as well. They are aware that Christian children are twice-born people and therefore need a healthy example who models wholesome humanity and spirituality. Their role model is Jesus Christ, the God-man.

The ministry is directed toward children six to fourteen years old living in single-parent families. The volunteer must be:

1. Eighteen years old or older
2. Willing to make at least a six-month commitment
3. Willing to spend three to six hours a week with the child

The CBB/BS commitment is shorter than that of the secular organization, but given the mobility of singles, it is more reasonable. For example, a college student may become a CBB/BS, but have plans to return home for the summer, which may be eight or nine months away. This would allow him to participate. The terms of the commitment can also be negotiated and renewed. Here are some other guidelines for the program:

1. *If the pastoral staff does not feel competent to start such a program, train CBB/BSs, oversee them, and hire a Christian professional from the community on an hourly or flat-rate basis.* Have him make a proposal as to type of program, training, supervision of workers, and fee for services. The church may find it possible to get professional services at a much lower price than hiring another associate minister or staff person. The type of professional who might run such a program would be a psychologist, social worker, or marriage and family therapist.

2. *Workers.* Advertise in the church for CBB/BS, and provide those interested with an interest-response card that does not commit them but lets them know when the next orientation is to be held.

3. *Orientation.* At the orientation, the program is explained to the respondents and an opportunity is given for them to ask questions and decide whether or not they want to be part of it. Those who do should be given an application. The form used by Big Brothers and Sisters of America may be used as a guide.[36]

   All Little Brothers and Sisters together with parents should attend the orientation. Everyone needs to know what is expected. After information about the program is given, parental concerns can be aired and feelings about the program and its goals can be shared.

4. *Christian Big Brother and Sister interview.* After the potential CBB/BS applies to become a worker, the program leader interviews the applicant to determine strengths and weaknesses and what type of child would be the best "match." This is also the time when an "inappropriate" applicant can be directed to another ministry. One essential feature of the screening process is a police-record check both in the current town of residence and the hometown. If the interviewer feels that the applicant should become involved, he or she is assigned to a training program.

5. *Home interview.* In addition to the CBB/BS interviewed, the parents and children interested in the program are also interviewed in their homes. This is a time when the program leaders are able to assess the child's interests and needs and the type of interaction the parent and child have.

6. *Training program.* This program should be designed to help the CBB/BS prepare for the kinds of problems he or she will be facing in the relationship. The applicants look at their own spiritual maturity, the needs and problems of their charges, and what support they can expect after the matches are made.

7. *Activities.* The Big-Little relationship is an individual one. Each pair are free to participate in whatever activities interest them. It is through activities that the CBB/BS shows the child he is loved and creates an atmosphere of trust in which the child can grow into a mature and responsible Christian adult. With the aid of the program leader, the CBB/BS be

comes friend, confidant, role model, problem solver, and guidance counselor.

8. *Contact with parent.* As much as possible a positive relationship should be built between the CBB/BS and the parent. It will help the parent monitor the Big-Little relationship and provide a better working relationship with the family. Sometimes the CBB/BS becomes friend and confidant to the parent as well.

9. *Follow-up.* It is the responsibility of the program leader to provide follow-up services to the Big-Little relationship after a match has been made. Any problems should be solved before they affect the relationship. A leader should be available as a supervisor at all times to give guidance to the CBB/BS.

10. *Evaluation.* At the end of the period of commitment the CBB/BSs and their charges evaluate their relationships and decide whether or not to continue for another period of commitment. It may be advisable for the program leader to interview each person separately, including parents.

11. *CBB/BS council.* This council is responsible, under the direction of the program leader, to plan and carry out group activities such as picnics, parties, and retreats. This gives all the workers an opportunity to get to know each other and share ideas.

In setting up the program the leader may want to check with philanthropic foundations as to whether funds are available for such a venture.

It is recognized that the key to establishing a program such as this is *leadership*. Take advantage of community resource people and use them to help put a program together and train church leaders.

Communication Workshop

While I was in the pastorate I led a number of communication workshops in my church. They were given this name because it is less threatening than "sharing group." People are interested in communication, but sometimes they are uneasy about sharing feelings, though this is a stated objective of the group.

The group is best led by a facilitator with some training in group dynamics. However, participants with spiritual gifts in this area can quickly learn the principles of facilitating such a group. After leading a group I would personally select promising members and ask them to co-facilitate new groups with me. I would also put them on a reading program of books on the group process. An information sheet on communication workshops is circulated to all interested persons. A sample is found in appendix G.

Group for the Widowed

The church has always had a place in its heart for widows. This concern has its origins in the Hebrew institution of *leviratus*—the marriage of an heirless widow to her brother-in-law after the death of her husband.[37] By the time of the Pastoral Epistles the custom of levirate marriage had fallen into disuse, and the church took on the support of "real widows" (*ontos cherai*), widows who could not be supported by relatives.[38]

Today widows generally are better off financially than New Testament widows. But they still have a need to deal with their grief. Widowers, though they may not reveal this as readily, have the same need.

The purpose of this group is to allow people to share with each other the meaning of being widowed. Out of the sharing process, supportive bonds are established with others who are also suffering and can understand. The individual is helped to develop insight and courage to deal effectively with grief and the practical demands of being alone again.

The philosophies of these groups differ. Some are therapy groups run by professional therapists who facilitate in-depth grappling with grief. Others are run by laypeople who have recovered from the death of spouses. Other lay group facilitators could be trained in the same manner described for the communication workshops. They would be chosen from existing groups and asked to co-facilitate new groups. They would also be assigned a reading program of good books on group process. The group leader should spend some time "debriefing" the co-facilitators after the group has met to explain the group process they have just observed.

With adequate screening it is possible to run a group with a mature widow or widower as a facilitator. However, it should be made clear that it is only a sharing group and that the facilitator is not to attempt to do therapy. It is one thing for the bereaved to volunteer what is on the surface and ready to come out and another thing to go through the pain of therapy and disclose deep feelings that are difficult to bring up and fraught with deep emotion. This does not mean that tears will not be shed in such a group. They will.

A group led by a professional facilitator would be made up of approximately twelve widows and widowers. It would run for a stated period to avoid repetitiveness—usually six to twelve sessions. The group should then disband and regroup with new members and any former members who wish to continue. Some of the former members may find that they have facilitative skills and could be used as co-facilitators in new groups.

After a brief introduction to the group and a statement of confidentiality, each widowed person is asked to narrate the events that led to the death of the spouse. Each describes the circumstances of the death (what kind of accident or the length and type of illness), where the spouse died, memories of the last days or weeks or months, the funeral and the first few days following it, and anything else they feel is significant about the experience. These are the most dramatic sessions of the group. It may take more than one session to hear everyone's emotion-filled story.

One of the important supportive features of the group is the recognition and acknowledgment of situations or feelings by other members of the group. As the process of identification unfolds, the pain is lessened. One woman in a widows group said, "After listening to each lady tell her sad story, it suddenly became clear that I wasn't alone any more. I found a place I belong. I am a widow and so are all the other ladies."[39]

By the time everyone has spoken, the group experiences cohesiveness. Whenever they get together for subsequent group meetings, it is like old friends getting together after a long separation. The occasion is not a happy one, but the depressing mood that marks the first session or two gradually lifts.[40]

Many of the women in a certain widows group had experienced

somatic problems in the first few weeks after the death of their husbands. All suffered sleeplessness, headaches, backaches, and general malaise. After the first meeting some reported their first good night's sleep. By the end of the sixth session, many more reported they were sleeping better. One woman who still had problems sleeping was philosophical about it. She said, "Now when I can't sleep, I know other women are going through the same thing and it helps." Facilitators have learned that there is no sure-cure formula for dealing with situational depression. But knowing that the feelings are a normal part of the grieving process makes them more bearable.[41]

The group also reveals how clumsy family members and friends are in handling the bereaved's grief. It is helpful to know that having family or friends who unintentionally appear thoughtless or cruel is a common experience among those who grieve.[42]

The group also provides identity for women who by tradition learned that they were spouses first, mothers second, and individuals last. In the same widows group, each woman began to develop her own identity by seeing herself as a unique person and dissociating herself from labels that were painful.

The group helped the women deal with guilt, anger, and other emotions common to their situation. By discovering they were not alone with these feelings and openly admitting them, they were able to exorcise their bad feelings.

One widow said of her group experience, "The group did much for me . . . to be able to talk it all out, all the sorrow, guilt, abandonment, and hurt from friends. There was so much inside of me that I couldn't express to relatives or friends, but with the group I could say it all."[43]

The church as a body along with the individual believers who constitute it has a key role in God's plan for a needy world. May our religion be "pure and faultless" as the apostle James describes it, not only because of what we don't do—worldliness—but also because of what we *do*. Not only do widows and orphans need our care, but single parents and their children need it also.

Appendix A

Women's Wages Compared With Men's*

TABLE A: The older women get, the wider the gap between their wages and men's wages grows

AVERAGE EARNINGS

Age	Men	Women	Women's Wages per $1,000 Earned by Men
18–24	$12,963	$10,213	$788
25–29	$18,031	$13,297	$737
30–34	$21,719	$14,398	$663
35–39	$24,802	$14,161	$571
40–44	$26,011	$13,798	$530
45–49	$25,673	$13,542	$527
50–54	$25,175	$13,239	$526
55–59	$25,273	$12,952	$512

TABLE B: Women's earnings relative to men's in various professions

WOMEN'S WAGES PER $1,000 EARNED BY MEN

Postal clerks	$939	Nurse's aides and orderlies	$822
Cashiers	$920	Textile operatives	$813
Security guards	$907	Stock handlers	$812
Packers and wrappers	$854	Physicians and dentists	$809
Editors and reporters	$850	College teachers	$803
Bartenders	$844	Social workers	$799
High-school teachers	$829	Cleaning-service workers	$756
Elementary-school teachers	$822	Social scientists	$749

*Reprinted from *Working Mother* magazine, October 1983.

237

WOMEN'S WAGES PER $1,000 EARNED BY MEN (cont.)

Computer programmers	$736	Engineers	$678
Cooks	$734	Sales clerks	$674
Waitresses	$720	Insurance agents	$671
Accountants	$712	Health administrators	$655
Lawyers	$710	Office managers	$655
Real-estate agents	$709	Personnel workers	$643
School administrators	$699	Blue-collar supervisors	$642
Bookkeepers	$694	Buyers	$623
Factory assemblers	$690	Advertising workers	$617
Office-machine operators	$688	Financial managers	$602

Appendix B

Emotional Experiences and Feelings

This chart of emotional experiences and feelings is especially helpful to fathers with custody, as explained in chapter 3.

CLUSTER 1: ACTIVATION

Sense of vitality, aliveness, vibrancy, an extra spurt of energy or drive
A special lift in everything I do and say; I feel bouncy, springy
I'm excited in a calm way
There's inner buoyancy
I feel effervescent, bubbly
Warm excitement
I seem more alert
A sense of being more alive
I feel wide awake
A sense of lightness, buoyancy and upsurge of the body
I seem to be immediately in touch with the world; a sense of being very open, receptive, with no separation between me and the world
Particularly acute awareness of pleasurable things, their sounds, their colors, and textures—everything seems more beautiful, natural, and desirable
There's an intense awareness of everything; I seem to experience things with greater clarity; colors seem brighter, sounds clearer, movements more vivid
I seem to sense everything and experience everything immediately
A sense that I'm experiencing everything fully, completely, thoroughly; that I'm feeling all the way
A strong sense of interest and involvement in things around me
I feel like singing

Cheerful, delighted, joyous, excited, hopeful, enthusiastic

CLUSTER 4: MOVING TOWARD

There is an intense positive relationship with another person or with other people; a communion, a unity, a closeness, friendliness and freedom, mutual respect and interdependence
I want to help, protect, please another person

239

A sense of empathic harmony with another person; in tune, sharing and experiencing the same feelings and thoughts

There's a sense of complete understanding of the other person

I want to feel with the other person, experience with the other person with every sense; to be psychologically in touch with another person

Realization that someone else is more important to me than I am to myself

I want to touch, hold, be close physically to the other person

I want to be tender and gentle with another person

I want to communicate freely, share my thoughts and feelings with everyone around

A sense of giving, doing something for another person

I want to make others happy

A sense of being wanted, needed

I feel soft and firm

A sense of trust and appreciation of another person

Sense of confidence in being with another person

There's a desire to give of myself to another person

Affectionate, tender, loving, compassionate, accepting

CLUSTER 7: COMFORT

There's a mellow comfort

A sense of well-being

A sense of harmony and peace within

I am free of conflict

A feeling of warmth all over

I am peaceful, tranquil, quiet

I feel like smiling

I feel safe and secure

I'm at peace with the world

It's a state of release

There is an inner warm glow, a radiant sensation

Sense of "rightness" with oneself and the world; nothing can go wrong

A sense of being very integrated and at ease with myself, in harmony with myself

I'm loose, relaxed

There is a general release, a lessening of tension

Everything—breathing, moving, thinking—seems easier

A sense of being carefree but within balance

I'm optimistic and cheerful; the world seems basically good and beautiful; men are essentially kind; life is worth living

I'm optimistic about the future; the future seems bright

I'm in tune with the world

My movements are graceful and easy, I feel especially well coordinated

I feel I can really be myself

Satisfied, warm, friendly, calm, awed, creative, peaceful, rested, hopeful, quiet

CLUSTER 10: ENHANCEMENT

I feel taller, stronger, bigger
I have a sense of sureness
A sense of being exceptionally strong or energetic
I'm really functioning as a unit
Muscle tone is suddenly enhanced
I feel strong inside
A sense of more confidence in myself; a feeling that I can do anything
A sense of being important and worthwhile
I seem to be functioning intellectually at a higher level
There is a sense of accomplishment, fulfillment
There are moments of tremendous strength

Confident, secure, strong, proud, eager, competent

CLUSTER 3: HYPERACTIVATION

My blood pressure goes up; blood seems to rush through my body
My body seems to speed up
There's an excitement, a sense of being keyed up, overstimulated, super-charged
There's a quickening of heartbeat
My heart pounds
My pulse quickens
The feeling begins with a sharp sudden onset

Angry, confused, alert, fearful, frantic, suspicious, horrified, alarmed, panicked, disgusted, peeved

CLUSTER 6: MOVING AGAINST

There is an impulse to strike out, to pound, or smash, or kick, or bite; to do something that will hurt
I want to strike out, explode, but I hold back, control myself
I want to say something nasty, something that will hurt someone
Fists are clenched
I keep thinking of getting even, of revenge

Critical, contemptuous, furious, irritated, resentful, betrayed, bitter, angry, vengeful, hateful, livid

CLUSTER 9: TENSION

My whole body is tense
There's tension across my back, my neck, and shoulders
I'm wound up inside

My face and mouth are tight, tense, hard
A tight knotted feeling in my stomach
I'm hypersensitive
I'm easily irritated, ready to snap
I have a sense of being trapped, closed up, boxed, fenced in, tied down, inhibited

Tense, frustrated, nervous, grouchy, impatient, boiling, irritated, annoyed, jealous

CLUSTER 12: INADEQUACY

A sense of being totally unable to cope with the situation
There's a sense of not knowing where to go, what to do
I feel vulnerable and totally helpless
A sense that I have no control over the situation
I seem to be caught up and overwhelmed by the feeling
Sense of being gripped by the situation
I want to be comforted, helped by someone

Self-conscious, anxious, powerless, overwhelmed, needy, vulnerable, helpless, tearful, awkward, inadequate, out-of-control

CLUSTER 2: HYPOACTIVATION

I feel empty, drained, hollow
I feel heavy, logy, sluggish
I feel understimulated, undercharged
All excitement, vitality is gone
I feel tired, sleepy
My feelings seem dulled
My body seems to slow down
A sense of being dead inside
I feel let down
I feel mentally dull

Bored, withdrawn, shallow, depressed, slow, gloomy, empty, isolated

CLUSTER 5: MOVING AWAY

I want to withdraw, disappear, draw back, be alone, away from others, crawl into myself
A sense of unrelatedness to others; everyone seems far away; I am out of contact, can't reach others
There's a lack of involvement and not caring about anything that goes on around me
A feeling of a certain distance from others; everyone seems far away
There is a sense of aloneness, being cut off, completely by myself
I feel aimless

As if I'm out of touch, seeing things from far away
A sense of wandering, lost in space with nothing solid to grab onto
A sense of being incomplete; as if part of me is missing

Indifferent, alienated, useless, defeated, isolated, apathetic, lonely, ugly, incomplete, cut-off, blah, withdrawn, uninterested, lost

CLUSTER 8: DISCOMFORT

There is a clutching, sinking feeling in the middle of my chest
There's a lump in my throat
A gnawing feeling in the pit of my stomach
An inner ache you can't locate
My heart seems to ache
There is a heavy feeling in my stomach
There's a heaviness in my chest
I have no appetite; I can't eat
There is a sense of loss, of deprivation
I can't smile or laugh
I feel as if I'm under a heavy burden

Grieving, hurt, disappointed, pitiful, heartbroken, aching, sad, heavy, pained

CLUSTER 11: INCOMPETENCE; DISSATISFACTION

Seems that nothing I do is right
I get mad at myself for my feelings or thoughts or for what I've done
I keep blaming myself for the situation
There is a yearning, a desire for change; I want things to hurry up and begin to change
A longing to have things the same as before
I begin to think about what I can do to change the situation
There is a sense of regret

Regretful, weak, blamed, angry-with-self, like-a-loser, incompetent, defeated, depressed, dissatisfied

Appendix C

Mediation Contract

WE AGREE to work with the assistance of the mediator whose name is signed below to try and resolve certain matters between us. These include:

☐ Responsibilities to child(ren) ages_____
☐ Support and maintenance for_____
☐ Fair and practical property division
   ☐ Jointly owned residence
   ☐ Household furnishings and personal effects
   ☐ Other_____

   ☐ Tax matters
   ☐ Insurance
   ☐ Other:_____

THE MEDIATOR AGREES:

1. To furnish mediation services at the rate of $_____.00 per hour for sessions, plus an administrative fee of $_____.00.
2. To draft any agreement which results from the mediation, but only if *both* parties so request, for a flat fee of $_____.00. This fee includes a reasonable number of redrafts and production of a final copy to be signed.
3. That he/she will not represent either party as an attorney, nor will he/she give legal advice to either or both parties.
4. To furnish any legal information (not legal advice) in a general and impartial way.
5. To encourage each party to have access to separate legal counsel, as appropriate.
6. To protect the confidentiality of the mediation and to refuse to testify or produce records in any legal hearing between the parties unless *both* parties consent in writing.
7. To furnish the parties with a current status sheet after each mediation session.
8. To be frank in assessing the probable success of the mediation.

244

THE PARTIES EACH AGREE:

1. To take part in the mediation in good faith and to respect any ground rules established by the mediator.
2. To furnish promptly, completely, and accurately to each other and the mediator all financial disclosure information requested by the mediator.
3. To instruct any attorney who represents either of us that we have agreed that the mediator may not be called as a witness, nor his/her records subpoenaed, in any court proceeding between us, unless we *both* agree in writing.
4. To pay all fees of the mediation promptly and to divide responsibility for those fees ☐ equally or ☐ in the proportion of _____ % by the husband and _____ % by the wife.
5. To commit to secure a legal opinion from separate legal counsel before the agreement is signed if the mediator drafts the agreement.

6. _____

   _____

   _____

   _____

   _____

   _____

IN WITNESS, this agreement to mediate has been signed by both parties and the mediator on this _____ day of _____, 198___.

_____

Husband

_____

Wife

_____

Mediator

Newspaper ads developed by the United Methodists to help churches reach single adults more effectively

Appendix E

What Kids Do After School*

DEAR PARENTS,
Please give this questionnaire to your school-age child, and if necessary, help him or her fill it out.

DEAR KIDS,
Please tell us about what you do after school by filling in the following questionnaire. If there's anything else you'd like to say, write it on another piece of paper. Get some help, if you need to.

A. How old are you?

Younger than six	☐	Ten	☐
Six	☐	Eleven	☐
Seven	☐	Twelve	☐
Eight	☐	Thirteen	☐
Nine	☐	Fourteen or older	☐

B. Are you:

A boy	☐	A girl	☐

C. Do your parents work? (Check one answer only.)

My mother does	☐	Neither my mother	
My father does	☐	nor my father does	☐
Both my mother and my father do	☐		

D. Who usually takes care of you after school? (Check one answer only.)

A sitter	☐
My older brother or sister	☐
Another relative	☐
Nobody, I take care of myself	☐

*Reprinted form *Working Mother* magazine, October 1983.

Nobody, I take care of myself and my younger brother or sister ☐
Other (tell us what you do): _____ ☐

E. Do you sometimes do any of the following things after school? (Check as
many as you want.)

Have a friend over ☐
Go to a friend's house ☐
Go to sports practice ☐
Go to an after-school club ☐
Go to an art or a music class ☐
Other (tell us what you do): _____ ☐

F. If you go home right after school, what do you do when you get there?
(Check as many as you want.)

Call my mother or father to check in ☐
Tell a neighbor or family friend that I'm home ☐
Do my homework ☐
Watch television ☐
Work on a hobby or project ☐
Walk the dog ☐
Start dinner ☐
Do other chores ☐
Other (tell us what you do): _____ ☐
I never go home right after school ☐

G. If you usually stay by yourself after school, when does a grownup get
home? (Check one answer only.)

In less than one hour   ☐   In about four
In about one hour   ☐   hours, or more   ☐
In about two hours   ☐   I never stay by
In about three hours   ☐   myself after school   ☐

H. Do you mind being home by yourself after school? (Check one answer
only.)

Yes, always   ☐   I never stay home by
Yes, sometimes   ☐   myself after school   ☐
No, never   ☐

I. Do you have a dog or cat?

Yes   ☐   No   ☐

J. When you're home alone after school, who do you call if you have a question or need anything? (Check as many as you want.)

Mother ☐	Other (tell us who you	
Father ☐	call): _____ ☐	
Grandparent ☐	No one	
Other relative ☐	I'm never home alone	
Neighbor ☐	after school ☐	
Family friend ☐		

K. How do you feel about your after-school arrangement? (Check one answer only.)

I like it the way it is ☐   I'd like to change it ☐

L. If you wish you did something else after school, what would it be? (Check as many as you want.)

I'd like to go to a friend's house more often ☐
I'd like to have a friend over more often ☐
I'd like to stay at school and play ☐
I'd like to have more activities (sports, clubs, music lessons, etc.) ☐
I'd like to go to a relative's house ☐
I'd like a relative to come to my house ☐
Other (tell us your choice): _____ ☐

M. What is the best thing about your afternoons? _____

_____

_____

_____

_____

_____

N. What is the worst thing about your afternoons? _____

_____

_____

_____

_____

_____

Appendix F

More Resources For Self-Help Groups

How to Grow a Parents Group by Diane Mason, Gayle Jensen and Carolyn Ryzewica, a complete guide to starting and maintaining a parents' group, is available from: CDG Enterprises, P.O. Box 97-B, Western Springs, IL 60558.

For guidance on setting up a child-care information-and-referral service, send a self-addressed, stamped envelope to: Bananas, 6501 Telegraph Ave., Oakland, CA 94609.

Family Focus, Inc., offers training and consultation for parent support and resource programs. Also available is a publication entitled *Creating Drop-In Centers: A Family Focus Model*. Write to: Family Focus, Inc., 2300 Green Bay Road, Evanston, IL 60201.

The International Childbirth Education Association, a resource center for existing and newly forming groups, coordinates a network of parenting groups throughout the country. Write to: Group Services Director, International Childbirth Education Association, Box 20048, Minneapolis, MN 55420.

For a brochure describing MELD's package of materials and services that can be purchased by community agencies wishing to serve first-time parents, write to: MELD (Minnesota Early Learning Design), 123 Grant St., Minneapolis, MN 55403.

Appendix G

Communication Workshop

This workshop teaches communication by doing. It is a group sharing the experiences of up to twenty people in which the members of the group are able to get varied reactions to their behavior, thought patterns, attitudes on life, and how they relate to others from people on their peer level. They discover through group sharing that their experiences are common to others. This is not a lecture or study group, and the emphasis is on feelings rather than opinions.

The workshop provides a sheltered environment that tends to give the individual social stability, acceptance, assurance, guidance and an opportunity for self-exploration and understanding in a sympathetic atmosphere.

The workshop is a unique blend of communication, training and encounter group principles used successfully for several years.

WHAT IS EXPECTED OF THE WORKSHOP PARTICIPANTS?

. All members are on a first name basis.
. All members of the group are accepted by the group by the very fact they are there.
. The group leader (and co-leader if one is used) is as much a part of the group as everyone else. He does not enjoy "diplomatic immunity."
. Everything said and done in the group is the property of the group. It is to be discussed with no one else outside the group.
. Each member of the group is committed to participating in every session that is scheduled. The presence of every member is essential to the success of the group.
. The group is interested in the feelings of its members as they relate to each other in the group and the manner in which they communicate these feelings.
. A successful group depends on the honesty of the group with each other and themselves. It is the responsibility of the leader to make sure that the group always functions with the best interest of every member in mind.

251

8. With the exception of the first session the group is not structured nor is there any signal to start. When the group gathers at the appointed time communication starts.

Resources for Single Parents

Information regarding resources in addition to those listed here may be obtained from the Institute for Christian Resources, P.O. Box 7494, San Jose, CA 95150.

Books

SINGLE LIFE

J. L. Barkas, *Single in America*. What makes a successful and happy single, and how long-lasting relationships can be coordinated with other achievements on the job and elsewhere. New York: Atheneum, 1980.

Allen Hadidian, *A Single Thought*. The freedoms and frustrations of the single life. Chicago: Moody Press, 1981.

Douglas W. Johnson, *The Challenge of Single Adult Ministry*. Not a "how-to" book, but a help for those who minister in determining what might make a ministry to singles effective. Valley Forge, Pa.: Judson Press, 1982.

Gien Karssen, *Getting the Most Out of Being Single*. How single women can enjoy their lives now rather than hoping for something better that may never come. Colorado Springs: Navpress, 1983.

Don Meredith, *Who Says Get Married?* How singles can find completeness in God and learn to build healthy, lasting relationships and get on with living a purposeful life now. Nashville: Thomas Nelson, 1981.

Susan Annette Muto, *Celebrating the Single Life*. How the Christian single can live as a fully human and fully Christian person. New York: Doubleday, 1982.

Dorothy Payne, *Singleness*. A book for single women with suggestions for ways to enjoy their singleness. Philadelphia: Westminster Press, 1983.

Stacy Rinehart and Paula Rinehart, *Choices: Finding God's Way in Dating,*

253

Sex, Singleness and Marriage. How to ward off temptation in dating and how to date with discernment. Colorado Springs: Navpress, 1983.

Lynn Shahan, *Living Alone and Liking It*. Affirms singleness and how to live alone. Los Angeles: Stratford Press, 1981.

Jim Smoke, *Suddenly Single*. Practical advice on picking up the pieces and starting over after becoming "suddenly single." Old Tappan, N.J.: Fleming H. Revell, 1982.

Jim Talley and Bobbie Reed, *Too Close Too Soon*. Relationships between men and women that have gone beyond the friendship stage. Nashville: Thomas Nelson, 1982.

Bruce Yoder and Imo Jeanne Yoder, eds., *Single Voices*. The life of singleness viewed by different writers. Scottdale, Pa.: Herald Press, 1982.

SINGLE PARENTING

Antoinette Bosco, *Successful Single Parenting*. Originally published under the title *A Parent Alone*. Help for the single parent as well as understanding to friends and family. Mystic, Conn.: Twenty Third Publications, 1979.

Sara Gilbert, *How to Live With a Single Parent*. How to anticipate and resolve problems in the single-parent family. New York: Lothrop, Lee & Shepard, 1982.

Sandra L. Hofferth, *Day Care in the Next Decade: 1980–1990*. Washington: Urban Institute Press (n.d.).

Cathie LeNoir, *Blessed Fools*. A single Christian mother with two daughters writing on the thesis that God still uses fools to accomplish His purpose. Bloomington, Minn.: Landmark Books, 1980.

Carol Vejvoda Murdock. *Single Parents Are People, Too!* Issues concerning single parents such as finances, social life, attitudes toward the ex-spouse, fathers with custody, and more. New York: Butterick Publishing, 1980.

Kristine M. Rosenthal and Harry F. Keshet, *Fathers Without Partners*. The nature of the father-child bond, especially after divorce. Totowa, N.J.: Rowman & Littlefield, 1980.

Morris A. Shepard and Gerald Goldman, *Divorced Dads*. Explained by subtitle: "How to keep on loving your kids after your marriage has ended." Radnor, Pa.: Chilton, 1979; New York: Berkley Books, 1980.

Harold Ivan Smith, *One-Parent Families*. How the church can minister to the hurts of single parent families. Kansas City: Beacon Hill Press, 1981.

DIVORCE

Gary D. Chapman, *Hope for the Separated*. Practical issues dealing with a separation that may end in divorce. Chicago: Moody Press, 1982.

Gary Collins, *Calm Down*. Deals with pressure, boredom, habits, depression, family tension, communication breakdown, and more. Chappaqua, N.Y.: Christian Herald Books, 1981.

John M. Haynes, *Divorce Mediation*. A book for people who are trying to help couples through divorce with a minimum of frustration and animosity. New York: Springer, 1981.

Darlene Petri, *The Hurt and Healing of Divorce*. The author's story of divorce after thirteen years of marriage and how she coped. Elgin, Ill.: David C. Cook, 1976.

LONELINESS AND OTHER EMOTIONS

Batsell Barrett Baxter, Harold Hazelip, and Joe R. Barnett, *Anchors in Troubled Waters*. Dealing with depression, stress, hostility, and other emotions. Grand Rapids: Baker, 1981.

Velma Darbo Brown, *After Weeping*. The grief process and living again after loss. Nashville: Broadman Press, 1980.

Craig W. Ellison, *Loneliness: The Search for Intimacy*. Help for those who suffer from loneliness and for those who help them. Chappaqua, N.Y.: Christian Herald Books, 1980.

Velma Darbo Stevens, *A Fresh Look at Loneliness*. A widow of seven years exploring loneliness and how the church can minister more effectively. Nashville: Broadman, 1981.

Ira Tanner, *Healing the Pain of Everyday Loss*. Hope for those who experience everyday losses that can be as devastating to peace of mind as loss through death. Minneapolis: Winston Press, 1980.

Alan C. Tibbetts, *Why Seek Ye the Dead Among the Living? A Guide for Widows*. Former army chaplain gives step-by-step guide for widows. Bryn Mawr, Pa.: Dorrance & Company, 1981.

CHILDREN

Neal C. Buchanan and Eugene Chamberlain, *Helping Children of Divorce*. Dealing with the trauma of those who are caught in divorce, particularly the children. Nashville: Broadman Press, 1981.

Ciji Ware, *Sharing Parenthood After Divorce*. The case for joint custody as the most sane and humane solution for divorced families, on the premise that children have the right to both parents as parents. New York: Viking, 1982.

Newsletters, Newspapers, and Magazines

Bulletin of Adventist Singles Ministries. Published at 5261 Sonora Way, Carmichael, CA 95608. A newsletter helpful to all singles groups.

Christian Single. Published by the Sunday School Board of the Southern Baptist Convention. Very informative.

Contact. Published by the Single Christian Fellowship International. Information about singles groups around the country, prayer requests of members, news items, and a Christian message. A list of members who wish to correspond is included.

Just for Families. Published by P & T Publications, Box 1968, Provo, UT 84603. Eight-page newsletter dedicated to building stronger families.

Key Intro. Box 8218, Rolling Meadows, IL 60008. Small tabloid billed as "the Christian Source for Christian Singles."

Marriage and Divorce Today. Published at 2315 Broadway, New York, NY 10024. A four-to-six-page weekly secular newsletter on all aspects of marriage, divorce, and the family, including singleness. Latest research and findings in the field.

Ministry Ideabank. Lutheran Center, 360 Park Ave. South, New York, NY 10010. Four-page newsletter sharing unique and successful ideas for a more effective ministry.

SALT Newsletter. A publication of *Solo* magazine "dedicated to producing practical help and ideas for those involved in the ministry with single adults." (Acronym for Single Adult Leadership Training.) Carries calendar of conferences for singles and training conferences for those ministering to singles.

Single i. Published by the Institute of Singles Dynamics, P.O. Box 11394 nsas City, MO 64112. Monthly newsletter offering news of what single oups are doing, ideas for ministry to singles, new books in print, and endar of conferences for singles.

Single Parent. Published by Parents Without Partners, 7910 Woodmont e., Bethesda, MD 20814. A secular, sometimes relativistic, monthly mag- ne with articles and news of importance to single parents. Very helpful for discriminating reader.

Solo. Published at P.O. Box 1231, Sisters, OR 97759. Billed as "the ristian Magazine for Single Adults." Helpful articles and news items from Christian perspective for single adults whether never married or formerly rried. Includes a "New Friends Directory"—a listing of subscribers who sh to get acquainted. Carries calendar of conferences for singles and train- conferences for those ministering to singles.

Today's Single. Published quarterly by the National Association of Chris- Singles (NACS), 915 W. Wisconsin Ave. Suite 214, Milwaukee, WI 33. Tabloid with articles on the single life.

esources by André Bustanoby

But I Didn't Want a Divorce. Written for the Christian who didn't want a orce but was divorced (or chose it) anyway. Deals with the biblical, psy- logical, and legal aspects of divorce and divorce recovery. Grand Rapids: ndervan, 1978, softcover.

Just Talk to Me. Directed to couples attempting to communicate more ctively in marriage, but applies to all situations that require more effective mmunication. Grand Rapids: Zondervan, 1981, softcover.

The Readymade Family. For those remarried, or planning to remarry, and blishing a "stepfamily." Stepfamily Test offered to those considering arriage and a stepfamily. Grand Rapids: Zondervan, 1982, softcover.

Being a Success at Who You Are: Personalities That Win. Formerly pub- ed under the title, "You Can Change Your Personality." Helps the in- dual evaluate personality type and what might be done to be more effective ho we are. Grand Rapids: Zondervan, 1985, softcover.

(Can Men and Women Be) Just Friends? Helps singles distinguish between ndship and intimate relationships and how to build both. Grand Rapids: dervan, 1984, softcover.

Notes

CHAPTER 1

[1]*Solo* (March-April 1982):38.

[2]*Current Population Reports,* "Population Characteristics," Series p-20, 381 (Washington: U.S. Bureau of Census, 1982): 21.

[3]*U.S. News and World Reports* (February 21, 1983): 54.

[4]*Current Population Reports,* "Population Characteristics," 2.

[5]*Marriage and Divorce Today* (August 1, 1983): 1.

[6]Ibid.

[7]Ibid.

[8]André Bustanoby, *But I Didn't Want a Divorce* (Grand Rapids: Zonderv 1978): 41.

[9]The number is most likely between 142,000 and 282,000. The figures based on a total prison population of 353,167 (82-83 Statistical Abstra of which 4 percent are women, and 42 to 80 percent of that number mothers. *See Social Work* (July 1980): 298. Extrapolated from these figu is the male population, of which 40 to 80 percent are estimated to be fathe

[10]*Social Work* (May 1979): 193-99.

[11]*Social Work* (November 1980): 347.

[12]Ibid., 439.

[13]Jacqueline Simenauer and David Carroll, *Singles: The New Americans* (N York: New American Library, 1982), 298.

[14]Ibid., 323.

[15]Ibid.

[16]Ibid.

[17]Ibid., 329-30.

[18]Ibid., 334.

[19]*Time* (January 4, 1982): 81.

[20]Barbara G. Cashion, "Female-Headed Families: Effects on Children Clinical Implications," *Journal of Marital and Family Therapy* (April 198 77.

[21]Ibid.

[22]Ibid.

[23]Ibid., 78.

[24]Ibid., 82.

[25]*Time* (January 4, 1982): 81.

[26]Ibid.

Ibid.
Ibid.
Ibid.
Ibid.
Ibid.
Ibid.
Ibid.
McCall's (May 81): 82.
Ibid., 92

CHAPTER 2

Harpers Bazaar (October 1983): 191.
Ibid., 192.
Provided by Bureau of Labor Statistics (U.S. Government, 202-376-6750, taken from Office of Management and Budget Poverty Guidelines as published by the Department of Health and Human Services).
Current Population Reports, "Money Income of Households, Families, and Persons in the United States: 1981," Series p-60, no. 137 (Washington: U.S. Bureau of Census, 1981): 22-23.
Marriage and Divorce Today (August 1, 1983): 1, 3.
Denis F. Johnston et al., *Social Indicators* (Washington: U.S. Department of Commerce, U.S. Bureau of Census, December 1980): 6.
Ibid., 64.
Ibid., 68.
Eunice Korfman, ed., *Families Today,* "Depression and Low-Income, Female-Headed Families" (Washington: U.S. Department of Health, Education and Welfare, DHEW Publication no. [ADM] 79-896, 1979): 326–28.
Ibid., 335.
Ibid., 337.
Ibid., 328.
Ibid., 341–42.
Ibid., 335.
Ibid.
Ibid., 339.
Marriage and Divorce Today (December 21 and 28, 1981): 1–2.
Current Population Reports, "Money Income of Households, Families and Persons in the United States: 1981," 1.
Working Woman (November 1983): 94.
Marriage and Divorce Today (February 1, 1982): 3.
Psychology Today (November 1983): 94.
Marriage and Divorce Today (December 5, 1983): 3.
Colette Dowling, *The Cinderella Complex: Women's Hidden Fear of Independence* (New York: Pocket Books, 1982).
Korfman, *Families Today,* 342.

[25]*Working Woman* (February 1984): 37.
[26]Ibid.

CHAPTER 3

[1]*Marriage and Divorce Today* (December 6, 1982): 1.
[2]*Social Work* (November 1982): 474-75.
[3]*Good Housekeeping* (November 1981): 84.
[4]*Social Work* (November 1982): 473. Various figures are reported, howeve
  Marriage and Divorce Today (August 1, 1983), 2, quotes census figures
  1,189,000 children under eighteen living with father only. *Current Popu
  lation Reports*, "Marital Status and Living Arrangements," series p—2
  no. 380 (Washington: U.S. Bureau of Census, 1982), 142, reports 679,00
  male householders (no wife present) with children under eighteen. Th
  breakdown is 148,000 married, wife absent; 88,000 widowed; 379,000 d
  vorced; 64,000 never married. The total children (their own) under eighte
  is almost 1.5 million (1,491,000).
[5]*People* (February 23, 1981): 76.
[6]*Social Work* (July 1976): 310.
[7]Ibid., 311.
[8]*Working Mother* (December 1983): 134.
[9]Ibid., 135.
[10]Ibid., 136.
[11]Fitzhugh Dodson, *How to Father* (Bergenfield, N.J.: New American L
  brary, 1974), 3.
[12]A warning is needed here. This book, among other materials used in r
  search, does not receive blanket endorsement. I disagree, for example, wi
  Dodson's view of spanking. The parent should read all books with tv
  things in mind: (1) We can learn from the unbeliever because he can I
  taught of God (Ps. 19:1-3; Rom. 1:18-20; 2:14-16; Acts 14:17); (2) th
  degree to which the unbeliever agrees with biblical principles is the degr
  to which his views are correct.
[13]*Social Work* (January 1978): 16.
[14]*But I Didn't Want a Divorce* (Zondervan, 1978) and *The Readymade Fami*
  (Zondervan, 1982).

CHAPTER 4

[1]*Marriage and Divorce Today* (August 30, 1982): 1.
[2]Ibid.
[3]*Marriage and Divorce Today* (August 22, 1983): 1.
[4]*Marriage and Divorce Today* (November 30, 1981): 2, 5.
[5]André Bustanoby, *The Readymade Family* (Grand Rapids: Zondervan, 1982
  118.
[6]This figure was extrapolated from *Current Population Reports*, "Populatic
  Characteristics."
[7]*Marriage and Divorce Today* (November 29, 1982): 1.

⁸Bustanoby, *The Readymade Family*, 19.

⁹*Single Parent* (October 1981): 14.

¹⁰Bustanoby, *The Readymade Family*, 119.

¹¹*Stepparent News* (July-August 1983): 3.

¹²*Marriage and Divorce Today* (January 17, 1983): 4.

¹³*Marriage and Divorce Today* (August 8, 1983): 3–4.

⁴*Marriage and Divorce Today* (March 28, 1983): 4.

⁵*Marriage and Divorce Today* (August 15, 1983): 3.

⁶Ibid.

⁷*Marriage and Divorce Today* (November 7, 1983): 3–4.

⁸*Current Research on Children: Birth Through Adolescence*, vol. 1, *Child and Family* (New York: Atcom, 1983), 72.

⁹Ibid.

¹⁰*Single Parent* (October 1983): 19.

¹Ibid., 20.

²Ibid.

³*Marriage and Divorce Today* (December 19 and 26, 1983): 1.

⁴Available from Blossom Valley Press, P.O. Box 4044, Mountainview, CA 94040.

⁵*Marriage and Divorce Today* (June 13, 1983): 4.

⁶*Dads and Moms*, Paul Lewis Publisher and Editor, P.O. Box 340, Julian, CA 92036.

CHAPTER 5

¹*Single Parent* (March 1981): 42.

²Sandra Kalenik and Jay S. Bernstein, *How to Get a Divorce* (Washington: Washingtonian Books, 1976): 39.

³Robin L. Franklin, "Child Custody in Transition," *Journal of Marital and Family Therapy*, vol. 6 no. 3 (July 1980): 285.

⁴Ibid., 286.

⁵Ibid.

⁶Ibid.

⁷Ibid.

⁸Ibid.

⁹Ibid.

⁾Joseph Goldstein, Anna Freud, and Albert J. Solnit, *Beyond the Best Interest of the Child* (New York: Free Press, 1980), 38.

¹*Woman* (February 1984): 70–71.

²*Marriage and Divorce Today* (February 1, 1982):1.

³*Marriage and Divorce Today* (May 16, 1983): 1.

⁸Barton E. Bernstein, "Lawyer and Counselor as an Interdisciplinary Team: Preparing the Father for Custody," *Journal of Marriage and Family Counseling*, vol. 3 no. 3 (July 1977): 30.

⁵Ibid., 29.

⁾*Single Parent* (January-February 1983): 38–39.

⁾*Marriage and Divorce Today* (December 20 and 27, 1982): 1.

18Ibid.

19Franklin, "Child Custody in Transition," 290.

20Ibid.

21Ibid.

22Ibid.

23Marriage and Divorce Today (March 28, 1983): 3.

24Marriage and Divorce Today (December 13, 1982): 4.

25Current Research on Children: Birth Through Adolescence, 74.

26Marriage and Divorce Today (July 26, 1982): 3–4.

27Marriage and Divorce Today (July 5, 1982): 3.

28Ibid., 3–4.

29Marriage and Divorce Today (November 28, 1983): 2–3.

30Single Parent (January-February 1981): 8–9.

31Current Research on Children: Birth Through Adolescence, 54.

CHAPTER 6

1Bustanoby, The Readymade Family, 122.

2Marriage and Divorce Today (May 16, 1983): 3.

3Marriage and Divorce Today (December 14, 1981): 2.

4Ibid., 3.

5Current Research on Children: Birth Through Adolescence, 29–30.

6Marriage and Divorce Today (March 26, 1984): 1.

7Single Parent (October 1982): 26–28.

8Single Parent (July-August 1980): 28.

9Ibid.

10Single Parent (October 1983): 21.

11Single Parent (November 1983): 15.

12Ibid.

13Ibid.

14Ibid.

15Ibid.

16Ibid.

17Marriage and Divorce Today (March 1, 1982): 1.

18Marriage and Divorce Today (June 14, 1982): 4.

CHAPTER 7

1Marriage and Divorce Today (August 1, 1983): 1.

2Current Population Reports, "Population Characteristics," 142.

3Judge Leon R. Yankwich, quoted in Dads Only (June 1983).

4Simenauer and Carroll, Singles: The New Americans, 320–21.

5Ibid., 317–18.

6Ibid., 318.

7Ibid.

8Time (January 4, 1982): 81.

[9]See Cornelius Van Til, *Common Grace* (Philadelphia: Presbyterian and Reformed, 1954), for a good discussion of this subject.

[10]*Time* (January 4, 1982): 81.

[11]Kristin A. Moore et al., *Teenage Motherhood: Social and Economic Consequences* (Washington: Urban Institute, 1979), 31.

[12]*Marriage and Divorce Today* (June 14, 1982): 3.

[13]*Current Research on Children: Birth Through Adolescence*, vol. 2, *Child and Teen Sexuality* (New York: Atcom, 1983), 17.

[14]Ibid., 26.

[15]Ibid.

[16]Moore et al., *Teenage Motherhood*, 11.

[17]*Social Work* (March 1978): 151.

[18]Ibid.

[19]Heather L. Ross and Isabel V. Sawhill, *Time of Transition: The Growth of Families Headed by Women* (Washington: Urban Institute, 1975), 107.

[20]Ibid.

[21]*Marriage and Divorce Today* (November 7, 1983): 3. It is noted that 58.6 percent of AFDC cases in Texas are paternity cases, 80 percent of which are uncollectable because the father is unknown.

[22]*Social Work* (November 1982): 484.

[23]Ibid., 485.

[24]Ibid.

[25]*Marriage and Divorce Today* (November 7, 1983): 3.

[26]*Marriage and Divorce Today* (February 8, 1982): 4.

[27]Ibid.

[28]Ibid.

[29]*Marriage and Divorce Today* (May 24, 1982): 4.

[30]Ibid.

[31]*Social Work* (July 1978): 311.

[32]Ibid.

[33]Ibid., 312.

[34]Ibid.

[35]Ibid.

[36]Ibid.

[37]*Single Parent* (June 1983): 28.

[38]Ibid., 313.

[39]*Family Life Today* (November 1983): 17.

CHAPTER 8

[1]*Single Parent* (April 1981): 5.

[2]Ibid.

[3]*Single Parent* (September 1983): 29. Approximately 100,000 widowers are raising 200,000 children under eighteen, and 665,000 widows are raising 1.2 million children under eighteen.

[4]*U.S. Catholic* (July 1983): 35.

[5]Ibid.

[6]Maxwell Maltz, *Psycho-Cybernetics* (New York: Bantam, 1973), ix.

[7]Larry Yeagley, "Coping With Grief," seminar notes at the Seventh-day Adventist General Conference (January 23, 1984): 3.

[8]Ibid., 6.

[9]Ibid., 7.

[10]Ibid., 5.

[11]Ibid., 4.

[12]Ibid.

[13]*Science News* (August 1981): 85.

[14]*U.S. News and World Report* (June 22, 1981): 47–48.

[15]Bustanoby, *The Readymade Family*, 16.

[16]*Parents* (January 1981): 34.

[17]*Single Parent* (November 1983): 25.

[18]*Current Research on Children: Birth Through Adolescence*, 20–21

CHAPTER 9

[1]*Working Woman* (November 1983): 131.

[2]*Ladies Home Journal* (January 1982): 69.

[3]Ibid., 69–70.

[4]This seventy-four-page pamphlet can be obtained from the U.S. Government Printing Office, Washington. Ask for DHHS Publication no. (OHDS) 80-30254, March 1980.

[5]*Good Housekeeping* (May 1983): 252.

[6]Kathy G. Ross, *A Parents Guide to Day Care* (Seattle: Self-Counsel Press, 1984), 11.

[7]Ibid., 12.

[8]*Good Housekeeping* (May 1983): 252.

[9]*Essence* (April 1981): 62.

[10]Ibid.

[11]*McCall's* (April 1981): 61.

[12]*Working Mother* (December 1983): 145.

[13]Ibid.

[14]*McCall's* (April 1981): 61.

[15]Ibid.

[16]Ibid.

[17]*Parents* (September 1982): 72.

[18]Ibid., 80.

[19]Ibid., 81.

[20]Ibid.

[21]Ibid., 82.

[22]Ibid.

[23]Ibid.

[24]Ibid.

[25]Ibid.

[26]Ibid.

[27]*Essence* (March 1982): 140.

[28]*Parents* (February 1982): 53.

[29]Ibid., 54.

[30]*Essence* (March 1982): 142.

[31]Ibid.

[32]Ibid., 167.

[33]Ibid.

[34]Ibid.

[35]*Education Digest* (February 1981): 15–16.

[36]*Essence* (March 1982): 142.

CHAPTER 10

[1]*Single Parent* (January-February 1982): 18.

[2]Ibid.

[3]Ibid.

[4]Joseph Bressler, Workshop on Depression, American Institute of Family Relations, Hollywood, California (February 1971).

[5]These figures are based on the *1984 World Almanac* (New York: Newspaper Enterprise Association): 915. It reports the rate of suicides per 100,000 population of each age group as follows: 0.8 for ten-to-fourteen-year-olds, 8.4 for fifteen-to-nineteen-year-olds, and 13 for fifteen-to-twenty-four-year-olds.

[6]*Marriage and Divorce Today* (August 15, 1983): 1.

[7]*Single Parent* (October 1982): 18.

[8]Ibid.

[9]Ibid.

[10]Ibid.

[11]Ibid.

[12]Ibid.

[13]Ibid.

[14]Ibid., 19.

[15]Ibid.

[16]*Single Parent* (September 1981): 21.

[17]Ibid.

[18]Ibid.

[19]*Parents* (November 1983): 105.

[20]Ibid., 129.

[21]Ronald A. LaTorre, *Sexual Identity: Implications for Mental Health* (Chicago: Nelson-Hall, 1979), ch. 6.

[22]Ibid., 94–95.

[23]*Parents* (November 1983): 107.

[24]*Single Parent* (December 1980): 8.

[25]Ibid.

[26]Ibid.

[27]Ibid.

[28]Ibid.

[29]Cliff Schimmels, *How to Help Your Children Survive and Thrive in Public School* (Old Tappan, N.J.: Fleming H. Revell, 1982).

[30]RIF Inc., Smithsonian Institution, 600 Maryland Ave. S.E./Suite 500, Washington, DC 20560.

[31]LaTorre, *Sexual Identity*, 7–12.

[32]Ibid., 14.

[33]Ibid., 27.

[34]Ibid., 26.

[35]Ibid., 64.

[36]Ibid., 65.

[37]Ibid.

[38]Ibid., 66.

[39]Ibid.

CHAPTER 11

[1]*Washington Post* (November 18, 1983): C5.

[2]Ibid.

[3]*Working Woman* (November 1983): 142.

[4]Ibid.

[5]Ibid.

[6]Ibid.

[7]Ibid.

[8]Ibid.

[9]Ibid., 145.

[10]*Single Parent* (May 1982): 20.

[11]Scmenauer and Carroll, *Singles: The New Americans*, 304.

[12]Ibid.

[13]*Washington Post* (November 18, 1983): C5.

[14]John Fischer, *A Single Person's Identity* (Palo Alto: Discovery Publishing, 1973), 1.

[15]For an extensive treatment on this subject see Bustanoby, *But I Didn't Want A Divorce*. The instruction to the Christian to remain unmarried does not apply in all cases.

[16]*Solo* (Fall 1983): 17. This material is based on André Bustanoby, *(Can Men and Women Be) Just Friends?* (Grand Rapids: Zondervan, 1984).

[17]*Single Parent* (October 1981): 23.

[18]Ibid.

[19]*Single Parent* (March 1981): 9.

[20]*Single Parent* (January-February 1981): 26.

[21]Ibid.

[22]Ibid.

[23]Ibid.

[24]Ibid., 27.

[25]Ibid.

[26]Ibid.

[27]*Single Parent* (July-August 1979): 6.

[28]Ibid.

[29]Ibid., 7.

[30]Bustanoby, *The Readymade Family*, 16.

[31]*Single Parent* (December 1979): 8.

[32]Ibid.

[33]Ibid.

[34]*Single Parent* (January-February 1983): 25.

[35]*Harpers Bazaar* (October 1983): 206.

[36]Ibid.

[37]Ibid., 246.

[38]Ibid.

[39]Ibid.

[40]Ibid., 206, 246

[41]Bustanoby, *But I Don't Want a Divorce*, 89–132.

CHAPTER 12

[1]Franz Delitzsch, *Biblical Commentary on the Proverbs of Solomon*, vol. 2 (Grand Rapids: Wm. B. Eerdmans, n.d.), 86–87.

[2]Lee Salk, *Your Child from One to Twelve* (Bergenfield, N.J.: New American Library, 1970), 21.

[3]Dodson, *How to Father*, 346–47.

[4]Ibid., 15.

[5]Salk, *Your Child*, 24–25.

[6]Dodson, *How to Father*, 26–27.

[7]Salk, *Your Child*, 36–37.

[8]Ibid., 37.

[9]Ibid., 38.

[10]Ibid., 68.

[11]Ibid., 69.

[12]Ibid., 74.

[13]Ibid., 99.

[14]Ibid., 101–2.

[15]Dodson, *How to Father*, 158.

[16]Bertram S. Brown, *When Your Child First Goes Off to School* (Washington: U.S. Department of Health, Education and Welfare, DHEW Publication no. [ADM] 76-304, 1975).

[17]Dodson, *How to Father*, 123.

[18]Ibid., 136.

[19]Ibid., 133.

[20]Ibid.

[21]Ibid., 143.

[22]Ibid., 146.

[23]Ibid., 148.

[24]Ibid., 157.

[25]Bustanoby, *But I Didn't Want a Divorce*, 111.

[26]Dodson, *How to Father*, 234.
[27]Ibid., 235–38.

CHAPTER 13

[1]Dodson, *How to Father*, 241.
[2]For more information on vocational testing and colleges, see André Bustanoby, *Everything You Need to Know About College* (San Bernardino, Calif.: Here's Life Publishers, 1983).
[3]Dodson, *How to Father*, 298.
[4]*Marriage and Divorce Today* (March 28, 1983): 4.
[5]*Marriage and Divorce Today* (January 23, 1984): 1.
[6]*Time* (June 8, 1981): 47.
[7]Ibid.
[8]Ibid.
[9]For more on communication, see André Bustanoby and Fay Bustanoby, *Just Talk to Me: Talking and Listening for a Happier Marriage* (Grand Rapids: Zondervan, 1981).

CHAPTER 14

[1]*Single i* (August 1983): 2.
[2]*Single i* (November 1973): 2.
[3]*Single i* (December 1983): 2.
[4]*Solo* (November-December 1979): 23.
[5]*Working Mother* (October 1983): 119–20.
[6]*SALT Newsletter* (January 1984): 1.
[7]Ibid.
[8]Ibid.
[9]*SALT Newsletter* (December 1983): 1.
[10]*SALT Newsletter* (January 1984): 1.
[11]Ibid.
[12]Ibid., 5.
[13]*Charisma* (May 1981): 33.
[14]Ibid.
[15]Ibid.
[16]Ibid., 34.
[17]Ibid.
[18]Ibid.
[19]Ibid., 35.
[20]Ibid., 36.
[21]Ibid.
[22]Ibid.
[23]Ibid.
[24]Ibid.
[25]Ibid.
[26]*Parents* (November 1983): 194.

27Ibid., 198.

28Ibid.

29Ibid.

30Ibid.

31Ibid.

32Ibid.

33Ibid., 200.

34For a copy of their directory write to Buckeye Singles Council, 92 Orchard Hill Ct., Gahanna, OH 43230.

35Unsigned, "Letters to the Editor," *California Southern Baptist* (n.d.).

36For a copy write to Big Brothers/Big Sisters of America, 117 South 17th St., Suite 1200, Philadelphia, PA 19103.

37Charles Caldwell Ryrie, *The Place of Women in the Church* (New York: Macmillan, 1958), 81.

38Ibid., 83, 142.

39*Social Worker* (January 1980), 63.

40Ibid.

41Ibid., 64.

42Ibid.

43Ibid., 65.

Index

About the Author

ANDRÉ BUSTANOBY, a marriage and family therapist living in Bowie, Maryland, is the author of seven books. The father of four, he is a former president and clinical member of the Mid-Atlantic Division of the American Association for Marriage and Family Therapy, and a graduate of Nyack College, Dallas Theological Seminary, and Azusa Pacific College.